Archaeological Oddities

Archaeological Oddities

A Field Guide to Forty Claims
of Lost Civilizations,
Ancient Visitors, and Other
Strange Sites in North America

Kenneth L. Feder

ROWMAN & LITTLEFIELD
Lanham · Boulder · New York · London

Published by Rowman & Littlefield
An imprint of The Rowman & Littlefield Publishing Group, Inc.
4501 Forbes Boulevard, Suite 200, Lanham, Maryland 20706
www.rowman.com

6 Tinworth Street, London SE11 5AL, United Kingdom

British Library Cataloguing in Publication Information Available

Library of Congress Cataloging-in-Publication Data

Names: Feder, Kenneth L., author.
Title: Archaeological oddities : a field guide to forty claims of lost
 civilizations, ancient visitors, and other strange sites in North America
 / Kenneth L. Feder.
Description: Lanham, Maryland : Rowman & Littlefield, An imprint of The
 Rowman & Littlefield Publishing Group, Inc., [2019] | Includes
 bibliographical references and index.
Identifiers: LCCN 2018043446 (print) | LCCN 2018048470 (ebook) | ISBN
 9781538105979 (electronic) | ISBN 9781538105962 (cloth : alk. paper)
Subjects: LCSH: United States—Antiquities—Guidebooks. | United
 States—Antiquities—Reproduction. | Indians of North
 America—Antiquities—Guidebooks. | Indians of North
 America—Antiquities—Reproduction. | Curiosities and wonders—United
 States—Guidebooks. | America—Discovery and
 exploration—Pre-Columbian—Miscellanea—Guidebooks. | Forgery of
 antiquities.
Classification: LCC E159.5 (ebook) | LCC E159.5 .F42 2019 (print) | DDC
 970.01—dc23
LC record available at https://lccn.loc.gov/2018043446

♾™ The paper used in this publication meets the minimum requirements of American
National Standard for Information Sciences—Permanence of Paper for Printed Library
Materials, ANSI/NISO Z39.48-1992.

Printed in the United States of America

Contents

List of Figures

Preface

What I Did on My Summer Vacations (and Intersessions, Spring Breaks, and Too Many Long Weekends to Count)

$\mathscr{I}$ am an archaeologist. I continue to be amazed at how frequently, after telling that to people who ask what I do, I get the response: "Ooo! I've always been interested in that!" I admit it's quite gratifying to hear from strangers that they are fascinated by my profession.

When I relate that common reaction to the students in my introductory archaeology course—the great majority of whom are enrolled simply for general education credit and are majoring in just about anything other than archaeology—I let them in on a little secret. I tell them that when most of them will be asked their majors or their professions after college—at a family function, a party, a bar, or on the bus—the great majority of them will *not* get a reaction like that. Sorry, but it's the sad truth; in the history of the world, when someone has been asked their college major or profession and they have responded "accounting," no one has ever said, "Ooo! I've always been interested in that." Oh well.

I think the interest most people express about archaeology rests in their assumption that archaeologists get to spend a lot of their time in remarkable places where extraordinary evidence of ancient human cultures can be found. They think we focus our professional lives on digging up incredibly cool artifacts, objects made all the more interesting because we are the first people to see or touch them since they were left in the ground hundreds, thousands, tens of thousands, or even more years ago. The Great Sphinx and ancient burial chambers (figure P.1), masterfully flaked spear points and remarkable art etched on rock surfaces (figure P.2), pottery shards, impressive cliff dwellings, monumental pyramids—that's what most people think of when they imagine the kinds of things archaeologists deal with on a daily basis.

This is the point in the conversation where you might think I am about to disabuse you of these romantic notions of what archaeology is all about and

iStock ID: 516505363; Credit: gbarm

Figure P.1. Splendid monuments like the Great Sphinx of Egypt (top) and intriguing structures like the Chun Quoit burial chamber located in Cornwall, England (bottom), are emblematic of the ancient worlds investigated by archaeologists.

Courtesy of the author.

Figure P.2. Artifacts, like this 1,600-year-old stone blade found in Granby, Connecticut (top), can inform archaeologists about the technology of an ancient people, and this petroglyph (art etched into a rock surface) in Nine Mile Canyon, Utah (bottom), can tell us about their artistic and even their spiritual lives.

Courtesy of the author.

then tell you how it really is. But I can't do that. What I've just told you about archaeology is, in large measure, true. We archaeologists do devote our careers to studying the amazing things and places I've just enumerated, but not simply because those things are beautiful or interesting or remarkable, or even because they are old. Our focus is on the amazing and engaging stories we can tell about past and also present cultures through the study of those beautiful, interesting, remarkable, and sometimes ancient things that people left behind. It's no wonder to me that most people are interested in that.

I have always been fascinated by human antiquity, and I have been lucky enough to have carved out a career in which I get to actually do archaeology and then write about my work (figure P.3). Granted, I need to hire an accountant to do my taxes, and I appreciate their diligent efforts. I don't want to rub it in, but nope, I've never told an accountant: "Ooo! I've always been interested in that." Sorry to all you accountants reading this guide.

Recognizing that many people find the study of the human past inherently fascinating, I have spent the better part of my career attempting to communicate to those fascinated nonarchaeologists the real stories of the human past as revealed by real archaeological research, through the books and articles I have written, lectures I have given, interviews I have provided on cable television documentaries, and even through my Instagram (ancientamerica50sites) and twitter accounts (@fiftysitesbook).

Figure P.3.   Excavating a 3,000-year-old tool-making feature in Barkhamsted, Connecticut. The white-haired guy is the author.

My most recent book reflects this precisely: *Ancient America: Fifty Archaeological Sites to See for Yourself* (Feder 2017). I refer to that book as a "time travel guide" to fifty of the most interesting archaeological sites in the United States, all of which are open to the public. The book is filled with information about ancient burial mounds (figure P.4) and cliff dwellings (figure P. 5), gigantic free-standing pueblos, spectacular rock art (figure P.6), monumentally scaled ground drawings, and more. If this sounds like a ploy on my part to convince you to buy that book, well, that's very perceptive of you.

Along with focusing some of my publications on real-deal archaeology, I have also devoted a significant part of my career to writing about the many misconceptions people have about what the archaeological record actually tells us about human antiquity. I have written fairly extensively on the topic of what is often called "fringe" or "pseudo-archaeology" with its claims of archaeological oddities including evidence of: ancient aliens visiting the Earth in antiquity and mating (you read that right) with proto-humans (to create our current species); those same aliens providing technological secrets to our ancestors, enabling them to build pyramids and other great monuments; residents of the Lost Continent of Atlantis spreading to all corners of the world and giving primitive people agriculture, writing, and principles of engineering; seafaring Europeans and Southwest Asians traveling to the Americas long before the voyages of Christopher Columbus or even the Norse and interacting with the Native People of the

Figure P.4.   Cemetery Mound, Marietta, Ohio; one of the sites highlighted in my book *Ancient America: Fifty Archaeological Sites to See for Yourself.*

Figure P.5.   Square Tower House Ruin, one of the breathtaking cliff dwellings enshrined in Mesa Verde National Park in Colorado; *Ancient America: Fifty Archaeological Sites to See for Yourself.*

New World. I have written two books that focus on these and many other varieties of fake or speculative archaeology: *Frauds, Myths, and Mysteries: Science and Pseudoscience in Archaeology*, 9th edition (Feder 2018) and *Encyclopedia of Dubious Archaeology: From Atlantis to Walam Olum* (Feder 2010). If it seems like, there he goes again, shamelessly flogging more of his books, you'd be wrong. I am very much ashamed, but I wouldn't mind it if you devoted an entire bookshelf in your home library to my books. In fact, I think that would be a terrific idea.

This leads to an explanation of my purpose and perspective in this book. In fact, as the cliché goes, it's kind of a funny story. In late 2016, soon after the aforementioned *Ancient America* was sent to the printers, I had a very nice conversation with Leanne Silverman, then my editor at the publisher Rowman & Littlefield, just sort of wrapping up and decompressing after a very busy year of site visits, writing, editing, and indexing. Half-jokingly, I am sure, Leanne asked: "Okay, Kenny, when would you like to start working on *Ancient America II: Fifty More Archaeological Sites to See for Yourself?*"

I was, needless to say, a little taken aback by the question. I was exhausted after finishing *Ancient America* and didn't really want to think about another book, at least not right away. Of course, I loved working with the folks at Rowman & Littlefield—Leanne has since moved on but she was a joy to work with—and I certainly enjoy visiting archaeological sites and then writing about

Figure P.6. I included many rock art sites in my fifty sites book, including those located at McKee Springs in Dinosaur National Monument (top) and the Great Gallery in Horseshoe Canyon (bottom), both in Utah.

Courtesy of the author.

them in an effort to encourage people to personally visit and experience these magical places for themselves. So I didn't necessarily want to turn Leanne down or sound like I hadn't already given it some thought, but, in reality, I hadn't given the idea of a follow-up book any thought at all.

So I panicked. Synapses fired in my exhausted brain leading to an epiphany—or maybe it was insanity, you decide. Again, only half-seriously, I said: "Well, Leanne, you know of my existing interest and publications related to archaeology at the fringes. How about this: instead of a book simply highlighting fifty additional legitimate archaeological sites, what if I were to start a project that combined my interest in fake and strange sites—here called archaeological oddities—with the approach of my fifty real sites book, and do an equivalent travel guide to those curious places and objects, explaining why popular interpretations of those sites and artifacts are not necessarily accepted by professional archaeologists, but are nevertheless fascinating and worth seeing for yourself?"

At that moment there was a dramatic and lengthy pause in the conversation. I distinctly remember thinking, "Oh well, Leanne is going to think that's a terrible idea for a book," while at the same time I thought, "But, you know, that might actually be a pretty good idea." At last Leanne broke the silence and responded, "Hey, that sounds like it might be a lot of fun." I was surprised by her reaction and, at the same time, excited about the prospect of what my fevered brain imagined could be an entertaining and sort of twisted version of my fifty sites book; a field guide to strange, weird, dubious, or just plain odd archaeological sites or archaeologically themed places here in the United States. With Leanne's encouragement, in a couple of months I had submitted a prospectus for the book and soon thereafter signed a contract with Rowman & Littlefield. You are now holding a copy of that book in your hands or on your tablet.

At least from an author's perspective, Leanne's notion that such a book might be a lot of fun was absolutely spot on. Researching, conducting site visits, and writing about the fascinating places highlighted in this book, in fact, were all great fun for me. My fondest hope is that reading about these places and maybe even visiting them for yourself is as much fun for you.

One final point. Though initially this book was going to focus exclusively on archaeological sites that have been misrepresented in popular media, I decided that a relentlessly negative book—a play-by-play debunking of every one of the places featured on these pages—just might not be the kind of fun Leanne and I had in mind. After all, there are in North America a fair number of whimsical, entertaining, and even silly examples of the use of archaeology in an attempt to amuse and maybe even inspire people. In those cases, there is no attempt to fool visitors or support any particular ideology. These sites were created to entertain and are intended to be fun or thought provoking. So, as you will see, there is an entire category of these just-for-fun sites highlighted in this book as well.

In the following chapter I will introduce you to the entire concept of "archaeological oddities." I'll provide my breakdown of the types of archeological oddities discussed in this book—technically, a taxonomy of site types—with detailed descriptions of what those sites are about and, where appropriate, why archaeologists are skeptical of the validity or accuracy of some of their more extraordinary interpretations. Next I will provide a very short bit of background about real archaeology in North America, offering the professional archaeological consensus on the culture history of North America. After that I will present forty entries, each focusing on a particular site or sites. So now, as musician and composer David Bowie might phrase it, it is time to "turn and face the strange."

Acknowledgments

A book is always a collaborative effort and I have many to thank who provided time, expertise, and photographs in my endeavor here. A nonexhaustive list of those to whom I am in debt includes: Thomas Bell, Don Burgess, Christine Muratore Evans, Amy Higgins, Kevin Howard, Doug Jenzen, Brad Lepper, Jean-Loïc Le Quellec, Phil Senter, and Joseph Wilson. Also, a special thanks to all the great folks at the Johnson-Humrickhouse Museum and, especially, the Tule River Indian Tribe for graciously sharing of one of their sacred sites.

Finally, I have been lucky enough to work with the fantastic crew at Rowman & Littlefield, both past and present. Thanks so much to Leanne Silverman (past), and Charles Harmon and Elaine McGarraugh (present). They graciously put up with all of my oddities.

Turn and Face the Strange

Facts are stubborn things; and whatever may be our wishes, our inclinations, or the dictates of our passion, they cannot alter the state of facts and evidence.

—John Adams

$\mathcal{M}$any of the sites highlighted in this book have been presented by their supporters as real game changers. These places, they assert, will inevitably force historians and archaeologists to rethink everything they think they know—about the sources for ancient migration to North America, the assumed isolation of Earth from extraterrestrial civilizations, the literal truth of the Bible, the survival of dinosaurs into the modern era, and about lost tribes, lost cities, and lost continents. Back to the drawing board, for you conservative, skeptical, close-minded scientists and historians! You need to rewrite your textbooks and make room in them for the existence of wandering tribes and peripatetic mariners (which may be a mixed metaphor), for incontrovertible evidence of ancient visitors to Earth from outer space, for biblical proofs, and the existence or persistence of creatures thought either imaginary or extinct.

Hey, if there's actual, physical, archaeological evidence for any of those and similar claims, I'm all in. Nobody I know in my discipline is opposed to data that will revolutionize what we know about human antiquity. Ultimately, however, it's all about that physical, archaeological evidence. Do any of the sites I showcase in this guide present us with evidence that rises to the level of proof for any of the game-changing claims?

I began this chapter with an epigram attributed to John Adams, a lawyer, an author, a diplomat, and, of course, the second president of the United States. While there's no hip-hop Broadway musical about him (*yet!*), he clearly was a very smart guy and his statement about the importance of facts was, I think, rather precocious for an eighteenth-century thinker. Whatever we might like to believe, however we might wish things to be, facts and evidence trump those beliefs and wishes. What Adams articulated in the above quote is a philosophy that resides at the core of the modern scientific method.

What Adams didn't consider in his epigram about facts, however, is that as stubborn as facts may be, people can be even more so. When facts contradict a longstanding perspective, a cherished belief, a desired outcome, a fervent wish, or a personal bias, people have an amazing capacity to ignore those facts, to massage them or, in the most extreme approach, just make up new ones more to their liking. The denial of genuine evidence, the embrace of claims that fly in the face of facts, and a susceptibility to fraud and fakery, is, rather unfortunately, extremely common. Perpetual motion machines, the Loch Ness Monster, artificially constructed monuments on Mars, haunted houses—the list goes on and on. Scientists ask themselves this question all the time: "Why do people believe so much nonsense that science can readily debunk?"

In this regard, my own discipline of archaeology may be more sorely afflicted than many others. Archaeologists have, for centuries, gathered facts about the human past. By discovering, excavating, and analyzing the fragmentary remnants of the lives lived by past peoples, we cobble together the facts of the human story. But not everyone is happy with those facts or the stories we can tell. Sometimes the stories that archaeologists reconstruct relate to times and places about which people already have a preferred narrative filled with preconceptions, misconceptions, and biases. When those preexisting beliefs about the human past collide with the results of actual archaeological research, things can get adversarial in a hurry. Please don't get mad at us, but archaeologists find no evidence for the Garden of Eden or for a universal flood (Cline 2007). Don't shoot the messenger here; I'm just relating the facts as we currently know them. Please don't be too disappointed when I tell you that the archaeological record does not show that extraterrestrial aliens arrived on our planet thousands of years ago, instructed the Egyptians in how to build pyramids (figure 1.1) or interacted with Native Americans who left us artistic depictions of these interstellar visitors. Really. These claims or beliefs may be fascinating and you might want to believe them, but they are not accepted by scientists for one simple reason: they are not supported by, and in many cases they are directly contradicted by, those "stubborn facts" Adams was talking about. The history of American archaeology in particular is rife with examples of the rejection of archaeological fact in favor of flummery. That rejection occurs in the form of misinterpretation and misrepresentation of actual evidence, as well as through the creation of fraudulent archaeological data.

I should add here that not all "fake" sites have been perpetrated to convince people of anything in particular. Perhaps precisely because archaeology inspires

Figure 1.1.   The pyramids at Giza, in Egypt, were the product of decades of hard work by ancient Egyptians, including examples of mistakes and solutions achieved through the very human process of trial and error. They were not the product of ancient aliens.
iStock ID: 177047347; Credit: WitR

so much speculation, its history and the pages of this book are also filled with parody sites that are intentionally odd and openly fake, sometimes entertainingly so (figure 1.2). Archaeological sites have sometimes been concocted entirely for the sake of entertainment. There also are examples of fake archaeological sites that are intended neither to fool nor to make visitors laugh. Those sites were created to inspire and move people, to make them think and wonder. We'll talk about a couple of those in this book as well.

I have already mentioned two of my own books on the subject of fringe or pseudo-archaeology (*Frauds, Myths, and Mysteries: Science and Pseudoscience in Archaeology* and *Dubious Archaeology*). This book is different, focusing on forty specific instances of the rejection of archaeological facts and the creation of new ones. On its pages I provide an inventory—a "greatest hits"—of misrepresentation and fakery, not always with ill intent, related specifically to American antiquity. I'll do this by serving as your tour guide in both a metaphorical and literal sense. You'll be able to visit most of the places highlighted in this guide. You can see for yourself the weird sites where fake artifacts were planted, museums where archaeological frauds are housed and on display, and places where you can personally marvel at the ability of the human mind to convince itself that something is what it manifestly is not.

Figure 1.2.   How could anybody not love a life-size replica of the 4,500-year-old Stonehenge monument, especially one made of styrofoam? Foamhenge in now located in Centerville, Virginia.

I divide up my greatest hits of archaeological fakery in North America into nine categories:

1. **Ancient Visitors: Written Messages.** Here we will visit sites where ostensibly ancient messages written in an Old World language have been found carved into rock, a sort of affirmation of "we were here" by visitors to North America in antiquity.
2. **Ancient Visitors: Stone Monuments.** Within this category are monuments made of stone—primarily dry-laid stone chambers and geometrically arranged slabs of stone—that are claimed to resemble similar monuments in the Old World.
3. **Ancient Visitors: Villages.** In this case, the archaeological ruins of entire settlements have been proposed as representing the colonies of these Pre-Columbian visitors from the Old World. We'll take a look at a few of those as well.
4. **Ancient Visitors: Aliens.** Have extraterrestrial aliens visited Earth in antiquity, schooling primitive humans in an early version of STEM (science, technology, engineering, and mathematics) education? Within this category we will visit sites where genuine and truly splendid works of ancient art have been interpreted as representing the eyewitness

depictions by America's first people of extraterrestrial visitors to North America in antiquity. While we're at it, we'll take a look at a site that's only about sixty years old where some claim an extraterrestrial spacecraft crashed, depositing debris and in so doing created an archaeological site.

5. **Lost Civilizations.** In far more elaborate examples of numbers 1, 2, and 3 above, the remnants of entire lost civilizations are alleged to have been found in North America. In this scenario, an entire colony of migrants—perhaps from ancient Egypt, Greece, Rome, or Tibet—settled in North America, interacted with Native People, leaving behind fabulous riches which, though once hidden from view, can now be investigated.

6. **Biblical Proof?** These are North American sites that have been interpreted as in some way providing physical evidence for the literal truth of an element of or story in the Bible.

7. **New Age Antiquity.** Focused in Sedona, Arizona, individuals with a New Age perspective have interpreted archaeological sites as residing at the core of powerful and mystical vortices, paranormal channels to other dimensions. We'll visit a couple of those sites. Hopefully, during our visit, we won't get sucked into an Earth-energy vortex. But, you never know.

8. **Unexpected Critter Depictions.** These are North American sites where ancient works of rock art have been interpreted as depicting animals that either were thought long extinct at the time of their depiction or whose very existence has not been confirmed by Western science. Think dinosaurs in the former case. Think Sasquatch in the latter.

9. **Follies.** Not every site visited in this guide is "serious-strange." Some are parodies where the intent by their creators was not to fool but simply to entertain, amuse, and even to inspire.

I will describe in more detail each of these categories of my taxonomy of archaeological oddities preceding each section of the book.

FORMAT

Using these nine categories of archaeological oddities from my typology, I'll present information about the forty sites highlighted in this field guide consistently using the following headings:

Archaeological perspectives. I'll include a short statement providing a general archaeological perspective concerning the misrepresentation, fakery, or out and out silliness involved with the site. This section will not be scolding or professorial, but amusing, entertaining, and informative.

Here's what we know. Essentially, this will be a "biography" of the artifact or site. I include a discussion of what we know about its discovery and investigation: When was it found? By whom? Who has excavated or investigated the place? How has it been interpreted?

Why are archaeologists skeptical? Here's where I provide specific evidence for fakery and even a bit of archaeological epistemology to explain the skepticism of the archaeological community. We know the **Cardiff Giant** is a fake because the perpetrators confessed and we have the absurd sculpture in hand. That's easy. We also are very skeptical of the **Kensington Runestone**, not because the Norse couldn't have made it to Minnesota in the fourteenth century and left a runic message about their exploits, but because archaeologists are very good at tracking the movement of people into and through an area. The material, archaeological evidence that would support the claim of a Viking presence in Minnesota in the fourteenth century, simply isn't there (more about that piece of archaeological epistemology in the next chapter).

Whodunit? Here I share a little detective work in sussing out the perpetrator(s) of each archaeological fraud or the names of those most closely related to purveying fantasies about real sites. In some instances (the **Cardiff Giant**), the identities of those who pulled off the fake are certain. In other cases (the **Davenport Tablets**), the evidence is equivocal.

Why? It is interesting in the context of this guide to attempt to figure out what motivated the perpetrators of archaeological frauds and to attempt to diagnose why people are so susceptible to hoaxes and the misinterpretation of archaeological data. In each case, I'll try to provide explanations for the sometimes passionate embrace of weird archaeological sites or the misinterpretation of genuine ones.

Fake-o-meter. Here I will rate the degree of "fakeness" of the site on a zero-to-five scale with zero being the rating for a legitimate site and interpretation and five being entirely bogus. I've included sites about which there is some remaining uncertainty concerning authenticity, and there's even a ringer, a site that is definitely the real deal, as an example of how archaeologists assess controversial sites and accept them when the evidence warrants it.

Getting there. I will here supply the directions necessary for you to visit the place where people unhappy with real archaeological evidence attempted to reinterpret it or even supplant it with a concoction of their own design.

Before beginning our journey through the universe of North American archaeological oddities, let's take a look at what archaeologists actually do know about American antiquity.

· 2 ·

Here's What We Know

*O*nce it was established that there were human beings in the Americas—it actually took a papal pronouncement in 1536 (Huddleston 1967) to confirm that those curious bipeds inhabiting the lands of what, not Columbus, but Amerigo Vespucci called a "new world" were, indeed, human beings who needed to be converted to Catholicism—European scholars began speculating about when those human beings arrived here and where they came from.

Since they were fully human, it was clear that they must have been children of Adam and Eve and, because of the biblical flood, they also must have descended from Noah through one of his three sons: Shem, Ham, or Japheth. For biblical literalists, the goal of science was to determine the identity of the offspring of which of the three sons of Noah had moved to America once the great flood waters had receded. The human migration to the New World, in this view, must have occurred within the last six thousand years because in 1650 Bishop Ussher, the Archbishop of Ireland, had calculated 4004 BC as the year that God created the universe.

Though Bishop Ussher's timetable turns out to be highly compressed, at least one seventeenth-century Spanish cleric, José Acosta, suggested the Native People of the New World were transplanted Asians who had entered the Americas after the biblical flood via some sort of land connection located between northeast Asia and northwest North America (Huddleston 1967). That was a very precocious suggestion, and Acosta turns out to have been fundamentally correct, though he was off by more than fifteen thousand years in terms of the timing of that migration.

In fact, archaeologists now recognize that the most likely port of entry into the New World for human beings was located exactly where Acosta suggested it would be located. Today, a strait (called the Bering Strait) of only about ninety miles separates the Seward Peninsula of western Alaska and the Chukchi Penin-

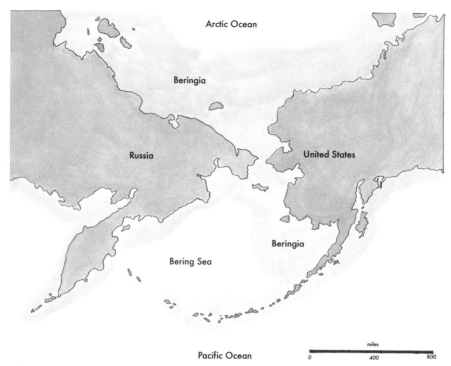

Figure 2.1. Intermittently between 40,000 and about 10,000 years ago, lowered sea level exposed a wide swath of dry land, creating a 1,000-mile-wide connection between northeast Asia and northwest North America. Animals and human beings in northeast Asia crossed this land "bridge," both in the interior and along the coast, and settled in North America.
Map by Jennifer Davis.

sula in far eastern Russia. During a period of maximum glacial expansion between about forty thousand and twelve thousand years ago, not only that strait but the entire area now under the Bering Sea was dry land, connecting the Old and New Worlds as the sea level lowered with so much ocean water tied up in glacial ice (figure 2.1). This dry land called Beringia stretched a thousand miles north to south providing, not just a bridge between two continents, but a vast plain allowing for the migration of millions of animals along with America's first people.

The scientific revolution following Darwin's (1859) publication of his seminal book *On the Origin of Species by Means of Natural Selection* was greatly affected by the recognition, at least by scientists, that for Darwinian evolution to work, the world must be ancient and changing, far older than the six thousand years that Bishop Ussher believed. This opened up a broad discussion of the actual age of Earth, where extinct species like dinosaurs fit into that expanding chronology, as well as the timing of the peopling of the Americas.

Even into the twentieth century, some scientists continued to believe that their arrival had been relatively recent. The general feeling, as championed by the Harvard anthropologist Aleš Hrdlička, a brilliant scientist without nearly enough vowels in his name, was that the Native People of the Americas had migrated here long after the end of the Pleistocene or "Ice Age" that occurred between 1.8 million and 10,000 years ago. Hrdlicka felt that this movement of people occurred substantially less than five thousand years ago. However, as archaeologists in North America began digging more deeply and into older deposits—and especially when a beautifully made spear point was recovered in the rib cage of the skeleton of a kind of bison known to have become extinct around ten thousand years ago—that pendulum swung, and by the 1960s a consensus was reached that placed the earliest human sites in the Americas in the period between twelve thousand and ten thousand years ago.

This view, sometimes called "Clovis First" (Clovis is the name applied to the culture that produced large stone spear points distinguished by channels or "flutes" chipped from both faces: figure 2.2), held fast for decades, but it always

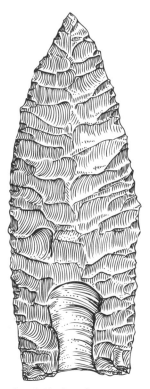

Figure 2.2.   Fluted Clovis points, stone spear points with a concave channel or "flute" on both faces, are found throughout North America dating to the period between 12,500 and 10,000 years ago. Though not the oldest artifacts found in the New World, Clovis represents the first widespread culture in the New World.
iStock ID: 502709647; Credit:IADA

had its critics, and after decades of discovery of sites that appeared to predate the twelve-thousand-year threshold, the Clovis First view has largely been abandoned by most, though not all, archaeologists. This overall shift of opinion has resulted from a growing number of pre-twelve-thousand-year-old sites that have been carefully excavated and accurately dated. For example, there's Manis, in Washington State, with a bone spear point lodged in the vertebra of a wooly mammoth dating to close to fourteen thousand years ago (Waters et al. 2011a); Meadowcroft Rockshelter in western Pennsylvania, a site occupied again and again beginning as much as sixteen thousand years ago (Adovasio et al. 1990); and the Debra L. Friedkin site in Texas with convincing dates of human occupancy exceeding fifteen thousand years ago (Waters et al. 2011b). Beyond this, of course if the people responsible for the sites just named entered the New World from the north and west, across a land connection between northeast Asia and northwest North America, well, it's a long walk to Pennsylvania and Texas and an even longer walk to places like the fourteen-thousand-year-old Monte Verde site in South America (Dillehay and Collins 1988). The initial arrival by human beings in Alaska must have occurred thousands of years earlier, and twenty thousand is a nice round number and a pretty good guess for their earliest entry into the New World.

This general date has received additional support from the genetic analysis of human remains found in the New World. An examination of both the DNA in the nuclei of human cells as well as in mitochondrial DNA (a form of DNA found in the mitochondria of cells and passed down only from mother to offspring) has shown that the earliest people in the Americas are most closely related to the people of northeast Asia and that their initial separation and subsequent divergence from their Asian forebears occurred about twenty thousand years ago (Moreno-Mayar et al. 2018; Rasmussen et al. 2014). This conforms nicely to archaeologically dated sites and the timing of Beringia. It's important to point out here that no DNA has ever been found in the ancient remains of Native Americans to suggest a population source or influx from anywhere but Asia (Raff and Bolnick 2015).

These earliest Americans adapted to the late Ice Age landscape of North America. Those living closest to the ice fields of the Pleistocene emphasized the large game—the so-called megafauna—that flourished in the tundra habitat, including wooly mammoths and mastodons, bison species far larger than the modern version, as well as horses and ground sloths (figure 2.3).

As climate changed following the Pleistocene, human groups already spread thinly across North America had to adapt to those changes in the flora and fauna that had dominated the landscape. There were no more wooly mammoths or mastodons, no more horses or giant ground sloths; entire species of bison became extinct. Over the course of a few thousand years the climates and plant and animal populations familiar to us in the modern world became

Figure 2.3.   The world of the late Pleistocene—the Ice Age—was far different from the modern world, filled with wooly mammoths, mastodons, giant ground sloths, and saber-toothed cats. This is the world the first Americans encountered and to which they adapted.
iStock ID: 536976819; Credit: CoreyFord

established, and people living in newly established habitats altered their adaptations to conform to the resources now available in their territories, setting the stage for the modern Native Peoples living in: the temperate woodlands of the northeastern United States; the hot and humid southeast; the coastlines of New England and the Northwestern United States and Canada; the arid semideserts and deserts of the Southwest; the grasslands of the northern plains.

The period following the Pleistocene is characterized by a diversification of subsistence strategies among the Native People of North America and a broad diversity of cultures. When Europeans arrived in North America, they did not encounter "Indians," a monolithic culture spread across the continent. They found, instead, as diverse and varied a group of cultures as that seen in Africa, Asia, or Europe living different lives, subsisting on very different food bases—including in some cases domesticated crops like maize (corn), beans, and squash, but also many more. Among the literally hundreds of different native groups, there were nomadic hunters and gatherers and sedentary farmers. Some lived in monumental apartment buildings of adobe, some in circular wigwams that could accommodate little more than a nuclear family, and some lived in enormous villages and even a city (Cahokia), whose populations peaked at ten thousand people (figure 2.4).

This isn't the time or place to provide a more detailed culture history of native North America; there are plenty of books that provide that, and even one that tells you how to visit some of the remarkable archaeological sites that reflect the vast array of native cultures (that would be my book, *Ancient America: Fifty Archaeological Sites to See for Yourself*, I've already mentioned that book at

Figure 2.4.   Monks Mound at the Native American city Cahokia is, by volume, the fifth largest pyramid in the world. Serving as the platform on which the ruler's house was constructed, it is a testament to the communal labor of the ancient city's population of more than 10,000. Cahokia was at its peak hundreds of years before European contact. It represents an entirely native North American civilization.

least once, but who's counting). Suffice it to say here, that in all of the archaeology done at the literally thousands of sites representing hundreds of different native societies in North America, there has never been convincing evidence produced for: the literal truth of the Bible; New Age interpretations of ancient sites; claimed visitation of North America by wandering Europeans, Africans, or Asians in the form of written messages, stone monuments, or entire villages produced by these visitors before the Norse exploration and short-lived settlement of North America about a thousand years ago; the presence of one or more non-native lost civilizations here in the New World; the presence of what amounts to a Peace Corps of helpful extraterrestrial visitors of North America in antiquity—or, well, ever; or the existence of large, hairy bipeds wandering the woodlands or plains of North America.

Most of the sites included in this field guide to North American archaeological oddities, however, are purported by some to provide the very evidence I have just denied exists. Well then, there's only one way to determine who's right about that. We need to visit these places and have a look at what the evidence actually shows. One important point before we proceed; whoever is correct in their interpretations of places like **Serpent Mound** and **Palatki**, **Gungywamp** and **America's Stonehenge**, **Dighton Rock** and the **Acton Stone Chamber**, it does not make these places any less interesting or important and, in keeping with my intention in this guide, it doesn't make these places any more or less worth visiting and experiencing for yourself.

THE SITES
(BY CATEGORY)

• 3 •

Category 1 Ancient Visitors: Written Messages

$\mathcal{A}$ number of the categories of archaeological oddities that I am using in this guide relate to claims of the presence in North America of foreign visitors or colonists in antiquity, some even of the extraterrestrial kind. It makes sense, therefore, to start our odyssey of the odd here, with claims that ancient people from Europe, Southwest Asia, or Africa arrived in the New World and left behind evidence of their presence. I'll focus in this section on the existence of written messages, so-called epigraphic artifacts.

Archaeologists recognize that different peoples bearing different cultures produce and use their own unique stuff. Their stuff—tools, cooking equipment, religious iconography, houses, burials, art, and the like—reflects their own unique traditions and doesn't look like the stuff produced by any other group. Archaeologists call that stuff a people's "material culture." That material culture, essentially, can be interpreted as the unique archaeological fingerprint of a particular human group.

When we're lucky, a lot of that material culture ends up in the ground, especially through discard and loss, it is preserved, and archaeologists find it. Elsewhere, I have compared archaeological fieldwork to detective work (Feder 2010). In detective work, forensic scientists collect material evidence of something that happened, perhaps only a day or so ago, and attempt to reconstruct events on the basis of that evidence. If we can say that detectives investigate the scene of a crime by collecting physical evidence, it's fair to say that archaeologists collect physical evidence in their broader investigation of the scene of a life lived by a group of people.

In many cases we can readily identify the group that deposited material evidence at a site because we can distinguish their stuff from the stuff left behind by other people bearing recognizably different material cultures. Similar to how a person's unique fingerprint can be used to identify him or her precisely in a criminal investigation, a group's unique material culture can be used to identify them precisely in an archaeological investigation. For example, the stuff made and used and which then became "archaeologized" (that's not a real word but I like the way it sounds) by Iroquois Indians of New York State in the seventeenth and eighteenth centuries or by the San People of the Kalahari Desert in southern Africa in the mid-twentieth century; by people of the Han dynasty of China in AD 200 or by the Maya of Mesoamerica in the sixth century AD; by medieval Norse in AD 1000 and by twenty-first-century Americans—each is unique, identifiable, and distinguishable from each of the others listed. You can't mistake one for another.

Explorers, intruders, immigrants, invaders, and colonists bring a subset their own, recognizably different stuff with them when they explore, intrude, migrate, invade, and colonize. Archaeologists are adept at recognizing the appearance of the new and intrusive material culture of groups moving into or through an area and, therefore, at recognizing the presence of these new folks exploring and colonizing a new (to them) territory.

Here's an obvious example. Archaeologists recognize the appearance of a new, nonlocal people entering into southern New England in the seventeenth century through the sudden appearance of a material culture very different from what was there before. In this example, the "new" material culture included glazed and wheel-made ceramics quite different from the nonglazed, coil-made pots of the native inhabitants of New England (figure 3.1). Archaeological work in New England also reveals the sudden appearance in the seventeenth century of previously unseen raw materials like iron and glass, neither of which had been part of the material culture of the people living in the region previously. That material culture is directly traceable to setters from Europe and, to reiterate, is recognizably different from the material culture produced by the Indigenous People. An archaeologist might say you just can't miss it, this rather sudden intrusion of a new and different material culture. Even if there were no definitive written documentation of the exploration and colonization of New England by people from Great Britain in the seventeenth century, the appearance of the material culture of those folks is a dead giveaway of their presence here (Feder 2018).

In another fascinating example of tracing intruders by their stuff, archaeologists have found a literal and figurative trail of artifacts including glass beads, brass bells, and iron tools left behind by Spanish explorers, including de Soto and his contingent of men when they traveled through the American Southeast in the early 1500s (Feder 1994). Like all people, these Spaniards left some of their stuff behind both accidentally—they lost stuff—and purposefully—by discarding broken or used-up objects as well as through trade with the Native

Figure 3.1. The ceramic technology and styles of the native peoples of New England (top) are recognizably different and distinct from those of the Europeans who settled in the Northeast in the seventeenth, eighteenth, and nineteenth centuries (bottom). Any archaeologist comparing the ceramics would recognize this and, even if completely unfamiliar with our local history, would conclude that a new and different people had entered the region solely on the basis of those technological and stylistic differences.

People. The Native People did not have glass beads or brass bells, for example, and those things only show up in sites in the American Southeast upon the Spanish arrival in the sixteenth century. Again, you can't miss the appearance of these out-of-place artifacts, and they are proof positive of the intrusion of a people different from the locals in the American Southeast.

This fundamental tenet of archaeology rests at the heart of archaeological skepticism concerning the validity of the artifacts we'll visit in this section (and much of what I say here generally applies to sections 2, 3, 4, and 5): none of these artifacts bearing ostensible messages in an Old World language were recovered from archaeological sites where items of everyday material culture would also have been found definitively proving the presence of ancient European or Asian or African visitors to the New World. The inscribed messages are all isolated phenomena not recovered in the broader context of a site that is clearly identifiable as belonging to travelers bearing the culture that used those scripts.

In other words and specifically, the writing on some of the stones we'll visit in this section has been identified as assorted forms of Hebrew, yet no ancient Hebrew artifacts of the kind recovered in excavations in Israel were found with the **Newark Holy Stones** in Ohio (Lepper and Gill 2000), the **Bat Creek Stone** in Tennessee (Mainfort and Kwas 1991), or the **Los Lunas Decalogue Stone** in New Mexico. No Norse artifacts of the kind and style found everywhere else they explored and settled, including Iceland, Greenland, as well as eastern North America (typical Viking house remains, soapstone spindle whorl, a ring-headed bronze pin), have been found in association with the **Kensington Runestone** in Minnesota (Kehoe 2005) or the **Heavener Runestone** in Oklahoma (Tompsen 2011). No diagnostic Old World artifacts—exhibiting a style consistent with an ancient Old World people or made of raw materials traceable to the Old World—were found alongside the **Davenport Tablets** in Iowa (McKusick 1991) or the **Grave Creek Stone** in West Virginia (Barnhart 1986). If ancient, seafaring Celts from Western Europe somehow managed to make their way to Picture Canyon in southeastern Colorado leaving messages etched into the walls of **Crack Cave**, they left no typical artifacts behind—they didn't discard or even lose anything—denoting their presence. The Templar Knights who, it is claimed, carved the image of a knight into a glacially weathered boulder in Massachusetts, left nothing else behind, and the written messages in several Old World scripts found on thousands of stone tablets that make up the **Michigan Relics** are similarly bereft of any other material evidence of the presence of interlopers in ancient Michigan (Halsey 2009). From an archaeological perspective, that's just an impossibility if the inscribed objects are genuine and found where they had been left in antiquity. Let's visit each of these sites in turn and examine the messages that are causing all the fuss.

1. CRACK CAVE, COMANCHE
NATIONAL GRASSLAND, COLORADO

Archaeological perspectives

The arrangement of lines etched into rock in Picture Canyon in the Comanche National Grasslands of far southeastern Colorado is an example of what is claimed by some to be an authentic message—in this case written in an ancient Irish script called ogham—left in North America by visitors to our shores long before Columbus arrived in 1492 and even before the Norse attempted to settle northeastern North America nearly five hundred years before Columbus, at around AD 1000.

Ogham was a form of alphabetic writing in Ireland dating to as much as two thousand years ago and most commonly found dating to the period between the sixth and ninth centuries AD. Altogether, about four hundred examples of ogham have been found primarily in Ireland and Wales (figure 3.2). Ogham

Figure 3.2.　A typical ogham message in England, consisting of an erect slab of stone with lines etched horizontally along the long axis of the rock.
From Green's History of the English People, 1874

ordinarily involved the use of an incised vertical line with shorter horizontal lines emanating from that vertical incision. Those individual horizontal lines were letters in an alphabet. Along with claimed ogham messages in Picture Canyon there also is, within the narrow separation in the bedrock today called Crack Cave, incised marks that appear to be illuminated by the sun during the spring and fall equinoxes, implying to some that those markings were part of a solar calendar (McGlone et al. 1993).

Genuine and ancient ogham in Colorado would be astonishing, implying the exploration and perhaps even the settlement of North America by people from western Europe—ancient Celts—long before Columbus. It also begs the questions: How did seafaring Celts end up so far from the sea in Colorado, and where is the trail of their archaeological sites leading from Colorado back to their maritime entry point to the New World?

Here's what we know

Picture Canyon is a lovely place, filled with evidence of its previous occupation by Native Americans. Tipi rings—circular clusters of stones used by Indians to hold down the margins of their tipis—have been found there along with household refuse including pottery sherds. There's also quite a bit of quite stunning rock art including petroglyphs and pictographs, and even combinations of the two: images incised into the rock that then were painted over (figure 3.3). This art—including depictions of bighorn sheep, antelope, horses, and human hunters—is believed to date to as recently as the seventeenth and eighteenth centuries, having been produced by members of the local Comanche tribe.

Another sort of art found in Picture Canyon consists primarily of incised lines. The most impressive of these is a cluster located in a shallow cave on the east margin of the canyon. It consists of a single horizontal line intersected at right angles by numerous vertical lines (figure 3.4). You can climb right up to it without too much trouble. It's actually pretty cool.

One interpretation presented for the panels of incised lines both in Picture Canyon and elsewhere in North America is that they represent examples of the aforementioned ancient ogham, proving the presence of Irish travelers to the New World in antiquity.

Okay, ogham's letters were made by short lines intersecting a long base line, so they share that in common with the petroglyph shown in figure 3.4. But not so fast. The image seen in figure 3.4 with a long, horizontal line intersected by short, vertical lines is off by ninety degrees from European ogham, with its long, vertical line intersected by a series of short, horizontal lines. Beyond this, the people who claim that petroglyphs like the one in figure 3.4 are written messages in ogham maintain that it is a unique variant of ogham that doesn't use

Figure 3.3.   An example of a painted petroglyph—a person with a spear in each hand—in Picture Canyon in southeastern Colorado (top). A stunning image of a horse, both etched and painted onto a rock wall in Picture Canyon, Colorado (bottom). As horses became extinct in North America at the end of the Ice Age and were only reintroduced after the Spanish entered into the Southwest in the sixteenth century, this image dates to no more than about 500 years ago.

Figure 3.4.   A petroglyph located in a little rock alcove in Picture Canyon. Though, like ogham, the image includes lots of shot lines intersecting a long one, unlike ogham, the long line is horizontal and the image toward the left appears to have antenna, giving the overall appearance of a centipede.

any vowels. All of those little lines are consonants, and it's the job of whomever is reading it to figure out, using his or her imagination, what the vowels are.

That's simply not true for genuine ogham in Europe. So, we have to accept the claim that ogham-literate Irish explorers arrived in the New World and they wanted to leave written messages, but, well, it had been such a long and tedious trip, they just decided to save some time and energy and not include any vowels. So, when William McGlone and Phillip Leonard translate New World ogham to read: "We are the people of the sun," and "The sun strikes here on the day of Bel" (McGlone et al. 1993), they are, in fact, making up about half of the letters. It's an interesting exercise, and you can make up lots of different and seemingly meaningful phrases, but it's not very convincing.

There actually are lots of examples of Native American rock art images in North America similar to the Picture Canyon example seen in figure 3.4. They're not messages in ogham; they're depictions of centipedes and millipedes (figure 3.5). In other Native American examples, the etched lines may be tally marks, a way of recording and keeping count of any one of a number of possible things: days or horses, for example. So, the interpretation of incised lines as ogham just doesn't hold up.

Figure 3.5. A rather obvious depiction of centipedes or millipedes. These petroglyphs are located in Moab, Utah. Depictions of many-legged insects are pretty common in the American Southwest.

Figure 3.6.   Peering into Crack Cave in Picture Canyon, Colorado, I was able to see one of the carved elements that some claim to represent part of an ancient European solar calendar.

How about the assertion that the sun illuminates the incised images located in the interior of Crack Cave as part of a solar calendar (figure 3.6)? Here's the deal. People usually will say that the sun rises in the East and sets in the West, but that's not true. Like a broken watch that's correct twice a day, the sun rises in the East and sets in the West, but only two days a year. Those days aren't random. They are the vernal (spring) and autumnal equinoxes. That means that any crevice in a rock wall that faces East or West will be illuminated by the sun, either at sunrise if it's facing East or sunset if it's facing West, two days during the year. The opening of Crack Cave, in fact, faces East. That's a product of geology—the positioning of the cliff—not human intervention. As a result, the illumination of the petroglyphs in the interior of Crack Cave may be entirely coincidental. Even if someone noticed that one particular spot on the interior wall of Crack Cave was briefly illuminated (somewhere between eight and twelve minutes) during sunrise a couple of days each year and marked the spot with a petroglyph, it doesn't mean much other than the unsurprising fact that the Native People of Colorado were perceptive. It certainly doesn't support the hypothesis that there were ancient Irish explorers of Picture Canyon.

Why are archaeologists skeptical?

Remember the discussion at the beginning of this section about how archaeologists recognize the appearance of a new people bearing a different culture in a region; it's all about finding evidence of their unique material culture, stuff that doesn't look like the material culture that was there before. And this is what resides at the core of archaeological skepticism of an ancient Irish presence in southeastern Colorado. If they, indeed, were the ones who left inscribed messages and calendars there in stone, they have to have been real neat freaks because they left nothing else behind: no artifacts typical of their culture, none of the kinds of things actually found by archaeologists working in Ireland. For most archaeologists investigating the possibility of new people moving into an area, the lack of any material culture reflecting their presence is a deal breaker.

There is one more thing, and it's a peculiar element underlying the interpretation of Crack Cave and a number of the other claims of the presence in ancient North America of Old World visitors. The peculiar element concerns their locations. One would expect that if seafaring travelers made it to the New World from the Old in antiquity, material evidence of those visits would be found near the sea; in other words, in coastal locations. Certainly that is true for much of the Norse evidence in Canada. Their one confirmed settlement is located on a peninsula on the island of Newfoundland.

So, in this context, it is mysterious in the extreme that Crack Cave is located in southeastern Colorado that is, at best, about seven hundred miles (straight line distance) from the nearest body of water, the Gulf of Mexico. That would have been one helluva trip for folks whose primary mode of travel was by ocean-going ships. This same peculiarity can be seen in the case of the **Heavener Runestone**, the **Los Lunas Decalogue Stone**, and, to a lesser extent, the **Kensington Runestone**. The locations of all of these inscribed artifacts are far removed from any possible maritime entry point for the maritime folks who are supposed to have left those inscribed messages.

As late as AD 1524, when Verrazano sailed into Narragansett Bay in Rhode Island where he moored his ship, he and his men traveled inland on foot only for a very few miles, never wanting to be too far from the only way they had of getting home. But in the case of Picture Canyon, some are suggesting that long before that, a hardy band of Irish travelers sailed across the Atlantic, into the Gulf of Mexico, moored their boat off the Texas coast, and then made a beeline to southeastern Colorado where they left a written message without vowels and a solar calendar whereupon they disappeared to history. Oh, and they left absolutely no archaeological footprint of their journey anywhere along the way. That is a neat trick. Unless we're considering the possibility of a parachute drop to Picture Canyon, it simply doesn't seem likely that these sites are what some claim them to be.

Whodunit?

Most of the incised and painted art located in Picture Canyon was produced by the Native Americans who lived in the area, perhaps primarily in the canyon itself. The graffiti written in Roman letters (modern English) that, in some cases, overlays that aboriginal art, was produced by recent European settlers and visitors.

Why?

The interpretation of some of the incised lines seen in Picture Canyon as ogham and the art in Crack Cave as astronomical note taking by those ogham-writing Irish visitors is championed by people who apparently think crediting European explorers makes for a more interesting story than that accepted by archaeologists and historians. In the view of those archaeologists and historians, the art in Picture Canyon was the product of the creativity of the Native People of Colorado, the Comanche and their immediate ancestors, for whom, by the way, there is ample evidence of their living there.

Fake-o-meter

Four.

Getting there

Getting there, of course, depends on where you're coming from. The biggest town near Comanche National Grasslands is Springfield, Colorado. Drive south from Springfield on Highway 287 for twenty miles. When you get to the town of Campo turn right (west) onto County Road J. Drive on County Road J for ten miles and then turn left (south) onto County Road 18. Take CR 18 for five miles, where you will see a sign directing you to turn right (south) to get to Picture Canyon. After the turn, drive for one mile to the parking lot. The hike is clearly marked from there. Most of the rock art is readily accessible and only takes a little exploring along established trails. Unfortunately, Crack Cave itself is gated and open only intermittently, but you can peer inside and see some of the rock art.

2. DAVENPORT TABLETS, DAVENPORT, IOWA

Archaeological perspectives

When English-speaking settlers spread from the Northeast to the American Midwest, they unexpectedly encountered the remains of sophisticated and monumental features built of earth. There were conical burial mounds up to seventy feet in height containing the remains of people and beautifully made artifacts, the grave goods intended for their use in the afterlife, perhaps. There also were large, earth-walled enclosures, containing as much as fifty acres of open space. Some were circular; others reflected a diversity of geometric shapes. Other mounds were earth sculptures in the form of gigantic representations of animals. There were bears and birds and, the most impressive of all, an effigy of a 1,350-foot-long snake (**Serpent Mound**). Other mounds were huge, truncated pyramids, flat-topped platforms as much as one hundred feet in height.

Many eighteenth-century English settlers were fascinated by these monumental features and wondered who had been responsible for their construction. A general aversion to giving credit to the most likely builders, the ancestors of the Native People of Ohio, Illinois, Indiana, Missouri, and so on, resulted in a period of speculation in which the mounds were credited to various Old World people: the Lost Tribes of Israel were a popular explanation, but, at one time or another, the mounds were credited to ancient Egyptians, South Asians, Greeks, Romans, and Scythians. Again, anybody but Native Americans. The mounds in Davenport, Iowa, though not particularly imposing, were raised to great importance in the debate when, in the winter of 1877, a series of stone tablets were found within one of them. The tablets appeared to have writing on them that could be traced to ancient people in the Old World. This brings us to the story of the discoverer of those tablets, the Reverend Jacob Gass.

Here's what we know

Reverend Gass was an outsider, a nineteenth-century immigrant from Switzerland to the community of Davenport, Iowa. From all that I can gather, he didn't exactly ingratiate himself among the locals—especially those who weren't German speakers—and was generally disliked. He especially appears to have rubbed people the wrong way concerning local archaeology.

Across the Midwest, including Iowa, people dug through ancient mounds, essentially mining them for artifacts. Before Gass moved to Davenport in 1868, there had been a number of excavations of sites in the area, reflecting a general interest concerning the age and cultural affiliations of the ancient earthen mounds that dotted the region. The hope was that some definitive, diagnostic artifacts would be found—for example, a tool made from a raw material and reflecting a style or technology not known to local Indians but common in the Old World. Perhaps a dig might reveal the presence of an inscribed object bearing a written language traceable to a culture and people in Europe or Asia. Such discoveries would solve the mound-builder mystery and allow for their identification as the features of an ancient culture from the Old World that had traveled to the New long before Columbus.

Iowa wasn't exactly the center of ancient mound-building cultures, and it isn't terribly surprising that the excavations in the area around Davenport had been relatively unproductive, providing no evidence that might solve the mound-builder mystery. This changed, however, after Reverend Gass arrived on the scene and, in 1874, hit archaeological pay dirt at Mound 3 located on the local Cook family farm. In that mound, Gass discovered a cache of finely made copper axes, copper beads, beautiful pottery, and carved smoking pipes. His excavations in 1874 put to shame the previous discoveries of arrow points and pottery shards that characterized digs in the area. Gass is rumored to have lorded his unique discovery over the locals, asserting that he had been successful in finding important artifacts because he wasn't afraid of a little hard work in his archaeological endeavors.

The results of this dig were published in the first volume of the *Proceedings of the Davenport Academy of Sciences* in an article written by R. J. Farquharson (1876), a local medical doctor with a deep interest in archaeology. The Academy was an organization that catered to local professional men, sponsoring lectures on scientific topics and conducting fieldwork, including archaeological excavations. If you were an educated man in greater Davenport in the late nineteenth century, you either already were a member of the Academy or you wanted to be.

Under the aegis of the Davenport Academy, Gass returned to excavate at the farm in January 1877, which is a bit strange. Cold air temperatures and frozen ground in the dead of a Midwestern winter do not create the best conditions for an archaeological dig. Gass explained the necessity of excavating in the winter as the result of a new tenant taking over farming operations at Cook's farm in the spring. The new tenant, word had it, would no longer be granting permission to conduct excavations on the property. Anyway, it is during this winter excavation that Gass and his crew, after literally pickaxing through a thick layer of frozen ground, discovered three amazing and utterly unexpected artifacts: two slate tablets bearing remarkable images and inscriptions that appeared to reflect a number of different Old World written languages along with a limestone tablet bearing images in relief of a person—who, disturbingly, is depicted with the sun in his crotch and a happy face on his chest—along with depictions of two animal effigy pipes, the Roman numeral VIII, and the Arabic number 8. The announcement of discovery appears in volume II of the *Proceedings of the Davenport Academy of Sciences*, dated January 26, 1877:

> A communication was read from the Rev. J. Gass, describing the discovery on the 10th inst. [?] of two inscribed tablets, in a recent further excavation of the mound on Cook's farm near this city, heretofore described in these Proceedings. (82)

Later in the same volume, Gass himself describes the discovery:

> Two inscribed tablets of coal slate (Plates I, II and III), which, with other relics from the mound, are now in the Museum of the Academy. The two

tablets were lying close together on the hard clay, in the northwest corner of the grave, about five and one-half feet below the surface of the mound, the larger one to the southward and the smaller one north of it. The smaller one is engraved on one side only, and the larger on both sides. (Gass 1876–1878: 96)

Why are archaeologists skeptical?

Of course, the discovery generated quite a bit of interest; perhaps a Swiss emigre had cracked the case of the mound builders of North America. But there were problems. The tablet with both sides inscribed possessed a hodgepodge of images. On one side there is a sun, a moon, three recumbent people (dead bodies?), apparent smoke rising from a fire surrounded by more than a dozen people holding hands, topped off with a bunch of random written, perhaps alphabetic characters (figure 3.7). On the other side are several unidentifiable animals, a few people (one of whom seems to be butchering a deer), plants, and one large tree (figure 3.8). The other slate tablet exhibits four concentric circles with im-

Figure 3.7. One of the Davenport Tablets, found in Davenport, Iowa, in 1877. The raw material is slate, precisely the same material used in the roof of the local house of prostitution. The images are a bizarre pastiche and bear no clear relationship to any ancient culture or language.

Figure 3.8.   This is the reverse side of the image seen in figure 3.7. There are images of trees, various animals, and maybe two horizontally positioned obelisks. Again, the "artwork" on the tablet cannot be traced to any ancient culture. It was a fake.

ages in each ring (figure 3.9). It has been suggested that this represents a zodiac. As can be readily seen, all of the drawings are amateurishly rendered, not much more than stick figures, the kind of thing you might expect in the notebook doodlings of a bored middle school student without any serious drawing skills. Its appearance is wholly unlike what you would expect in an authentic artifact.

The lettering on the first tablet, rather than conveying any coherent message in a single Old World written language, instead exhibited characters that appeared to be Roman and Greek. About a hundred years after its discovery, marine biologist Barry Fell (1976) claimed that he could also identify characters in Egyptian, Phoenician, and Iberian languages on the large, slate tablet. This, of course, makes no sense in a genuine artifact intended to convey a readable message—a prayer, a land claim, a bit of history. Imagine a message in which some words were in English, some in French, one in Portuguese, and another in Chinese. It makes no sense and seems to reflect a scenario in which someone is simply trying to make Gass appear to be foolish if he embraces the authenticity of an object bearing a meaningless and apparently random series of unrelated characters from entirely different written languages.

Cyrus Thomas (1894), who was hired by the Smithsonian Institution to investigate the mystery of the mounds and to draw conclusions regarding their age and origin, examined photographs of the Davenport Tablets and declared them to be frauds in the pages of *Science*, then and now the preeminent science magazine in North America (Thomas 1885).

It is also important to point out that in Gass's report of the excavation to the Davenport Academy, he described the soil above the finds as "loose" and mentioned that human bones in the mound were scattered about. That sounds suspiciously like a disturbed context for the tablets, like someone had recently dug into the mound to plant them there. Furthermore, the limestone tablet with the VIII and 8 inscriptions was reported to have been found in a little crypt made of loosely fitted stones located at the base of the mound. All of those present upon its discovery testified that the little crypt was devoid of anything other than the tablet; there had been no infilling from the soil that surrounded the crypt during the, perhaps, two thousand years it had supposedly lain there. Cyrus Thomas in the above-mentioned *Science* commentary mused on the improbability of this if the crypt was authentically ancient. Water seeping through the soil of the several feet of mound above the crypt for a couple of thousand years certainly would have caused it to fill with dirt. This also would seem to support the hypothesis that the mound had been broken into not that long before Gass's dig and the fake objects had been inserted.

With all of the other issues raised about the context of discovery and the bizarre inscriptions, ultimately the raw material on which the inscriptions were made was a dead giveaway. Rather than being an exotic material brought in from afar by those artistic and literate Roman/Phoenician/Egyptian/Greek/Iberian travelers to Iowa (perhaps they came for their famous corn?), it was precisely the same raw material that roofed a building very nearby the Davenport Academy building. The zodiacal slate actually exhibits the nail holes where it would have been attached to the subroof (see figure 3.9). Seriously. The fact that the building with the slate roof was known as a house of prostitution isn't necessarily relevant, but it's a juicy tidbit nonetheless.

Figure 3.9. Called "the Zodiac," for a presumed astrological connection, this tablet actually bears nail holes that match those on the slate tiles of Davenport's nineteenth-century house of prostitution. There could hardly be clearer evidence that the artifacts were fake.

Whodunit?

There is a smoking gun—however imperfect—concerning the tablets in the form of a confession by an individual who claimed to have personally participated in the fraud. Archaeologist Marshall McKusick (1991; his book is the gold standard treatment of the Davenport Tablets) was able to track down an admission in which the confessed conspirator—Judge James Willis Bollinger, who died in 1951—revealed that, indeed, members of the Academy disliked Gass intensely. In his recorded confession, he stated: "We had no respect for Reverend Gass because he was the biggest windjammer and liar and everyone knew he was. We wanted to shut him up once and for all" (cited in McKusick 1991:

125). Bollinger explained that he and his buddies, all members of the Davenport Academy, hoped to make Gass appear foolish by fabricating the inscriptions and then planting them in the mound, expecting that he would find them and gullibly accept them as genuine, which seems to be exactly what happened. All of that makes sense, but, there is a serious problem. As McKusick points out, Bollinger was only nine years old in 1877 when the hoax was perpetrated. It is extremely unlikely that he was personally involved and, therefore, his account is not firsthand. So much of the confession rings true, however, it is at least plausible that Bollinger heard the story as an adult member of the Davenport Academy from one or more of the conspirators and injected himself into the tale to add importance to his role. So, Bollinger obviously didn't participate in the conspiracy but may have heard the story from someone who did. Maybe.

Most researchers today do not believe that Gass was the one responsible for creating and then planting the fraudulent tablets. He was, instead, their target. Though we may never know exactly who the perpetrators were, almost certainly it was other members of the Davenport Academy.

Why?

If, as seems probable, the perps were other members of the Davenport Academy, their likely motive was to embarrass and even humiliate Gass, just as Bollinger asserted. Gass was a foreigner and a newcomer; he was overbearing, overconfident, and thought he was a much better archaeologist than local people whose discoveries paled in comparison to his. What better way would there have been to put him in his place than by fabricating a very cheesy looking artifact or two—but artifacts that would seem to be momentous in their implications concerning a topic that fascinated so many people—and then positioning them in the mound where Gass would almost certainly find them? In this scenario, as often happens, the purported discovery would be of immense scientific import, captured so much attention that the perps elected not to pull the trigger on the hoax, concerned that instead of humiliating Gass, a tide of public anger would turn on them.

Fake-o-meter

The Davenport Tablets were a cheesy fraud. Five.

Getting there

The Davenport Tablets are on permanent display at the Putnam Museum in Davenport, Iowa. It's a terrific museum and, even though the tablets are fake, the modern curators have embraced them as a wonderful and important part of local history. The larger of the two tablets—the one with an inscription on both faces—was long ago split along a cleavage plane in the slate. This enables the museum to display both faces of the artifact simultaneously. The images on the tablets are silly—I've already used the word *cheesy* only because it's the best word to describe them—but well worth a look. The museum is located at 1717 West 12th Street in Davenport, Iowa. It's open seven days a week (check the website for hours and holidays: http://www.putnam.org).

3. DIGHTON ROCK, BERKLEY, MASSACHUSETTS

Archaeological perspectives

The forty-ton sandstone boulder now known as Dighton Rock has been protected from the elements since 1973. Now ensconced in a glass-walled enclosure within its own, dedicated museum, the rock originally lay in repose very nearby in the middle of the Taunton River in Massachusetts. The Taunton is a tidal stream whose level rises and falls with the ebb and flow of the tides in Narragansett Bay. In its original location, Dighton Rock was fully submerged during periods of high tide, only to reappear twice daily, as if by magic, when the tides lowered.

Each time it would reappear, the multiple and overlapping inscriptions on Dighton Rock were exposed to view, a fact first recorded by white settlers to the region in about 1680. In an area with some, but certainly not a substantial, amount of rock art, that discovery inspired a rising tide of speculation about what those inscriptions meant, how old they were, and who left them behind on the large boulder in the river. Was it ancient Phoenician visitors to America, who thousands of years ago left behind a statement that effectively says "we were here"? Perhaps the rock bears a message from Thorfinn Karlsefni, a Viking who may have passed the rock on his way to establish a settlement on Vinland (Newfoundland in Canada) in the early eleventh century, following that island's exploration by Leif Ericson (see the **L'anse aux Meadows** entry in this book). Or does the inscription on Dighton Rock record the melancholic cry of an early sixteenth-century Portuguese navigator, Miguel Corte-Real, a brief record of a doomed search for his brother Gaspar who had disappeared on his own nautical expedition into the Atlantic in 1501 (Delabarre 1936)? Edmund Burke Delabarre (who was not an archaeologist or historian but a psychology professor at Brown University in Rhode Island) was so enamored of the notion that a sixteenth-century Portuguese navigator was responsible for the inscription, he dedicated his 1928 book on the subject to that navigator, Miguel Corte-Real, identifying him as the "First European dweller in New England." Or was the inscription on Dighton Rock, after all, merely a marvelous example of Native American picture writing, perhaps the record of a religious ceremony or maybe of a historical event?

Here's what we know

The existence of a large rock in the Taunton River covered with inscriptions was noted by the colonist Cotton Mather—he of Salem Witch Trial fame (well, infamy)—in a sermon of "thanksgiving" that he gave in 1689. In that sermon, Mather described a "mighty rock" in the river and said it was "deeply engraved" with what he called "strange characters." In that sermon, Mather correctly and unambiguously identified the authors of those "strange characters" as the "Indian people."

Of course, that was the simplest answer, and though Mather was wrong about the existence of supernatural, malevolent witchcraft, he almost certainly was right about the Dighton Rock inscriptions. Take a look at the rock as a whole (figure 3.10). Unfortunately, much of the rock art is so weathered as to be indecipherable. Regular submergence in the waters of the Taunton River for hundreds of years has not been kind to preservation of the petroglyphs etched into the surface of the stone. Nevertheless, after playing with my photos a bit and boosting the contrast, you can make out a pretty clear depiction of an antlered animal (figure 3.11), in this part of the world almost certainly a white-tailed deer. There are also a couple of anthropomorphs, humanlike beings, with round faces, circular eyes and mouths, and armless and legless geometric forms for bodies (figure 3.12).

While the rock is covered with other markings, it's extremely difficult to make out what those markings may have actually been depicting when they were freshly made. There certainly does not appear to be writing on the stone identifiable as an ancient Old World script; no Phoenician, no Viking runes, no numbers, or, for that matter, messages in Portuguese. Nevertheless, ever since

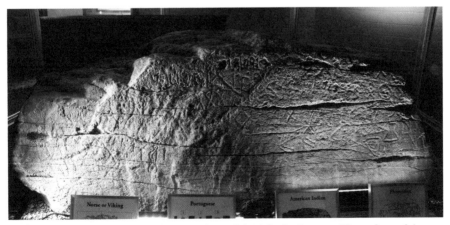

Figure 3.10.   Broad view of Dighton Rock. No longer in the Taunton River, the rock is now housed in its own museum. It is covered with petroglyphs, all of which are very clearly Native American.

Figure 3.11.   An antlered quadruped on Dighton Rock.

Mather shared his definitive judgment identifying the creators of the images on Dighton Rock in the late seventeenth century, a sequence of speculations has been offered about authorship of the inscriptions. Researcher and author Douglas Hunter's (2017) book, *The Place of Stone: Dighton Rock and the Erasure of America's Indigenous Past*, is a marvelously detailed account of Dighton Rock, and he enumerates and explicates the many lame attempts made to connect it to an Old World people in antiquity.

Why are archaeologists skeptical?

So why didn't it end there, with Dighton Rock highlighted in books about New England Indians or Indian rock art instead of in a book with "oddities" in its title? Perhaps one reason for the rejection of Mather's lead in recognizing that the petroglyphs on Dighton Rock were the work of local Indigenous People can be traced to the fact that, while many European immigrants to America were at least aware of the existence of Native American rock art including petroglyphs (inscribed) and pictographs (painted) in the American West, not many were aware that such things exist in northeastern North America as well. Indeed, there is an abundance of petroglyphs and pictographs in the American Southwest, especially in New Mexico, Arizona, Utah, Nevada, and southern California. However,

Figure 3.12. A ghostly, humanlike figure appears on Dighton Rock.

though not found in protrusion, there is rock art in much of the rest of the country as well as in Canada: beyond those Southwestern states just mentioned, I have personally examined Native American rock art in Washington, Minnesota, Ohio, North Carolina, Georgia, Vermont, and Massachusetts. Rock art in New England in general and Massachusetts specifically may not be nearly as common and as well known as it is in the Southwest, but it's certainly here; in fact, researcher and author Ed Lenik (2002; 2008) has written two entire books on the subject of American Indian rock art in northeastern North America.

As a result, archaeologists are skeptical of a non-Indigenous source for the inscriptions on Dighton Rock since they conform well with Indigenous rock art found elsewhere in New England. No external source is necessary to explain it. Add to this the fact that:

1. There is no clear evidence of non-native symbols on the rock.
2. There is no identifiable actual writing on the rock beyond modern graffiti.
3. There isn't any consensus among those who believe the rock bears written messages in a non-native language about what those messages state, much less what language is reflected on the rock.
4. There is no archaeological evidence for the existence of non–Native People in New England before Europeans moved into the region in the seventeenth century (see the introductory essay that opens this section of the book).

So yes, there is great skepticism on the part of historians and archaeologists that Dighton Rock is anything but a boulder bearing ancient Native American rock art imagery.

Whodunit?

The small museum in which the rock is housed conveniently provides reconstructions of what the inscriptions would have looked like when fresh to match what some past interpreters thought they saw. Of course, those reconstructions are entirely different and reflect, not so much what's really there, but what they wanted to see to support their interpretation. Douglas Hunter (2017) insightfully explains this interesting aspect concerning the speculations about the source and origins of the inscriptions on Dighton Rock. He sees the sequence of these interpretations as a microcosm reflecting the sequence of speculations about who may have arrived in the New World in antiquity. In other words, when Vikings were popular, this is when people began seeing Norse runes on the stone. When, in the greater world of archaeological speculation, it was popular to wonder about the presence of ancient visitors to the New World from the Middle East, the inscription on Dighton Rock was read as Phoenician. So, in answering "whodunit" we need to point fingers at different thinkers at different periods of American history, each of whom wished to make a material connection between ancient America and peoples known from Old World history.

Why?

Why have people taken what is most reasonably interpreted as a wonderful example of Native American rock art and used its imagery in the manner of a Rorschach test in the search for evidence of ancient exploration of the New World? Hunter (2017) maintains that it's all about cultural erasure and appropriation. By this he means that explorers and colonists of the New World were caught in a conundrum when they encountered artifacts or features in the New World that reflected great intelligence and sophistication on the part of the Indigenous inhabitants. Many of those explorers and colonists were firmly committed to the notion that the Native Peoples of the New World were neither intelligent nor sophisticated. To them, the existence of beautiful rock art, elaborate and well-made artifacts, and monumental constructions (specifically, the earthworks of the American Midwest and Southeast) simply didn't jibe with their assumptions about the limited capabilities of Indigenous People. A well-respected nineteenth-century expert in Native American culture, George Catlin (1838), assured skeptics that American Indians did, in fact, carve images into stone. His examination of Dighton Rock led Catlin to conclude "they are the works of Indian hands," and he maintained that he had seen "many similar productions in the western country." But because of the bias of so many, Catlin's conclusions went largely unheeded. Hunter (2017: 162) chillingly labels this effort to deny credit to Indians for their artistic creations "retroactive ethnic cleansing," part of an effort to deny the essential humanity of the Native People of the New World. Other people were capable of etching images onto rock. In this biased view, Indians were not, so the art on Dighton Rock needed to be credited to someone else.

Finally, a bit of ethnic pride comes into play in the interpretation of Dighton Rock by some members of the Portuguese community. Just as we will see ethnic boosterism on the part of Scandinavian Americans concerning the Kensington Runestone, there is great pride taken in at least the possibility that a Portuguese navigator actually made it to New England more than one hundred years before the British settlers arrived to establish the Plimouth colony. There is no question that the Corte-Real brothers alluded to at the beginning of this entry were real people and, indeed, brave sailors. As Douglas Hunter (2017: 1) describes it, several hundred people of Portuguese descent made a pilgrimage to Dighton Rock in 2011 to honor the memory of Gaspar and Miguel and to celebrate what they referred to as "500 years in southern New England." Those five hundred years were calculated on the basis of the date "1511" claimed to be visible on the surface of Dighton Rock adjacent to the name "MIGUEL COR-TEREAL" and nearby four crosses. The fact that most people don't see any of these inscriptions should not be interpreted by anyone as a slap in the face of those brave Portuguese explorers.

Fake-o-meter

As a wonderful example of Native American rock art in Eastern North America: zero. As the written inscriptions of some other group: five.

Getting there

Dighton Rock is located, as previously noted, in its own little museum in the appropriately named Dighton Rock State Park in the town of Berkley, Massachusetts (just south of the larger community of Taunton). The park entrance is located on Bayview Avenue in Berkley. Enter the park on 3rd Avenue (which oddly then becomes 2nd Avenue) and take that to the parking lot. Dighton Rock is housed in the white building near the lot and butting up against the Taunton River. There is one complication in seeing Dighton Rock; although the park is open seven days a week, the museum is open only by appointment. Call 508-822-7537 for access. I know it's a pain, but I've never had any trouble seeing the rock, and in my experience the State Park folks have been very helpful and accommodating.

4. WESTFORD KNIGHT, WESTFORD, MASSACHUSETTS

Archaeological perspectives

Two pieces of art, half a world away, lie at the heart of this oddity. We begin in Scotland at the fifteenth-century Rosslyn Chapel in Roslin, Midlothian. The chapel was built by the Scottish earl William Sinclair. If you've read the novel or seen the movie *The Da Vinci Code*, this is the very church where the Holy Grail is supposed to be hidden. However, this entry isn't related to the Grail but to a work of art in the Rosslyn Chapel that is asserted by some to represent a New World crop, corn.

Archaeological evidence for the movement of a plant species from one place to another on our planet preferably includes actual fragments of the plant: seeds, pits, nut fragments, that sort of thing. Pollen may also provide firm evidence for such a movement. Finding plant parts or plant pollen far removed from where the species originated represents solid evidence for the movement of that plant into a new territory.

That brings us back to "corn," labeled that by the European explorers who first encountered it because they didn't know what else to call it. To them, "corn" was a general term for any seed crop; wheat, rye, oats, and barley were merely different varieties of corn. Maize—we'll use the more technically correct term—is a New World cultigen that today is grown all over the world and serves as one of humanity's most important food crops for feeding people and their livestock. It did not begin its spread beyond the Americas until after Columbus brought samples back with him late in the fifteenth century, perhaps as early as 1493, and certainly by 1496.

Rosslyn Chapel in Scotland was built in the middle of the fifteenth century, so about fifty years before Columbus's first voyage and, therefore, before anyone there would have known about maize. However, over one of the windows in the chapel are carvings that some have suggested are, in fact, depictions of corn cobs (figure 3.13). Despite the complete lack of supporting archaeological evidence—

Figure 3.13. The carvings along one of the windows in Rosslyn Chapel in Scotland are claimed by some to be of the Native American crop, maize (corn). Two problems arise in this interpretation: the chapel was built fifty years before Columbus brought back knowledge of maize to the Old World and, well, it doesn't really look like maize.

Wikicommons/Kjetil Bjørnsrud.

no kernels, no cobs, no pollen—some take this to mean that a Scottish explorer visited the New World before Columbus and before the chapel was built and either brought back samples of maize or had recorded a detailed description of the crop and its imagery was incorporated into the chapel building. Some people even claim to know who that explorer was: the Scottish earl Henry Sinclair, and here's the connection; his grandson William built Rosslyn Chapel. Supporters of this claim further believe there is evidence of Henry's visit in the second piece of art alluded to at the beginning of this entry and our focus here: the Westford Knight in northern Massachusetts.

Here's what we know

That some sort of petroglyph or carving had been incised into a glacially striated boulder in Westford, Massachusetts, was first noted in 1873 in the book titled *A Gazetteer of the State of Massachusetts*. Within the context of a general discussion of the geology of the state, with an emphasis on economically valuable rock types, the author notes for the town of Westford:

> The mineral called "andalusite" is found here; and an immense ledge which crops out near the Centre has upon its surface ridges furrowed in former times by glacial forces. There is upon its face a rude figure, supposed to have been cut by some Indian artist.
>
> (https://archive.org/stream/gazetteerofstate00innaso/gazetteerofstate00 innaso_djvu.txt)

Ten years later, the carving was noted again, this time in a town history:

> A broad ledge, which crops out near the house of William Kittredge, has upon its surface grooves made by glaciers in some far-off geological age. Rude outlines of the human face have been traced upon it, and the figure is said to be the work of Indians.
>
> (https://archive.org/stream/historytownwest01hodggoog/historytown west01hodggoog_djvu.txt)

So, undeniably, in the late nineteenth century, local people had noted the presence of a "rude" carving on an exposed piece of bedrock located in Westford, Massachusetts, crediting local Indians for the artwork. That Indians might have incised a petroglyph in Massachusetts isn't terribly surprising. Though, as noted previously, rock art is more common in the American Southwest—we've just visited a terrific example, **Dighton Rock**, also in Massachusetts (Hunter 2017). As a result, no one, at least initially, made much of a fuss about the Westford image.

Then, about sixty years later in the 1940s, along came William Goodwin, who is a key player in the interpretation of **Mystery Hill** (now called **America's**

Stonehenge) in New Hampshire as a Pre-Columbian settlement of Irish monks. Here's where it gets weird; Goodwin (1946) mentions the Westford carving and even includes a sketch of it in his book, *The Ruins of Great Ireland in New England*. But it's not a "rude figure" or the "rude outlines of a human face" anymore. Goodwin identifies and depicts the image very clearly as "a broken sword . . . an ancient symbol of a warrior's death" (figure 3.14). From crude figure to obvious sword in less than one hundred years is quite a jump, isn't it? Here's my photograph of the stone as it looked in 2009 (figure 3.15).

Next up is Frank Glynn, a long-time member of the Archaeological Society of Connecticut, an organization of which I am a member; I even once was its president, but long after the tenure of Mr. Glynn. Glynn visited Westford in the early 1950s and remarkably saw far more—and in far more detail—than

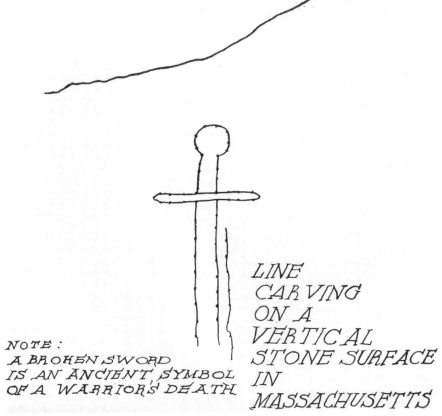

NOTE :
A BROKEN SWORD
IS AN ANCIENT SYMBOL
OF A WARRIORS DEATH

LINE
CARVING
ON A
VERTICAL
STONE SURFACE
IN
MASSACHUSETTS

Figure 3.14. Dating to the 1940s, William Goodwin's drawing of the so-called Westford Knight in Westford, Massachusetts, shows little more than the incomplete sword that is still visible on the rock. There is no detailed depiction of a Templar Knight, as some later observers have claimed.

Public domain.

Figure 3.15.   This is what the Westford Knight image looked like when I photographed it in 2009. The rock is now partially encased in plexiglass. The only clear image is of an incomplete sword.

anyone had before. So certain was he of his interpretation, he helpfully (I'm being sarcastic here) chalked it in, just in case no one else could make out what he could. Glynn's heightened ability to perceive the image on the rock allowed him to see a fully decked-out, helmeted, medieval knight holding a sword along with a shield that no one had seen before. And that I can't see today.

Why are archaeologists skeptical?

To begin, when rock art is exposed to the elements, it weathers. There's *less* to see every year. Think about the designs and epitaphs etched onto old gravestones. Sadly, they are subject to freezing and thawing and, especially in recent years, the ravages of acid rain. I am fascinated by old grave markers in New England and have witnessed this weathering over just the few decades I have been examining them; some of the same individual stones whose epitaphs I could read a little more than twenty years ago are now indecipherable. But the Westford petroglyph, rather miraculously, appears to have improved through time, getting fresher every year with new elements appearing that previously had gone unnoticed. In truth, this simply isn't possible. The new imagery on the Westford Knight stone either has been recently added or is entirely imaginary, and probably a bit of both.

Whodunit?

The most likely explanation for the Westford Knight is this: along with still visible natural and parallel striations left by the glacier as it moved over the bedrock in Westford, there very well may have been a Native American petroglyph on the exposed boulder, as noted in the late nineteenth century. At some point subsequent to that, someone *added* imagery to the boulder using a punch technique where a metal rod or awl was placed against the rock and then hit with a hammer. That series of punches was made in the shape of a sword, at least part of one. A rumor in town, admittedly unsubstantiated, is that a couple of local kids were actually seen making the sword, and the reason the sword is incomplete is because they were told to stop in midcarve. The knight in all his regalia resides only in the imagination of Frank Glynn. Other images—for example, a boat, which I could not discern on my visits—may have been added later.

Why?

If, in fact, a couple of teenage boys superimposed the punched sword image over much older, native rock art sometime in the nineteenth century, well, who knows what motivates teenage boys? Of far greater interest is the question: Why do people want to see the ancient image of a medieval knight in Massachusetts?

And not just any knight, and here's where we finally get back to Rosslyn Chapel. Some believe they actually know the identity of the mysterious knight in Westford: Sir James Gunn, who was in the employ of the Scottish earl Henry Sinclair.

How does Gunn get to Massachusetts and leave his image carved in a rock? According to one story, Henry Sinclair voyaged to the New World with his band of knights in AD 1398. If this were true, it might have been Sinclair who, upon his return to Scotland, inspired his grandson to include images of maize—a crop he might have seen in the New World a little less than one hundred years before Columbus—during his construction of Rosslyn Chapel (see figure 3.13).

It's an interesting hypothesis, but not so fast. There's a long list of alternative facts we have to accept in order to support the identification of an image on a rock in Massachusetts with a particular Scottish knight and then use this to explain some plant carvings in a chapel in Scotland:

1. We have to accept the debunked claim that in 1398 Nicolò and Antonio Zeno of Venice sailed to the New World with the earl Henry Sinclair (Lucas 2013). That story was revealed in 1558 by one of their descendants in what is called the Zeno Narrative. That descendant, also named Nicolò Zeno, claimed to have read the narrative when he was a child, whereupon he destroyed it, and only later recognized its historical value and then reconstructed it from memory (http://www.jasoncolavito.com/blog/the-zeno-brothers-fantastic-voyage). He would have had to have a photographic memory. With this in mind, why are we even talking about this anymore? Historians are almost unanimous in declaring both the narrative and an associated map to be fake.

2. If Sinclair and the Zeno brothers—and hundreds of other knights as related in the narrative—really did travel into the Atlantic, we have to accept the thoroughly speculative claim that they made it to North America. By the way, nothing like that is suggested in the text of the Zeno Narrative. And there's the pesky problem of a lack of any archaeological evidence of a merry band of medieval knights traipsing around Massachusetts in the fourteenth century.

3. In the narrative, the expedition was captained by a prince named Zichmni, not Sinclair. But believers in the truth of the story have to assume that possibly, maybe, based on an error in translation or transcription, Zichmni really was the Scotsman Henry Sinclair.

4. The next assumption we have to accept is that one of Zichmni/Sinclair's knights etched James Gunn's image onto a rock in Massachusetts, perhaps as a memorial, because a coat of arms no one other than Frank Glynn can see and, in truth, doesn't actually exist on the rock, represents Gunn's.

5. We have to accept the unsupportable interpretation that the Rosslyn Chapel plant carvings represent convincing evidence of a familiarity with maize in mid-fifteenth-century Scotland.

Once you catch your breath from all of this speculating, you can read the Zeno Narrative for yourself here: http://www.jasoncolavito.com/voyage-of-the-zeno-brothers.html. It's pretty clear that the cartographer responsible for the map in the narrative didn't even do a very good job of depicting lands known to him, much less locate North America anywhere on that map. Good luck finding North America there. Oh, and there's no mention or description of a maizelike crop encountered by the Zenos in the territory they ostensibly explored. The carvings in Rosslyn Chapel have been examined by botanist Adrian Dyer; his verdict: they're not maize or any other New World plant (http://www.bbc.co.uk/religion/religions/christianity/places/rosslynchapel_1.shtml).

Ultimately there is a sort of weirdly beautiful symmetry to all this. To explain the meaning of an image that doesn't actually exist (the invisible medieval knight on a rock in Massachusetts), supporters make reference to a fake story about an ancient voyage that never took place in which there's no explicit claim of the discovery of or travel to America and in which the captain leading the expedition has a completely different name. Finally, we are asked to believe that this story shows how the maize that's really not maize ended up carved in stone at a chapel in Scotland. Seriously. It really is sort of breathtaking in its weirdness.

Fake-o-meter

Five.

Getting there

Punch 17 Depot Street, Westford, Massachusetts, into your GPS or cell phone mapping app. The rock itself is now in a glass coffin, and there's a stone marker telling the story of the image from the perspective of a true believer. Finally, there's a recumbent bronze sculpture of James Gunn in repose immediately adjacent to the incised rock (figure 3.16). If you're supremely dedicated to the Zeno Narrative, drive up to Halfway Cove in Nova Scotia where there's a marker located at the ostensible landfall made by Sinclair in Canada. Yeah, there's no real evidence there either of his voyage to the New World.

Figure 3.16.   Based on the image in figure 3.15, the friends of the Westford Knight commissioned this imaginative sculpture of a knight, presumably Sir James Gunn, who was in the employ of the Earl of Sinclair. It is claimed, with very little supporting evidence, that Sinclair and his band of merry men visited America nearly a century before Columbus. Oh, and they brought back corn to Scotland and that corn was artistically rendered in Rosslyn Chapel (see figure 3.12).

5. MICHIGAN RELICS, MICHIGAN

Archaeological perspectives

Imagine the following scenario: You are selling me something for exactly one dollar. I hand you the bill, but something just doesn't seem right about it to you. The paper doesn't feel normal, the color seems off, and, omg, the *United* in *United States of America* is misspelled! "*Untied* States of America?" Seriously? Oh, and the image of George Washington looks quite a bit less like George and more like Weird Al Yankovic. Of course, you reject the fake bill and hand it back, accusing me of trying to pass a counterfeit. I protest—and listen to my argument: "Oh no, it certainly can't be fake. I have a thousand of them." Wait, what? One fake thing might be fake, but if there's a lot of them, they must be legitimate? How does that bit of reasoning work? A fake dollar bill is worth nothing. Do the math; a thousand times nothing is still nothing. We shouldn't be surprised to find that counterfeiters of all kinds—of dollar bills or of ostensibly ancient artifacts—are diligent and industrious and more than capable of cranking out lots and lots, even thousands upon thousands, of crappy fakes. That's how they make their money. The fact that there's a lot of them lends no support at all to their authenticity.

Nevertheless, you will sometimes hear this argument presented concerning large assemblages of even very obviously fake antiquities: "There are so many of them, no one could possibly have made them all." Such an assertion is both absurd and indefensible, yet it has been proposed as strong evidence for authenticity of the Ica Stones in Peru, the **Burrows Cave** assemblage in Illinois, and the Michigan Relics (obviously enough from Michigan) discussed in this entry.

Here's what we know

According to the story told by James O. Scotford, he found the first of what were to be called the Michigan Relics when he was digging fenceposts in October 1890 on property located near Wyman, Michigan. The object in question appeared to be a clay cup unlike anything he or the locals had seen in any Indian mound site in the area (Halsey 2009). Inspired, Scotford began actively looking for more artifacts, resulting in an avalanche of discoveries that ignited the interest, first of local folks, but then of people all over the United States. A consortium of individual investors, with Scotford at its core, even formed a company, the purpose of which was to control archaeological excavations and to monetize the discoveries. Most of these initial finds—the so-called first series—were clay objects, pots, small boxes called caskets, and tablets, many of which had been inscribed with written messages that appeared to be in ancient Old World languages, including cuneiform-like symbols (figure 3.17). Cuneiform is the earliest

Figure 3.17. One of the Michigan Relics. Along with the image of a baby being handed to a king, there are a bunch of impressions that, I assume, are supposed to be part of a written language.

written script known from Mesopotamia and dates to more than four thousand years ago. If the writing on the first of these Michigan Relics was authentic and ancient cuneiform, this would prove the presence of ancient Mesopotamians in Michigan and cause a rewrite of American history because, well, Michigan.

Scotford possessed an uncanny, almost supernatural ability to find these out-of-place relics and seems to have been involved in all of the discoveries either by actually excavating them or by leading people to spots—small earthen mounds and "tree throws," places where trees had toppled over creating a pit where the roots had been—where the relics could be found. A former Michigan Secretary of State, Daniel Soper—who, as it turns out had resigned that post after being accused of embezzlement—joined with Scotford and became the man responsible for marketing the artifacts. To add to the cast of characters, Father James Savage became intimately involved in the relics, purchasing a large number of them, especially the copper objects, and singing their praises to a fascinated and not terribly skeptical public.

As time wore on, the artifacts became more abundant, increasingly elaborate, linguistically diverse, and the raw material repertoire expanded to include slate and a lot more copper. Some of the imagery on the tablets appeared to be related to the Old Testament of the Bible. For example, one tablet depicts a scene that appears to include Noah's Ark, another the Tower of Babel.

Discoveries of more relics continued unabated at least through the second decade of the twentieth century (figure 3.18). You may see assertions on the internet that there were, all told, tens of thousands of individual objects found in Michigan that can be categorized under the Michigan Relics heading—with inscriptions in assorted ancient Old World scripts, depictions of Bible stories, and myriad other images that screamed out Old World antiquity, including crowns and castles. This likely is an exaggeration, but whoever had been cranking out the relics was no slouch; researcher Richard Stamps (2001) estimates that there may have been as many as three thousand of them (and Stamps states that he has personally examined about one thousand of the objects).

So, what are we to make of the Michigan Relics? Do they provide evidence of the presence of ancient travelers from the Middle East especially, visiting Michigan in antiquity, being especially prolific about making artifacts, and then leaving a tremendous number behind? Well, not so fast; let's not rewrite the history books just yet.

Why are archaeologists skeptical?

There is so much wrong with the Michigan Relics, it's almost too easy to debunk them. Ironically, a number of Mormon scholars investigated the relics, hopeful, perhaps, that their authenticity might provide evidence for the historicity of stories in the Book of Mormon, specifically those concerning the presence of

Figure 3.18. Another of the Michigan Relics. I'm sorry, but these all look to me like the doodlings of a middle school student who's designing torture devices for a faux Medieval role-playing game. It does not look like an authentic ancient artifact.

Courtesy of Thomas Bell, EyeWonder Media.

ancient people from the Middle East living in America. In fact, one of those scholars, James Talmage (1911: 8), was explicit on this point: "Indeed, if the Michigan Relics are what they purport to be, they would furnish strong external evidence of the main facts set forth in the Book of Mormon narrative." Ironically, and to their great credit, some Mormon researchers have diagnosed the relics as complete bunk and provided strong arguments and evidence proving that it was all a humbug (Talmage 1911; Stamps 2001). We can add the voice of Michigan archaeologist John Halsey (2009) to the list of people to whom thanks is due for deconstructing and debunking the Michigan Relics.

So, what was wrong about the Michigan Relics? A lot:

1. James Scotford, as noted, appears to have been involved with every discovery related to the relics. He's always there in the front row either finding relics himself or directing people to places where they might discover them. Well, it's easy to impress people with your skill at finding artifacts when you're the one who planted them in the first place.
2. Many of the objects found initially were clay. Just dried clay, not fired ceramics. Think about that. All you need to do with dried clay is add water to reconstitute the soft, raw clay. An unfired clay pot, tablet, or casket curing in the soil of Michigan for a few thousand years—in fact for just a couple of years—will soak up more than enough moisture from the surrounding soil to regain its original "smooshiness." The original Michigan Relics made of clay simply could not have retained their shape in the wet soils of Michigan for very long. By the way, when this was pointed out to the discoverers, the next round of clay-based objects all were fired ceramics. That is not a coincidence; the forger or forgers learned their lesson and simply improved on their fakery.
3. The raw material used to make the copper artifacts was identified as modern copper. Stamps (2001: 223) identifies it as "commercial copper stock," unlike the copper from which ancient artifacts would have been made.
4. Richard Stamps's (2001) detailed analysis of the Michigan Relics reveals with certainty that they were manufactured using modern tools.
5. The writing on the Michigan Relics is a hodgepodge of ancient scripts. They are the equivalent of a person writing a bunch of random characters from the Roman alphabet, Cyrillic, Japanese, Hebrew, and Egyptian, and maybe throwing in a cute emoji or two. It's complete nonsense. As researcher James E. Homans pointed out in 1961, the inscriptions on the Michigan Relics "mean nothing at all" (cited in Stamps 2001: 230).
6. The images inscribed on the slate, copper, and clay relics are laugh-out-loud bad. Researcher Miriam Brooks likens them to images you might see in a newspaper comic strip and characterizes the style as: "a class of

art, in which, if an ancient should have indulged, he would most as-
suredly have been put to death" (as cited in Talmage 1911: 29). Yikes!
Francis Kelsey (1908: 59) in the *American Anthropologist* describes the
relics as "unsophisticated" and suggests that whoever was responsible
"did not know enough about genuine relics of any class to make intelligent imitations." The end result, Kelsey states, is "jumbled together in
the manner of a child." Kelsey then goes on to liken the Michigan Relics
to the **Cardiff Giant**, the giant petrified man from before Noah's flood
and the subject of an entry in this book.

7. Thom Bell (2011), who produced a documentary about the Michigan
   Relics (*Hoax or History: The Michigan Relics*, http://eyewondermedia
   .com/content/michigan-relics), submitted one of the baked clay artifacts
   for luminescence dating, a technique commonly used in archaeology to
   determine the age of ceramics. The result: the artifact had been fired
   sometime in the early twentieth century, precisely when it was "discovered." It cannot be an ancient artifact; it's modern.

8. Okay, now here's a spoiler, a smoking gun that makes all of these other,
   already nail-in-the-coffin proofs that the Michigan Relics were bogus,
   almost beside the point. There was an eyewitness, someone with no
   agenda and nothing to gain or lose, who actually saw Scotford fabricating fake relics. That witness was Walter Wyman, an agent charged
   with purchasing American Indian artifacts intended for display at the
   World's Columbian Exposition, also known as the Chicago World's
   Fair of 1893. As noted earlier, the local people were hoping that the
   relics would be purchased and everyone involved would make a financial
   killing. The problem is, Wyman showed up at James Scotford's house
   unannounced, and was shown into the basement where Mr. Scotford
   was busy fabricating—wait for it—more Michigan Relics! Scotford
   made no attempt to hide what he was doing, going so far as to offer
   some of the pieces for sale to Wyman, who demurred (Halsey 2009).

9. And there's this: Scotford's stepdaughter, Etta Riley, signed an affidavit
   about her stepfather's role in the Michigan Relics in 1911, asking that
   it not be released until after the death of her mother (rather obviously,
   Scotford's wife) to save her from embarrassment. The affidavit reads:

   > I have seen and witnessed the preparation of plates in slate, clay, and
   > copper, which plates have afterward appeared as purported archaeo-
   > logical finds. I know that James Scotford makes and prepares tablets
   > of stone, hammered pieces of copper and pieces of clay, simulating
   > works of ancient art, and that he buries such and afterwards digs
   > them up as per demand. (Halsey 2009)

Bam. Done. Mic drop.

Whodunit?

I am neither a lawyer nor a judge, and most of what I know about the judicial system I've picked up by watching the various versions of the *Law and Order* franchise. While I don't know whether James Scotford could be tried and convicted in a modern courtroom, he certainly seems to have been the industrious crafter of the Michigan Relics. Daniel Soper was the money man and marketer—the CFO or "Chief Financial Officer"—of the Michigan Relics business. The Catholic priest James Savage, perhaps naively and as a result of his interest in the biblical themes of some of the artifacts, gave Scotford and Soper cover, a patina of just enough legitimacy and deniability to deflect at least some of the skepticism generated by the relics.

Why?

After a careful and in-depth investigation, I have come up with the following three key motivations behind the Michigan Relics:

1. Money.
2. Money.
3. More money.

Pretty clearly, it became known that a representative from the planned World's Columbia Exposition in Chicago in 1893 was buying archaeological artifacts for display at the fair. What better way to make a quick buck than to make artifacts in your basement that were even better than authentic archaeological specimens related to the actual inhabitants of America, the Indians? Simply fabricate fakes that appeared to turn the history of our continent upside down! When that plan disintegrated, a backup, a "plan B," was hatched to market the artifacts more broadly to a public desperate for a fabulous tale of Old World cultures related to the people of the Bible—ancient Mesopotamians, Egyptians, Greeks, and Romans. I imagine that the fact that this would appeal in particular to Mormons was a happy accident. The Church of Jesus Christ of Latter-Day Saints acquired about eight hundred of the relics for study and display at their Salt Lake City Museum. Ultimately, they donated those objects to the Michigan Historical Museum. Other individuals and institutions (Alma College in Michigan) retain ownership of the relics.

Fake-o-meter

Five. Maybe six, if there was a measure that high.

Getting there

Unfortunately, though several years ago some of the Michigan Relics were on display for a year at the Michigan Historical Museum, they no longer are. The next best thing to actually seeing the artifacts was a virtual exhibit that accompanied the museum exhibit. But that website is no longer hosted. The good news is that nothing ever dies on the internet. You can still access the virtual exhibit through the Way Back Machine at this address: http://web.archive.org/web/20140824194156. The aforementioned documentary, *Hoax or History: The Michigan Relics* (http://eyewondermedia.com/content/michigan-relics), is a great resource as well.

6. KENSINGTON RUNESTONE, ALEXANDRIA, MINNESOTA

Archaeological perspectives

Some people like to argue. That's okay; perhaps I am one of those people. But even I find occasion to step back a bit and consider the sometimes negligible significance of what I argue about with other people. Take the Kensington Runestone, a slab of greywacke—a hard sandstone—ostensibly found in north-central Minnesota by a local farmer, in 1898. A message in ancient Norse runes had been etched onto its surface and sides. The date specified in the inscription itself: AD 1362.

People argue about it a lot. That argument focuses on its authenticity: Does the Kensington Runestone provide proof that the Norse made it as far west as Minnesota by the middle of the fourteenth century? If genuine, it would certainly be a remarkable artifact, expanding the Norse world by quite a distance. Kensington is more than 2,800 miles west of a verified, Pre-Columbian North American Norse site, **L'anse aux Meadows**, for example, and you can't sail the entire way from Newfoundland to Minnesota; there's quite a bit of an overland walkabout, so the demonstrable abilities of the Norse at seafaring would have been of little help for a large part of the trip. So sure, I'm skeptical, as are many, but by no means all, archaeologists, historians, and linguists about the inscription's authenticity and whether it provides reliable evidence that the Norse made it this deeply into North America 130 years before Columbus.

Nevertheless, it is important to point out that if the Kensington Runestone were to turn out to be genuine, an authentic artifact left in Minnesota by an expeditionary force of Norsemen more than 650 years ago, it wouldn't change all that much about what we already know concerning the Norse in North America. We already know, definitively, that the Norse were in the New World more than a thousand years ago. The discovery and excavation of L'anse aux Meadows in 1960 was a very big deal, confirming the basic story of the Greenlander's and Eric the Red's sagas. As mentioned, if the Kensington Runestone is the real deal, its existence would greatly expand the geography of the Norse incursion into North America, but the larger issue, the incursion itself, is already proven. No clichéd rewriting of textbooks would be called for, maybe just a footnote.

Here's what we know

Back to the artifact itself: its existence was first reported by Olof Ohman, a Swedish immigrant farmer living in Solem, Minnesota, in the nineteenth century. By his own telling, he was clearing land on his farm in 1898 when he found the 202-pound inscribed slab embraced by the roots of a tree (figure 3.19). Ohman claimed to not recognize the language used in the inscription but understood that it might be an important artifact. Copies of the inscription began to circulate and, though many experts declared it to be a forgery, the inscription was translatable by those familiar with Viking runes. At the time, Kensington was the town nearest to Ohman's farm, and the artifact became known as the "Kensington Runestone." The message on the stone told a compelling though brief tale:

> Eight Götalanders (Swedes) and 22 Northmen (Norwegians) on (this?) acquisition journey from Vinland far to the west. We had a camp by two (shelters?) one day's journey north from this stone. We were fishing one day. After we came home, found 10 men red from blood and dead.
>
> Ave Maria save from evil.
>
> There are 10 men by the inland sea to look after our ships fourteen days journey from this peninsula (or island). Year 1362.
> (on the side of the stone)

Why are archaeologists skeptical?

This book is not the proper venue for an in-depth academic argument about the authenticity of the writing on the Kensington Runestone: Are there anachronisms that indicate the inscription was carved far more recently than the date suggests? Are there rune forms on the stone that prove authenticity because no one in the nineteenth century could have known about them? Does the degree of weathering of the inscription show that they were carved hundreds of years before the discovery date of 1898? All of these questions have been asked and various claims made. (See especially Scott Wolter [2009]; for a more reasoned argument supporting authenticity see Alice Beck Kehoe [2005].)

Figure 3.19. The famous Kensington Runestone housed in a museum that also houses the Chamber of Commerce in Alexandria, Minnesota. The message on the stone tells the story of a band of Norsemen visiting the area whereupon several are attacked and killed by local people. The date on the stone: 1362 (AD).

From the perspective of an archaeologist, a focus on the rune forms or estimates of their age based on weathering (which is an exceptionally inaccurate dating method for lots of reasons) ignores a fundamental problem. Where's the rest of the stuff a party of Norse explorers would necessarily have brought with them and left behind? There simply is no other ordinary archaeological evidence for the existence of the Norse in Kensington or, for that matter, anywhere else in Minnesota in the 1300s comparable to the ordinary archaeological evidence found for a Norse presence in Newfoundland in the early 1000s and scattered throughout northeastern Canada for that same period (Sutherland 2000). And it's not for lack of trying. Excavations have been carried out in the vicinity of the Runestone in 1899 and 1964. Further archaeological testing in the general area was conducted in 1981 and 2001 (Kehoe 2005). Archaeologists found nothing that could be ascribed to ancient Vikings. The Minnesota contingent of Norse New World explorers must have gotten fastidious about leaving behind a trail of material culture—fire hearths, broken tools and weapons—because they didn't lose, discard, or put away for safe keeping anything that might betray their presence. That just isn't possible from an archaeological perspective. Those Norse explorers would not have behaved like thieves in the night, covering their tracks and eliminating every piece of evidence testifying to their presence, and yet, beyond the Runestone, there is no such evidence.

Archaeologists know that's not how cultures work. It makes no sense to us that a group of interlopers in a region, bearing a material culture wholly unlike that of Native People, could have passed through, make camp in numerous places, and never lose or discard any of that unique material culture for archaeologists to find 650 years later. As shown in the introduction to this section of the book, that just doesn't seem likely.

Whodunit?

If the Runestone is real, we are pretty sure "whodunit"; it would have been the Swedes and Norwegians who survived the expedition. If it's fake, the perpetrator is uncertain. Olof Ohman is usually accused as being the responsible party and may have had the requisite knowledge of runes; he was in possession of a book that discussed runes. Was Olof responsible? Possibly. Ultimately, we don't know whodunit.

Why?

Even without definitive proof that the Runestone had been the brainchild of Olof Ohman or one of his neighbors, a motive for perpetrating just such a fraud is easy to suggest. Consider this: today the Kensington Runestone is on display at a building that serves as a museum and the Chamber of Commerce

Figure 3.20.   That's me doing my best Vanna White impression as I'm pointing to the Kensington Runestone.

in Alexandria, Minnesota. When you walk in, the first thing you see is a desk loaded with brochures for restaurants, motels, and all manner of tourist-related activities and services. The Runestone is to the right, encased in glass in a place of honor, positioned almost worshipfully, alone in the center of the room, like the body of a recently deceased president in the Capitol rotunda in Washington, D.C. (figure 3.20).

Related bric-a-brac is on sale at the museum, including a license plate frame emblazoned with the statement, "Alexandria; Birthplace of America." That's wrong on so many levels. Even if the Runestone is a genuine artifact of the Norse exploration of the American Midwest, it's dated to more than three hundred years later than L'anse aux Meadows and—this is no minor point—it's something like twenty thousand years too late to be the "birthplace of America" because Native Americans have been on the continent for about that long.

But that's not the point of the license plate frame, I think. Its message is to those Italians who think their ancestor discovered America, the Spaniards who think they birthed America by establishing a settlement in St. Augustine in Florida, or those Brits who think Jamestown and Plimoth represent the roots of the American tree. Ha! The Norse beat you all to the punch right here in north-central Minnesota!

It is impossible to know for sure if the desire to establish Nordic priority in the New World and the attendant enhancement of ethnic pride that followed

THE KENSINGTON RUNE STONE

ON THIS SPOT WAS FOUND A STONE DATED 1362
RELATING THE STORY OF A BAND OF THIRTY MEN
AMBUSHED ON THE SHORE OF A LAKE ONE DAYS
JOURNEY NORTH OF HERE. HISTORIANS HAVE
IDENTIFIED THESE INTREPID MEN AS THE PAUL
KNUTSON EXPEDITION SENT INTO THE WEST IN 1355
BY KING MAGNUS ERIKSON OF NORWAY AND SWEDEN

8 GOTES AND 22 NORWEGIANS ON
EXPLORATION JOURNEY FROM
VINLAND OVER THE WEST WE
HAD CAMP BY 2 SKERRIES ONE
DAYS JOURNEY NORTH FROM THIS STONE
WE WERE AND FISHED ONE DAY AFTER
WE CAME HOME FOUND 10 MEN RED
WITH BLOOD AND DEAD AVE MARIA
SAVE FROM EVIL
HAVE 10 OF OUR PARTY BY THE SEA TO LOOK
AFTER OUR SHIPS 14 DAYS JOURNEY
FROM THIS ISLAND YEAR 1362

STONE FOUND BY   TABLET PLACED
OLOF OHMAN 1898   1948

Figure 3.21. This historical marker is located at the spot where Olof Ohman claims he found the Kensington Runestone in 1898. The message on the marker reflects a belief in the authenticity of the stone.

was the inspiration for the Kensington Runestone. However, it is pretty clear that it serves that purpose today. And after all, Minnesota's NFL franchise isn't called the Dolphins, the Eagles, or the Patriots. And they certainly aren't the Minnesota Celtics. They're the Vikings, so it is not to be unexpected that ethnic pride might play a role in local support for the Runestone.

The Olof Ohman farm is now a public park, and there is a monument marking the spot where Ohman discovered the artifact (figure 3.21). There is a multimillion-dollar development plan in the works for the farm, which includes a museum focused on the Runestone. So yes, local people take the unfulfilled tourism potential of the Kensington Runestone very seriously.

During my visit, a gentleman approached me as I read the message on the monument at the Ohman farm. He began to read it as well and, with pride evident in his demeanor, he leaned over to me and asked, "Are you Scandinavian?" thinking he was sharing a moment with a countryman visiting a sacred place where Scandinavians had given birth to America. I had to admit that, alas, I was not. At that he just shrugged his shoulders and walked away.

Fake-o-meter

Let's give this one 4. There is a slight possibility that it's genuine.

Getting there

The Runestone is located at the Runestone Museum at 206 Broadway in downtown Alexandria, Minnesota. You can see Ohman's home, farm, and the monument erected at the purported find spot of the stone at Runestone County Park, 8755 County Road 103 SW, Kensington, Minnesota. Just follow the road signs heralding, of course, the "Viking Trail."

7. LOS LUNAS DECALOGUE STONE, LOS LUNAS, NEW MEXICO

Archaeological perspectives

The Los Lunas Decalogue Stone bears a purportedly ancient inscription of the Ten Commandments written in an archaic version of Hebrew. If genuine, it would imply that a band of ancient Jewish explorers and settlers were traipsing around New Mexico long before the voyages of Christopher Columbus. Did I say it was in New Mexico? Yeah, I think I did.

The stone itself is an estimated eighty-ton basalt boulder, a dark, dense, volcanic rock tucked into a natural stone alcove located at the base of Hidden Mountain, about sixteen miles west of the town of Los Lunas (figure 3.22).

Figure 3.22. Hidden Mountain, outside of Los Lunas, New Mexico. The Los Lunas Decalogue Stone bearing a version of the Ten Commandments is tucked away in a little alcove on the side of Hidden Mountain.

Figure 3.23.   The Los Lunas Decalogue Stone. The angle of the inscription conforms with the longest dimension of the stone.

Eroding basalt boulders and outcrops are scattered all over the place at the base of the mountain. On a naturally flat, vertical face of the rock in question, an inscriber has, indeed, etched nine lines of text in a language that has been identified as Paleo-Hebrew or Phoenician (those two languages were very similar and closely related). The inscription was positioned so as to take advantage of the longest dimension of the rock, enabling the inscriber to produce the longest possible lines of text. As a result, the writing is angled, conforming to the orientation of the long axis of the rock, at about 30 degrees clockwise from the horizontal (figure 3.23).

Basalt tends to be gray or black, but whoever produced the inscription took advantage of the fact that exposed surfaces of volcanic rock in the area commonly develop a thin brown or tan weathering rind or patina, sometimes called a "desert varnish." He or she scratched partway into that layer, exposing a lighter layer beneath and producing a message in white letters.

Here's what we know

The story behind the discovery of the Los Lunas Decalogue Stone is a hot mess. One person credited at least with making the stone's existence public was Frank Hibben, a professional archaeologist who taught at the University of New

Mexico. Hibben was largely well respected and did important research, but there is an unfortunate stain on his reputation. Hibben was associated with the excavation of Sandia Cave in New Mexico. He believed that the occupation of that cave produced evidence for the oldest human settlement found in North America, dating to as much as twenty-five thousand years ago. Hibben's claim occurred at a time when the oldest sites in North America were half that age, so that was a very big deal. Unfortunately, subsequent reexamination of the cave has called Hibben's work there as well as his conclusions into serious question. Fairly or not, that casts a pall over his testimony about the discovery of the Decalogue Stone.

Anyway, according to a 1996 interview, Hibben claimed to have been brought to the inscribed stone by an older gentleman sometime in 1933. That man, who was not named in the interview, told Hibben that he remembered first seeing the stone in the 1880s, when he was a young boy (https://manvsarchaeol ogy.wordpress.com/2012/11/10/the-mystery-of-the-decalogue-stone/).

That's interesting, but there are problems with that story. In another interview, a former mayor of Los Lunas told people that *he* was the one who had been shown the stone back in the 1920s or 1930s by a man who said he first saw it fifty or so years earlier than that (http://www.tabletmag.com/jewish-arts-and-culture/125339/the-mystery-stone). That sounds a lot like Hibben's story. Which version, if either, is correct? Or maybe they both are? No one knows.

Why are archaeologists skeptical?

Remember, the existence of the inscription, claimed by its believers to be possibly as much as a couple of thousand years old, wasn't brought to anyone's attention until about 1933, less than one hundred years ago. How is it that nobody saw or commented on it before that? The original Los Lunas land grant dates to 1716, and it was a substantial enough community to be named the county seat in 1876. So, there are plenty of settlers in the area long before 1933, yet no one reported the existence of the inscription before that. That's a big problem for an artifact purported to have been reposing west of Los Lunas for a couple of millennia.

So what do we have? A large basalt boulder with the Ten Commandments inscribed in an archaic version of Hebrew or Phoenician shows up, maybe in 1933, maybe fifty years before that, in the dry desert of western New Mexico. Before 1933 (or maybe the 1880s), apparently the only ones to see the stone were jackrabbits—the ancestors of the ones I saw on my hike to the site—and they're not talking. Or, just maybe, no one reported it earlier because it wasn't there yet. That would seem to be a quite reasonable explanation.

Then there's the writing on the stone. Linguists have pored over the inscription and argued about its authenticity. Are the letters correctly formed; are the spellings right? Is the punctuation appropriate? That sort of thing. (See http://www.chafer.edu/files/v14no2_los_lunas_decalogue_stone.pdf)

As I've noted previously, I'm skeptical that this form of analysis alone can ever be definitive concerning an inscription's authenticity. My take on this is, well, if the inscription is poorly written and filled with errors, that might mean it's fake, but it also might simply mean that a genuinely ancient inscriber simply wasn't very good at writing. I can show you some undergraduate essays with spelling, punctuation, and grammar so terrible you might conclude they can't possibly be authentic. But they aren't fake; they're just bad. Then again, even if the writing in the Los Lunas inscription is technically perfect, that doesn't prove it authentic; it might just mean that whoever faked it did a very good job. Even if we accept the 1880s date, there likely were knowledgeable people in the late nineteenth century who could have produced the inscription.

More important from an archaeological and geological perspective is the degree of weathering on the inscription when compared to Native American petroglyphs just a few feet away. While it's exceptionally difficult to determine the chronological age of an inscription based on the degree of weathering, it's quite a bit easier to put inscriptions or petroglyphs in age order if they are side by side. In the case of the Los Lunas inscription and rock art, it's pretty telling; the genuinely ancient rock art is much more highly weathered than is the Paleo-Hebrew inscription. Compare my photograph of the nearby petroglyph of some sort of animal (figure 3.24) with a closeup image of the inscription (see figure 3.25). It's clear. The lettering in the inscription is crisp, fresh, and even cuts through what appears to be rather recent bits of erosion (technically, exfoliation of the patina). There has been no subsequent patination on the surface of those exfoliations, so not a lot of time can have passed since they popped off.

Figure 3.24. Native American petroglyphs are located adjacent to the Decalogue Stone. Note how the petroglyph, genuine and ancient, exhibits far more weathering than does the inscription, indicating that the inscription probably is much more recent.

Figure 3.25.   Close shot of part of the inscription. The inscription is carved into the brown surface patina of the volcanic rock and it continues into the black subsurface, indicating that the weathering that exposed the interior of the rock happened before the inscription. As there is virtually no repagination of the basalt, the "exfoliation" of the patina must be fairly recent and the inscription must be even more recent than that.

That suggests that the inscription postdates that erosion, again implying that the Hebrew letters are fairly recently carved and far more recent than what we see in the nearby rock art.

Finally—and I've presented this argument previously for other written messages discussed in this section of the book: no one has ever found artifacts or habitation sites in the American Southwest that can be identified as reflecting the material culture of ancient Jewish explorers or settlers. There are no remnants of ancient synagogues, no mezuzahs, phylacteries, or anything else for that matter. The wandering Jews of ancient New Mexico, if they existed, must have been obsessively neat, never losing or disposing of anything for archaeologists—or anyone else, for that matter—to find.

In truth, it is a near impossibility for an ancient people to have been in New Mexico, taken the time to inscribe the Ten Commandments in Hebrew on a boulder during their journey, and not leave behind (through loss or discard) any mundane evidence of their presence in the region. Remember the discussion in the opener for this section about how archaeologists use the unique nature of every group's material culture—their stuff—to identify their presence in the archaeological record? Put bluntly, an incursion of Jews into New Mexico two thousand years ago could not have been the equivalent of an episode of the TV show *Naked and Afraid*, where people are dropped into a new territory with only a handful of tools to assist them. Real people bring lots of elements of their unique material culture with them when they explore or settle a new territory, and they leave an identifiable, recognizable, and culturally diagnostic trail as they pass through. If, as is the case here, there is no evidence for the mundane, every day, utilitarian pieces of material culture a group of visitors or immigrants or invaders would necessarily have brought with them, archaeologists are going to be very skeptical about the possibility of their presence.

Whodunit?

We really don't know, but there are at least a couple of stories that percolate in the area. Some point to Mormons, specifically, members of an all Mormon military battalion who were in the region in the 1840s during the Mexican-American War. Maybe, but that still begs the question: Why did no one report the existence of the inscription until 1933? Another explanation points to a couple of places along the trail past the stone and toward the Hidden Mountain summit where you can find rocks tagged: "Eva and Hobe 3-13-30." Some believe that those were the names of a couple of University of New Mexico students who were the actual hoaxers, which at least would fit with a 1933 date for the earliest supposed eyewitness accounts of the inscription's existence. No one has ever been able to even verify their existence, so that explanation cannot be confirmed. Ultimately, this is an instance in which the question, "Whodunit?" simply can't be answered with any degree of certainty.

Why?

Of course, without a confession or smoking gun definitively identifying the perpetrator, it's almost impossible to come up with a certain explanation for why they did it. Was it a student prank aimed at Hibben? Possibly. The Book of Mormon maintains that Israelites were in North America long before Columbus, so it is plausible that a Mormon was responsible for the inscription, producing fake evidence for the Book of Mormon or just having some fun, never thinking that anyone would take it all that seriously. Maybe. The bottom line: we can't determine if the inscription was a prank, a fake intended to prove a religious point, just someone screwing around, or if there was some other purpose. With that in mind, we just can't answer the question: Why did they do it? But it's in a starkly beautiful setting, the hike is pretty easy, and it's fun to visit and contemplate just how strange people can be. And if you're lucky, you'll encounter some cool jackrabbits like I did.

Fake-o-meter

Five.

Getting there

The Los Lunas Decalogue Stone is located off of Route 6, about sixteen miles west of the center of Los Lunas, New Mexico. From Route 6, turn left onto the road that leads to the Los Lunas dump (it's signposted). Almost immediately, you'll pass over a set of railroad tracks and then drive over a bridge that spans a wash. Before you reach the entrance to the dump (there's a kiosk in front of you), you'll see a gate on the left. Park anywhere out of the way and walk southeast on the dirt road that begins at that gate. In about one-third of a mile, there's a subtle trail that branches off to the right (south). After about one-third of a mile on that trail, you'll reach a barbed wire fence and a gate. Pass through the gate and walk to the right (west) along the fence line. In less than one-tenth of a mile the trail turns left (southwest) and ascends the flank of Hidden Mountain. You'll begin seeing black basalt boulders with arrows recently scratched onto them as you follow up the very short trail to the Los Lunas Decalogue Stone. I should point out that the relatively recently etched arrows show about as much subsequent weathering as do the letters on the Decalogue Stone itself, indicating that they're not that different in age. The Decalogue Stone is tucked into a little alcove in front of you. Look around at the native rock art. If you are so inclined, when you've finished there, continue hiking up the trail to the summit, where you'll see the remains of stone structures, some more rock art, and the Eva and Hobe graffiti.

8. NEWARK HOLY STONES, NEWARK, OHIO

Archaeological perspectives

I was passing through the security line at the Dayton, Ohio, airport in January 2013, returning home to Connecticut after giving a lecture at the wonderful SunWatch Village, an outdoor museum dedicated to a one-thousand-year-old archaeological site in western Ohio. Following the lecture, archaeologist Brad Lepper, a great friend and colleague at the Ohio Historical Society, presented me with a wonderful gift, a ceramic replica of one of the Newark Holy Stones, a notorious, nineteenth-century archaeological fraud crafted to prove an ancient Jewish presence in, of all places, Newark, Ohio. I loved it and made sure the false artifact replica was safely packaged in bubble wrap in my carry-on luggage for my trip home.

Heading home, I dumped my belt and shoes, along with the usual junk in my pockets, into one of those plastic bins they provide you at the beginning of the airport security line, placing it along with my travel bag on the conveyor belt, and I walked through the metal detector and waited. Then everything stopped. At first, I didn't understand why a group of three TSA agents had congregated around the x-ray machine, speaking in hushed tones, while looking at my bag. It was initially mysterious and a bit disconcerting when they then waved me out of the line, opened my carry-on, with gloved hands reached in to find something, picked up the bubble-wrapped artifact, unwrapped it, and then confronted me with the cheesy knockoff of an archaeological fraud. "Sir," one of the agents seriously intoned. "Can you please explain what this is?"

Omg! There I was, pulled out of a security line at an airport because I was carrying a copy of one of the fake Newark Holy Stones! This could only happen to me. "It's kind of a funny story," I responded while nervously laughing. And then I told them the tale of the Newark Holy Stones, a shortened version of what I am about to tell you here. The best part of the experience: the agents were transfixed by my telling of the story. One of the agents, a young woman, asked if I would mind if she took notes. I told her of course she could, and she pulled a small spiral notebook out of her back pocket and began note taking. It was like I was in my university lecture hall. When I had finished, one of the agents admitted that, you know, it's the Dayton airport and nothing ever happens here, but this had been her most interesting job experience. Ha! So, what are the Newark Holy Stones, and what's all the fuss?

Here's what we know

David Wyrick was one of those nineteenth-century thinkers alluded to earlier in this book—like Jacob Gass in Iowa in relation to the Davenport Tablets— who was fixated on the question of the identity of the people who had built the earthworks that seemed ubiquitous in his native Ohio. That fascination led to his conducting excavations of mounds in an attempt to discover artifacts that might help to solve the mystery and prove who, exactly, those mound builders were. It was during a dig at a small, circular enclosure mound on the outskirts of Newark, Ohio, in August 1860 that Wyrick thought he had found a game-changing object, an artifact that would prove definitively who the mound-building people were and where they had originated (for a superb summary of the story, see Brad Lepper and Jeff Gill's [2000] article, "The Newark Holy Stones" in the magazine *Timelines*). While excavating a pit in the center of the enclosure, Wyrick uncovered a piece of polished, yellow sandstone in the form of a plumb bob with four flat, triangular faces. Called the Keystone because of its triangular shape, this artifact was interesting and unique, but of far greater significance was the fact that there were inscribed messages on each of those

Figure 3.26.   The Keystone, the first of the Newark Holy Stones found in an ancient Indian mound by David Wyrick in Newark, Ohio, in 1860. The Hebrew inscription turned out to be an anachronism compared to the probable age of the mound in which it was recovered. It was written in a modern version of Hebrew and, therefore, a bad fake.
Ben Croghan. Courtesy of the Johnson-Humrickhouse Museum.

four faces, and the messages were written in Hebrew (figure 3.26). It was my replica of the Keystone that got me into hot water at the security checkpoint at the airport in Dayton, Ohio.

Like most people even today, we recognize Hebrew when we see it, but cannot read or translate it. Sensibly, Wyrick took the object to someone who could, the Reverend John McCarty. McCarty provided the following translations for the four inscriptions on the artifact Wyrick had recovered at the mound site: "the Laws of Jehovah," "the word of the Lord," the Holy of Holies," and "the King of the Earth." That seemed incredibly important and impressive. Fortunately, Charles Whittlesey, one of Ohio's preeminent prehistorians, was in Newark at the time, examined the object, and immediately declared it to be a fake; the object had been found in a very shallow pit and, of greater importance, whoever had manufactured the artifact had made a fundamental error—the version of Hebrew in which the inscriptions were written was of a modern vintage (Lepper and Gill 2000: 19). Oops.

Chastened but undeterred, Wyrick continued in his quest to find an artifact in a mound that would more clearly and definitively prove the identity of the builders. In an apparently miraculous coincidence (well, it was no coincidence at all) considering all of the ongoing excavations aimed at answering this same question, just five months later and only a few miles away from the first discovery, none other than John Wyrick—what an incredibly lucky researcher!—found another inscribed artifact, this one in black limestone, with an abridged version of the biblical Ten Commandments written in an appropriately archaic version of Hebrew and bearing a bas-relief carving of a man who is, in all likelihood, Moses (figure 3.27). This artifact was labeled the Decalogue and, just wow. Forget the Keystone, was this the artifact that once and for all would solve the mound-builder mystery and identify the responsible culture and people as wandering Jews, perhaps members of one or more of the Lost Tribes of Israel who settled Ohio more than two thousand years ago? Well, not so fast.

Figure 3.27. Five months later and just a few miles away, Wyrick found this stone, the Decalogue, engraved with the Ten Commandments in an appropriately ancient version of Hebrew. The carver of the Keystone learned his lesson and did a better job the second time around. Nevertheless, experts in ancient Hebrew have declared it, too, to be a fake.
Ben Croghan. Courtesy of the Johnson-Humrickhouse Museum.

Why are archaeologists skeptical?

Think about it. An investigator everyone knew was interested in solving the mystery of who built the mounds of the New World gets very lucky and finds an artifact with a Hebrew inscription in an Ohio mound. But that artifact turns out to be an obvious fake, written in an anachronistic script for the period in question. Then, miracle of miracles, just a few months later that very same investigator, digging just a few miles away, finds another inscribed artifact, also in Hebrew, but this time in a far more temporally appropriate version of the language. That's quite a coincidence. Doesn't it seem reasonable to suggest an alternate explanation, that when the plumb bob object was dismissed and disavowed because of the inappropriateness of the writing, whoever crafted it learned from his or her mistake and made a more convincing one?

After more than two centuries of archaeological research in the American Midwest in general and Ohio in particular, no mundane evidence of an ancient Jewish settlement has been found. There are no village sites, traditional Jewish burials, houses of worship, religious artifacts, or anything else that you would expect to be found at an ancient Jewish settlement. Considering the thousands of sites excavated by archaeologists in the American Midwest, especially in the past few decades applying sophisticated remote-sensing technology, the lack of anything beyond a couple of Hebrew inscriptions, one of which is demonstrably fake, explains our skepticism concerning the authenticity of the Newark Holy Stones.

As for the validity of the inscription on the Decalogue which, to the untrained eye, appears to be dramatically more reasonable than the one on the Keystone, Frank Moore Cross, one of the twentieth century's preeminent authorities on the Hebrew language, characterized it as a "grotesque" forgery (as cited in Lepper and Gill 2000: 20).

One more thing: I'll leave it to you to decide whether the following is a coincidence. When David Wyrick died, his headstone was made of a raw material that appears identical to—even the same thickness of—the Decalogue Stone.

Whodunit?

Having been a central figure in the discovery of both of the Newark Holy Stones, David Wyrick is an obvious suspect in this case. However, based on egregious errors Wyrick made in transcribing the inscriptions for publication, it would appear that his knowledge of Hebrew was simply not up to the task of concocting the frauds in the first place. This leads us to another suspect who played a significant role in promulgating the notion that the Newark Holy Stones were proof of an ancient Jewish source for the mound-builder societies of the American Midwest: Reverend John W. McCarty, the first person fluent in Hebrew to translate the Keystone. But what would have been Reverend McCarty's motive?

Why?

Brad Lepper and Jeff Gill (2000) suggest a reason for McCarty's involvement, and it is steeped in the religious and racial politics of nineteenth-century America. Remember, the Holy Stones were revealed in the summer of 1860, less than one year before the beginning of the Civil War, a period during which there was rampant speculation not only about who the Native People of the Americas were, but also the nature of the relationship between the various "races" of human beings. Essentially, there were supporters of "monogenesis," the idea that all of the people on our planet descended from the same Adam and Eve and, as a result, were all part of one human family. "Polygenesis" was predicated on the belief that God had created different races of human beings entirely separately, the equivalent of different species of animals. We humans, therefore, were not all closely related members of the same family marked by only superficial differences including skin color, but separate species with entirely different inherent abilities and potentials. In line with their perspectives, most monogenesists opposed slavery while many polygenesists thought the enslavement of some "inferior" peoples (people of color, of course) by the superior products of God's creation (white Europeans, of course) was entirely natural and defensible.

The Reverend Charles McIlvaine (1839: 11), bishop of the Episcopal Church in Ohio and the Reverend McCarty's superior, was a firm believer in monogenesis. Asked to write the preface of the book *An Inquiry into the Origin of the Antiquities of America* by John Delafield, McIlvaine characterizes the unity of humankind as "forever settled." And get this: McIlvaine went on in that same preface to predict that artifacts will surely be found in America that will lend further support to the connection between the Native People of the New World and those discussed in the Bible, lending further support for the monogenesis perspective.

Lepper and Gill point out that the discovery of artifacts in America inscribed in biblical Hebrew, bearing a version of the Ten Commandments no less, was nearly made to order to lend evidentiary support to McIlvaine's hypothesis. What better way to curry favor with the bishop, therefore, than to be involved with the discovery and interpretation of just such an artifact? In this view, McCarty had the knowledge and the motive to produce the Newark Holy Stones which, with the unwitting (perhaps) help of Wyrick, he brought to McIlvaine and, ultimately, the world. It's an interesting take on the Holy Stones and provides a convincing explanation for their rationale.

Fake-o-meter

Five.

Getting there

The Newark Holy Stones can be seen at the Johnson-Humrickhouse Museum in Coshocton, a lovely little town in central Ohio. The museum is really quite wonderful, and it's more than worth the trip to actually be in the presence of artifacts that caused so much controversy and that, ultimately, may have been well intended as evidence to support the unity of all of the races of humanity and, in so doing, as proof that the enslavement of any one of those human groups was counter to the Bible.

9. HEAVENER RUNESTONE, HEAVENER, OKLAHOMA

Archaeological perspectives

Look, you are probably aware that the Norse—commonly called the Vikings—were a peripatetic people. I love having the opportunity to use that word: *peripatetic*. It means, literally, "traveling from place to place." And the Norse, indeed, were proficient and peripatetic sailors, especially during what is called the "Viking Age," between the late eighth through the middle of the eleventh century AD. Norse exploration, especially, of the North Atlantic was fueled by the quest for resources and places for settlement.

There is indisputable historical and archaeological evidence for this. The Norse sailed down the west coast of Europe; explored England, Ireland, and Spain; and made it as far as the north coast of Africa. They traveled east from there into the Mediterranean, where they explored Italy and even made it to Egypt. The Norse also traveled south along a number of navigable rivers through Russia, emerging in the Black Sea. Especially where there was an ocean or navigable rivers, the Norse were fearless and dedicated travelers, explorers, and colonists.

Not confined only to coastal exploration, they also traveled the open sea and settled Iceland in about AD 860, Greenland in 978, and North America by 985 (see the entry for **L'anse aux Meadows**). And yes, true to the stereotype, they weren't exactly the friendliest of visitors and neighbors. For example, when they "discovered" Iceland there were Irish monks already living there, but the Vikings didn't feel compelled to share the place with those monks. So they killed them. In their first personal encounter with the Native People of the New World, they found eight "Skraelings," as they called them, hiding under four hide boats. They immediately killed seven of them. The other Skraeling got away. You know the old saying: "We shoot first and ask questions later." The Viking variation on that policy was "we shoot first and, hey, we just killed these guys so it's pointless to ask any questions at all." Needless to say, the Viking encounter with the Skraelings wasn't the start of a beautiful friendship between Europeans and Native Americans.

So yes, we know that the Norse made landfall in the New World—at least in northeastern Canada—about five hundred years before Columbus. The evidence on this point is unambiguous (L'anse aux Meadows), and archaeologists and historians are not surprised to find substantial evidence of their presence there (Sutherland 2000).

But seriously: Heavener, Oklahoma? Heavener is located more than 350 miles as the crow flies from the nearest substantial body of water, the Gulf of Mexico, and more than 230 miles from the navigable Mississippi River. How in the world could a maritime culture that did the bulk of their exploring over water make it to Oklahoma? And no insult intended to Oklahomans, but why in the world would they want to go there? Yet if the Heavener Runestone discussed here is authentic, it means that, not only were the Norse in Oklahoma hundreds of years before the Columbus voyages, they settled there, leaving a written boundary marker in a runic script. But is the Heavener Runestone a legitimate ancient Norse artifact or a fake? Let's see.

Here's what we know

The story of the Heavener Runestone begins with a letter to the "Smithsonian Institute" (that's an error on the part of the writer; it's the "Smithsonian

Figure 3.28. Norse runes found on a stone slab in Heavener, Oklahoma. Translated variously, there is no evidence whatsoever of a Norse presence in Oklahoma in antiquity.

Institution," not "Institute") dated March 24, 1923. It was written by a local school teacher, C. F. Kemmerer, on the stationary of the Heavener Masonic Lodge. Kemmerer wrote:

> While exploring the neighboring county in the vicinity of Heavener recently our party chanced upon a large rock on the face of which was carved some curious characters which none of us were able to decipher.

Kemmerer went on to supply a "rough sketch" of the "curious characters" and encouraged the Smithsonian to become involved in "solving the quotation riddle." While there are indications that the inscribed stone had been seen previous to this, the Kemmerer note appears to be the earliest written record of its existence (figure 3.28).

The type of runes seen on the stone have been identified as Elder Futhark, which dates in Scandinavia between the second and eighth centuries AD. Though translations vary, the Heavener Runestone is generally thought to read "GNOMEDAL," which could be a person's name (G. Nomedal) or the term *Gnome Valley*. Other translations change one of the runes to make the inscription read Glome dal, the Valley of Glome (the valley owned by Glome). Take your pick.

Why are archaeologists skeptical?

As I've pointed out elsewhere in this book, as an archaeologist and not a linguist, I am not especially confident in the value of using the accuracy—or lack of accuracy—of an inscription to determine definitively whether or not an artifact is authentic. Of course, egregious anachronisms in a written inscription can be a dead giveaway that it simply can't be the real deal; for example, reference to a place that had not yet been discovered or named when the inscription ostensibly had been written. In most other instances, the argument can go either way: there are so many mistakes, the inscription can't be real, or the mistakes show that it wasn't fake because a faker would try to create the most accurate inscription possible.

For what it's worth, Swedish runic expert Henrik Williams at the University of Uppsala has carefully examined the Heavener Runestone and concluded that it is highly unlikely that it is an authentic bit of ancient Norse writing (Wallace 2015). Also, Lyle Tompsen, who wrote his master's thesis focusing on the Heavener Runestone at the University of Leicester in England, concluded that the runic forms on the Heavener Runestone are simply not authentic for the period when Elder Futhark was in use (Tompsen 2011).

Fair enough, and both Williams's and Tompsen's argument seems pretty strong to me. Combine that with the pretty much outlandish notion that the maritime Norse would appear in, of all places, eastern Oklahoma, and you can understand my skepticism. But there's an even more important basis for my skepticism. Remember, I'm an archaeologist and I need material, archaeological evidence to be convinced of the presence of the ancient Norse in Oklahoma, not just a one-off Runestone.

As I discussed earlier and, you might fairly say incessantly, in this book, when people enter into, pass through, and even settle in an area, they leave behind a culturally diagnostic trail. Just as they did in Greenland, Iceland, and Vinland, if Vikings were living in Oklahoma in antiquity, settling in, and even marking their property they would have lost, discarded, or hidden away for safe keeping bits and pieces of their material culture: iron boat rivets, bronze pins, sheep wool, part of a halberd (a Norse battle axe/spear), and more. No such artifacts have ever been found in Oklahoma or, in fact, anywhere in the American Midwest. The very artifacts listed have indeed been found in northeastern Canada. That lack of the common, everyday objects left behind by the Norse and readily identifiable as Norse and not Native American is pretty much a deal breaker for the claim that they were living in Oklahoma in the ancient past.

The folks who cling to the hope that the Heavener Runestone is authentic certainly realize that the lack of any archaeological evidence is a serious issue. In fact, nearby to where the Heavener Runestone is housed, there is a small cliff wall of shale and sandstone. Based on no evidence in particular, the signage for the rock wall suggests:

> The vertical ledge of sandstone that overlies this shale does create an over-hanging mass of rock that *may* have the appearance of a cave opening. *If* such an overhang existed in the past it *could* have provided shelter. *If* the cave

actually existed, the floor *might* provide evidence of Viking habitation in the area. (Italics, mine)

If you're playing at home, that's two "ifs," a "may," a "could," and a "might" in those three sentences. Well, as the old saying goes, "If wishes were fishes, we'd all cast our nets in the sea." But wishes aren't fishes and there's no actual evidence whatsoever for a Viking settlement near the Runestone. Enough said.

Whodunit?

Lyle Tompsen, cited above, suggests that the Heavener runes likely were produced in the late nineteenth or early twentieth century, probably by an individual of Scandinavian descent. Scandinavian immigrants were living in the area by the nineteenth century, and some were employed by the railroad in Oklahoma during that period. Many Norse knew runes, and it's not much of a stretch to ascribe the Runestone to one of them.

Why?

In this case, there likely was no ill intent, no desire to fool anyone. The inscriber may simply have been making a sort of nationalistic, Scandinavian statement and maybe just having some fun, like graffiti artists from time immemorial. In this scenario, which, I admit, is entirely speculative, a Scandinavian immigrant with an imperfect knowledge of Elder Futhark found a large boulder with a flat rock face just a couple of miles from town. He thought it would be great sport to carve some runes, a kind of "we were here" statement about Scandinavians. Mr. Kemmerer finds it, naively reports it to the Smithsonian as the real deal, and the rest is history.

Oh, and one more thing. The people of Heavener are proud of their town's contribution to a discussion about who settled America in antiquity. You know a community is all-in concerning their homegrown archaeological artifact when they even brag about it on the sign leading into town (figure 3.29). The Runestone was, for years, administered by the State of Oklahoma in a state park. When they abandoned the park for financial reasons, the town of Heavener stepped up and took it over. The town didn't really have the money to keep the park open, so a group of locals adopted the park in which the Runestone is located in a very commendable grassroots movement for historic preservation. The Heavener Runestone doesn't have to be ancient to be important and worthy of preservation as a part of local history. I met one of those folks when I visited. She was working the ticket counter and store and more than happy to tell you about her personal commitment to the Heavener Runestone. She was there with her dog and her baby. It's a family affair and, even though it's a modern fake, good for her.

Figure 3.29.   Sign posted on the outskirts of downtown Heavener. Clearly the people of Heavener are proud of their connection to the inscription.

Fake-o-meter

Five. But that's no reason to not swing through Heavener if you're ever in eastern Oklahoma and see it for yourself.

Getting there

Heavener is about as far east as you can get in Oklahoma without actually slipping into Arkansas. Interstate Route 40 provides access from Fort Smith located a little more than thirty miles north of Heavener. The Heavener Runestone Park is located at the end of Route E1460.

10. BAT CREEK STONE, LOUDON COUNTY, TENNESSEE

Archaeological perspectives

Like the **Newark Holy Stones** in Ohio, the Bat Creek Stone was, for many, a perfect artifact, just exactly what was hoped for when it was discovered in 1889.

Its perfection has to do with how its existence seemed to relate to a major question raised by the presence of human beings already in the New World when Europeans arrived in the late fifteenth century: How did those New World Natives fit within a biblical framework? That fundamental puzzle was accompanied by other questions: Where did the Indians come from, how did they get to the New World, when did they get here, and did they encounter other colonists who may have already been here? Any artifacts that might relate to those important questions drew the rapt attention of anyone interested in the human history of America. The Bat Creek Stone, found in a burial mound in Tennessee, was just such an artifact.

Here's what we know

The Bat Creek stone itself is a flat, roughly rectangular piece of a soft, black rock called siltstone, about 11.4 centimeters long and 5 centimeters wide. Across one surface there are eight, possibly nine, inscribed characters (figure 3.30).

The best source for the story of the discovery, analysis, and history of claims related to the Bat Creek Stone is the Robert Mainfort and Mary Kwas 1991 article published in the *Tennessee Anthropologist*. The stone was recovered while excavating a mound in 1889 by John W. Emmert, who was, at the time, a field assistant for the Smithsonian Institution's Bureau of American Ethnology

Figure 3.30. The Bat Creek Stone, in Tennessee, bears a message in an archaic version of Hebrew.

(BAE) Mound Survey. That federally funded project was explicitly designed to definitively identify the people responsible for constructing the thousands of diverse earthworks—burial mounds, enclosure mounds, effigy mounds, and platform mounds—found in profusion across the American Midwest and Southeast. Was it Indians who built those mounds—the ancestors of the modern Native People encountered by European explorers and colonists of the New World—or was it someone else entirely?

And herein lies the great ostensible mystery underlying the Bat Creek Stone: the artifact was, according to Emmert, recovered in a pristine context, undisturbed and in situ (which is just a fancy, Latin way of saying, "in place"; in the original location where it was placed in the ground). Emmert recorded that the inscribed stone was found at the base of a burial mound in which there also were the skeletons of nine people. The stone was found beneath the skull of one of those nine skeletons along with two "copper bracelets," a drilled fossil, a copper bead, a bone tool, and some wood preserved by having been in contact with the copper (copper tends to help preserve organic material in the soil where it might otherwise decay). If it truly was found in situ, then the inscribed stone was placed when the mound was constructed and the people buried therein—and that appeared to be a very long time before its excavation by Emmert.

Emmert excitedly alerted his boss, Cyrus Thomas, an ornithologist who had been placed in charge of the entire BAE Mound Survey, about his momentous discovery. Thomas examined the stone and believed the inscription was written in the Cherokee Indian language invented by the Cherokee scholar Sequoyah in the 1810s and 1820s. Thomas felt that the stone lent strong support to his belief that the direct ancestors of the living Cherokee had been the mound builders and that, therefore, their mound building had continued into the early nineteenth century, after Sequoyah had developed the Cherokee alphabet.

Unfortunately, and rather embarrassingly for Thomas, it appears that he was reading the inscription upside down! Obviously, the Bat Creek Stone had not been written in Cherokee. Here's where it gets really interesting: in the 1970s, the inscription came to the attention of Cyrus Gordon, a professor of Mediterranean Studies at Brandeis University in Massachusetts. Reading the inscription right side up, he identified it as a version of Hebrew dating to about AD 100. The translation reads something like "Holy to Yahweh," "Yahweh" being the name of God used in the Old Testament of the Bible. The inscription, therefore, was an ancient version of Hebrew, and if Emmert was correct—and honest—in his report that the artifact was found in an undisturbed context, it was at least as old as the mound, strongly implying that ancient Jews had been in Tennessee.

Why are archaeologists skeptical?

An authentic artifact bearing an inscription written in a nearly two-thousand-year-old version of Hebrew found in an undisturbed context beneath a skeleton in an ancient burial mound in Tennessee would certainly be a game changer in our understanding of who built the mounds. The key word here is *authentic*. But the inscription's authenticity is highly questionable. Certainly one of the world's preeminent experts in "Paleo-Hebrew," Frank Moore Cross (at the time, Hancock Professor of Hebrew and Other Oriental Languages at Harvard and the debunker of the Hebrew seen on the Newark Holy Stones), deconstructed each of the letters in the inscription, declaring six of the eight to be "impossible" for Paleo-Hebrew. Not surprisingly, based on his analysis he declared the inscription on the Bat Creek Stone to be a fake. Further, a possible template from which a faker may have crafted the Bat Creek Stone inscription has been identified on page 169 of Robert Macoy's book, *General History, Cyclopedia, and Dictionary of Freemasonry* published in 1870 (figure 3.31). The Bat Creek Stone inscription certainly looks like a rough version (with errors) of the Masonic illustration, with the right letters in the correct order (read from right to left).

Ohio State University economist Hu McCulloch supports the authenticity of the Bat Creek inscription, but archaeologists are generally not swayed by the radiocarbon date he derived for the wood found in the burial mound in which the inscription was recovered. That date indicates that the wood found in the mound is close to two thousand years old, and McCulloch believes that this is strong evidence for the authenticity of the artifact and its placement in a Tennessee burial mound two thousand years ago. There's a big problem with that line of reasoning. The date applies to the wood found in the mound, but if the inscription is fake and the object was inserted into the mound, the dated wood

ANCIENT CHARACTERS OF THE INSCRIPTION.

HOLINESS TO THE LORD. An inscription worn on the forehead of the High-Priest, as described in Exodus xxxix. 30: "And they made the plate of the holy crown of pure gold, and wrote upon it a writing like to the engraving of a signet, HOLINESS TO THE LORD."

Figure 3.31.   A page from the book *General History, Cyclopedia, and Dictionary of Freemasonry* bearing what appears to be the template for whomever carved the message on the Bat Creek Stone. The book was published in 1870. The Bat Creek Stone was discovered 1889 in a genuinely ancient burial. Do the math.
Public domain.

bears no relationship to the artifact. I might be able to sneak my first, late, and lamented iPhone into a mound with a legitimate two-thousand-year-old carbon date but, as old as my first iPhone might be, it isn't nearly that old. In other words, the carbon date derived for the wood recovered in the mound may bear as much relationship to the inscribed stone as the dated wood in my hypothetical example applies to my iPhone.

Finally, the bracelets found in the burial—in reality brass, and not copper—are of an alloy of copper and zinc. That's incredibly odd because no alloyed metals are found in aboriginal North America. Native Americans in North America utilized "native copper," where the metal was found in nearly pure, natural seams and used as is, needing no smelting for its recovery (though heat was applied to make the material more malleable when tools were being manufactured). But bronze and brass, both alloys in which copper was a major constituent, are not known from aboriginal, precontact archaeological sites in North America (the Inca, in South America, did make bronze). That would imply that the brass bracelets were also placed into the mound as part of a broader scheme to make it appear that the burials did not belong to Native People. The metal itself cannot be used to definitively date the Bat Creek bracelets; brass with similar metallurgical proportions (about two-thirds copper, one-third zinc) was made between two thousand years ago and right up into the nineteenth century.

Just as important from an archaeologist's perspective—and I apologize for repeating myself here, but it bears repeating—I can assure you that had there been a roving band of Hebrew explorers or colonists traipsing around Tennessee a couple of thousand years ago, they would have left an archaeological trail consisting of considerably more of than a couple of brass bracelets and an inscribed tablet. Those roving Hebrews, had they been here, must have lived somewhere, collected food, perhaps planting crops, discarding broken and used-up tools, and simply lost stuff along their way. Archaeologists in Tennessee have excavated thousands upon thousands of test borings in their search for archaeological sites and in their excavation of hundreds of those discovered sites and never have they found an ancient camp, village, or town attributable to ancient members of the Lost Tribes of Israel. As we've seen, the same can be said for the **Newark Holy Stones** in Ohio and the **Los Lunas Decalogue Stone** in New Mexico. These objects, as elaborate as any of them may seem (and the Bat Creek Stone is the least elaborate of these examples), are all reasonably simple knockoffs, one-offs that might have taken no more than a few hours to produce, with absolutely no archaeological context relative to an ancient Jewish presence in the New World. All of the handwaving about linguistics, epigraphy, metallurgy, and radiocarbon dates don't—and can't—negate that fundamental archaeological fact.

Whodunit?

In truth, there is no smoking gun that would allow us to definitively conclude whodunit. Robert Mainfort and Mary Kwas make a strong case for John Emmert being the perpetrator. He had professional challenges resulting from a documented drinking problem and was at one time fired by the BAE. Certainly his value as an archaeological fieldworker jumped considerably by finding amazing and truly game-changing artifacts, including one with an inscription. But here again, there is no definitive answer to the question: Whodunit?

Why?

As we've already seen, the Bat Creek Stone was one of a handful of artifacts found in the nineteenth and early twentieth centuries (including the **Newark Holy Stones** and the **Los Lunas Decalogue Stone** discussed in this book) that fulfilled both the expectation as well as the desire to be able to support a simple, biblical explanation for the existence of people in the New World.

As noted previously, in past centuries virtually all Europeans took the Bible literally and thought that it presented a perfect and inclusive history of the world and its people. All human beings—including any previously unknown groups encountered during the Age of Exploration—descended from Adam and Eve (who lived in the Garden of Eden, which must have been somewhere in the Middle East). Beyond this, since the Bible states that virtually all of Adam and Eve's descendants were killed in a great flood, everyone alive in the world must be descendants of that universal flood's only human survivors: Noah and his wife, their three sons, and their sons' wives.

Along with speculating about which of Noah's sons was the founder of the American Indian lineage, Europeans recognized that there were historical peoples who had gone missing between the time of the Bible and their present, groups who simply dropped out of the historical record. One of the most intriguing of the presumed missing groups included the so-called Lost Tribes of Israel. In the Old Testament of the Bible, the patriarch Jacob is said to have fathered twelve sons, and each of those sons became the progenitor of a separate tribe. Through migration, expulsion, warfare, and intermarriage, ten of those tribes historically disappeared and, in so doing, became a very convenient source of and explanation for the Native People of the New World. In one bold stroke, the existence of people in the New World could be traced, explained, and positioned firmly in the context of the Old Testament of the Bible. Any artifacts, therefore, that might seem to identify American Indians as Jews were embraced by many European thinkers and that, ultimately, may have supplied the motivation for the perpetrator of the Bat Creek hoaxed inscription and an explanation for why many people embraced the artifact as both genuine and genuinely important.

Fake-o-meter.

Five.

Getting there

The Bat Creek Stone is held by the Smithsonian Institution. I saw it where it is currently on loan: the Museum of the Cherokee Indian, 589 Tsali Boulevard, Cherokee, North Carolina. Modern speakers and readers of the Cherokee language are certain at least that the Bat Creek message is not in their language.

11. GRAVE CREEK STONE, MOUNDSVILLE, WEST VIRGINIA

Archaeological perspectives

As we've already seen in this section, artifacts have been found in North America that bear inscriptions ostensibly left by ancient European or Southwest Asian visitors to our shores. In most cases, for example the **Heavener** and **Kensington Runestones** as well as the **Los Lunas Decalogue Stone** and the **Newark Holy Stones,** both skeptics and believers recognize the written language on the artifacts (Viking runes at Heavener and Kensington; Hebrew in the case of Los Lunas and Newark). They even agree, for the most part, on what the inscriptions say. The primary arguments about these artifacts focus on their age (are they really Pre-Columbian?) and the identity of their inscribers.

This, however, is not the case for the Grave Creek Stone (sometimes called the Grave Creek Tablet). Found in 1838 during the commercial excavation of a two-thousand-year-old burial mound in West Virginia, it's almost impossible to get two researchers even to agree on what language is reflected in the marks carved on the stone, much less what those marks actually say. At this point, we might as well identify the writing on the Grave Creek Stone as being Klingon—you know, the written language of the aggressively warlike villains on the original *Star Trek* television series. What might the Grave Creek Stone say in Klingon? It's probably something like: "We met the locals. Didn't like them. Ripped their hearts out of their chests and then stomped on them while they were still beating. Until they weren't beating anymore." That's those crazy Klingons for you.

But what was the Grave Creek Stone really? What are its implications for the nineteenth-century mound-builder mystery? Let's explore those questions.

Here's what we know

Grave Creek Mound is a very impressive two-thousand-year-old conical burial monument made of piled earth located in the city named, not coincidentally,

Figure 3.32.   The Grave Creek Mound, a nearly 70 feet high, 2,000-year-old burial mound located in Moundsville, West Virginia.

Moundsville in far western West Virginia (figure 3.32). The name assigned to the Native American culture responsible for its construction is Adena. The Adena people subsisted primarily on the rich, wild plant and animal foods available in the major river valleys of the Mid-Atlantic and Midwest. The Adena traded extensively for raw materials, including obsidian (natural, volcanic glass) from the West, shell from the Gulf of Mexico, and raw copper from Michigan. The Adena appear to have developed a stratified social system, and their leaders were honored upon their deaths by being interred in sometimes enormous burial monuments made of piled earth. These monumental mounds are found across the American Midwest and are concentrated in Ohio, Illinois, and Kentucky. Grave Creek Mound is arguably the largest and most impressive of the Adena burial mounds with a height of nearly seventy feet and a diameter of about 240 feet at its base.

Many Midwestern burial mounds, especially the smaller ones, were destroyed by being plowed over to make the land more convenient for farming. Some were broken into for the often finely made objects—the so-called grave goods—placed in the graves of Adena leaders. A very few were excavated by scientists eager to study the lifeways of the ancient people of North America.

Perhaps as a result of its great size, the Grave Creek Mound was preserved—at seventy feet you couldn't simply remove it with a horse- or ox-drawn plow. There also is some evidence that the owner of the property on which the mound was located hoped to preserve it for study. Whatever the case, the mound was excavated in 1838.

Certainly, no one conducting archaeological excavations in the early nineteenth century adhered to modern standards of mapping, record keeping, and preservation, so it is impossible to know the exact circumstances of the discovery of the unique object found in the Grave Creek Mound, a small, flat pebble that appeared to have a written inscription on one of its faces (figure 3.33). Even more problematic is the fact that the excavation of the mound wasn't sponsored by a museum or university with researchers experienced in conducting archaeology. Instead, the Grave Creek Mound excavation was a commercial enterprise; it was, in essence, not so much an archaeological dig as it was a mining operation for antiquities. The only prerequisite for digging a part of the mound was cash; any curious individual could purchase permits to dig the mound. The expectation, encouraged by the folks selling the permits, was that there were vast archaeological riches entombed in the great burial mound, rivaling, perhaps, those found in the tombs of Egyptian pharaohs.

Though there were archaeological "riches" in the form of pottery shards, copper bracelets, and beads, there was nothing like the gold and silver objects found in ancient tombs in the Old World. Though many were disappointed by their haul of objects, one artifact found in the excavation appeared to be uniquely important: the aforementioned flat, polished sandstone pebble with an incised inscription on one of its faces (see figure 3.33). This was labeled the Grave Creek Stone or the Grave Creek Tablet.

Figure 3.33. Mining the site for hoped-for riches, this small pebble bearing an incomprehensible message in no identifiable language was found. Even true believers in the stone's authenticity couldn't agree on what it said or even in which language it was written.

Almost as soon as it was discovered, there was controversy concerning its authenticity. The Native People of North America north of Mexico had no written language, and the Grave Creek Stone certainly had writing on it (Barnhart 1986). If it were authentic, clearly a literate people had been responsible, showing conclusively, at the least, that a foreign people had explored the New World long before Columbus and, perhaps, that they stuck around long enough to have constructed a monumental burial memorial for a deceased comrade.

Why are archaeologists skeptical?

The term *provenience* has a very specific meaning and significance in archaeology. It represents the precise location—horizontal and vertical—of an object found at an archaeological site. When we excavate a site, we necessarily take it apart. In essence, ironically, we erase all of the important spatial data provided at a site by the very act of recovering artifacts and removing them from their spatial contexts in the ground. It's analogous to the challenge faced by paleontologists when they find the skeleton of a dinosaur. The bones of the extinct beast may be articulated; that is, in their correct anatomical positions. Those anatomical data are crucial to reconstructing what the animal looked like, but in order to recover the bones, paleontologists usually need to remove each of them from their original spatial contexts, thereby erasing their preserved anatomical positioning.

Excavating an archaeological site is analogous to that. When archaeologists remove each artifact from its original location, we eliminate its spatial contexts and associations—where it was found, with what nearby, and in which layer. Just like paleontologists, we are obsessive about mapping, drawing, and photographing each object before we recover it. This allows us to, in a sense, reconstruct all of those spatial contexts and associations back in the lab.

Nobody, including many experienced archaeologists, was doing a particularly good job of this key element of record keeping at archaeological sites in the early nineteenth century. At a commercial dig like the one conducted at Grave Creek, it was even worse. The result here is that there are no records of the exact context of the discovery of the inscribed stone. We simply don't know its provenience with any certainty. As historian Terry Barnhart (1986) states, when researchers interviewed those present at the mound when the tablet was discovered (unfortunately, sometimes many years after the fact), there are gross inconsistencies and contradictions in their testimony, not only about where the inscribed stone was found (in the mound itself during excavation or accidentally in the dirt already excavated?) but also in who found it in the first place. Without very exacting records of the precise provenience of the Grave Creek Stone upon its discovery, we can't really say if it was an artifact recovered in an authentically ancient layer or only recently added to the soil, making it a simple fraud. So, an analysis of the archaeological context of the discovery of the Grave Creek Stone cannot prove the artifact is authentic or not because we really have no record of the context of its recovery.

Next, when we examine the language in the inscription, the tablet becomes even more problematic. Here's the thing: no two scholars could agree even on which language was represented (Libyan, Phoenician, Celtic, or what?), and when it came to the actual translation, forget about it.

For example, in an article about the **Davenport Tablets**, for comparison, the medical doctor R. J. Farquharson (1876–1878) noted these three wildly varying translations of the Grave Creek Stone:

1. "Thy orders are laws, thou shines in thy impetuous clan, and rapid as the chamois."
2. "The chief of emigration who reached these places (or island), has fixed these decrees forever."
3. "The grave of one who was murdered here; to revenge him may God strike his murderer, suddenly taking away his existence."

I'm not kidding. Those are all "translations" (there I go with scare quotes again) of the exact same handful of markings on the Grave Creek Stone as determined by three different scholars (again, look at figure 3.33). Some people accuse me of being a bit snarky in my writing and, guilty as charged. But it's hard not to include a little snark in this case. Equally disparate translations of the stone and differing identifications of the language represented abounded and continued right up through the late twentieth century.

As Farquharson (who actually believed the tablet was authentic, though how I cannot imagine) admitted: "These three different renderings of the same sentence by these learned men are doubtless interesting, but it must be admitted that they are also somewhat embarrassing" (106).

Somewhat embarrassing? Trust me; if your high school foreign language teacher asked you to translate a sentence into English and you came up with three wildly different translations and couldn't even decide the identity of the language you are attempting to translate, well, that teacher wouldn't conclude that your work was "somewhat embarrassing." You're going to more than "somewhat" flunk the assignment. Your teacher would be skeptical that you knew what you were doing and, I think, extreme skepticism concerning the authenticity of the inscription on the Grave Creek Stone is equally warranted.

Whodunit?

In a public presentation (that unfortunately remains unpublished), researcher David Oestreicher (2008) suggested that the Grave Creek Stone was planted by Wheeling, West Virginia, native Dr. James W. Clemens, the primary figure behind the money-making scheme to sell what amounted to mining rights to the burial mound. He pointed out in the same presentation that he had found the likely source for the inscription on the tablet: a book written in 1752 by a Spanish historian titled *An Essay on the Alphabets of the Unknown Letters That Are Found in the Most Ancient Coins and Monuments of Spain.* Oestreicher found some of the exact sequences of markings found on the Grave Creek Stone in that book so, in his estimation, the book served as the model for the nonsensical, fraudulent Grave Creek Stone inscription.

Why?

If Oestreicher's hypothesis is correct, then the motive was simply part of an effort to reignite interest among those who might be willing to pay for the opportunity to dig at the mound once it became apparent that no great riches were to be found therein. Though no pharaoh's treasure would be found, at least there was the possibility of discovering important and, no doubt monetarily valuable, evidence of an Old World presence in ancient North America.

Fake-o-meter

Five.

Getting there

The bad news is that you cannot see the original Grave Creek Stone; it was lost sometime in the late nineteenth century. The good news is that the Grave Creek Mound still exists in all its glory and sits adjacent to the wonderful Delf Norona Museum that has a very informative display about the excavation of the burial mound and the discovery and interpretation of the inscribed stone. Though, for my taste, that display is a little too credulous concerning the authenticity of that inscription, there is a nicely made replica you can view. Hey, why not try your hand at translating it. Your translation won't be any worse than those of the "learned men" who attempted it in the nineteenth century.

Grave Creek Mound is about as far west as you can get in West Virginia, only fifteen minutes south of Wheeling, just east of Route 2 at 801 Jefferson Avenue in downtown Moundsville, West Virginia.

Category 2 Ancient Visitors:
Stone Monuments

𝒯he same fundamental issues discussed in the opener for the previous section (Ancient Visitors: Written Messages) applies when we consider stone structures including the **Acton** and **Upton Chambers** in Massachusetts (Chartier 2007), the **Peach Pond Stone Chamber** and **Balanced Rock** in New York State, **Newport Tower** in Rhode Island (Godfrey 1951), and the **Druid Hill Stone Circle** in Massachusetts.

In a sense, the lack of any artifacts beyond the monuments themselves is an even greater problem than such a lack was in the case made for written messages, where it already was pretty much a deal breaker. Unlikely as it may be, a brief message etched into a rock might have been accomplished by an individual person working for a relatively brief time with little expectation for a sizable assemblage of artifacts at the spot of the inscription. In comparison, for stone monuments—chambers and stone circles—to have been built, there would likely have been a substantial investment of time and their construction would probably have required the participation of a group of people. This combination of time and population makes it even more likely for there to be an archaeological record composed of lots of mundane stuff, the material culture of the folks who lost and discarded that stuff as they busied themselves by building the monument.

One more thing. I have heard people respond to my archaeological take on this by saying, well, these were sacred monuments and would have been kept pristinely clean, so no artifacts should be expected. That isn't a very strong, informed, or persuasive argument. There's an entire archaeological subfield called church archaeology in which archaeologists excavate and recover plenty of lost and discarded material among the ruins of churches that were, rather obviously, sacred structures (Rodwell 1989). No, there really ought to be artifacts found among, within, or in the vicinity of the stone monuments to be visited here, and the cultural source of those artifacts and their dating would provide strong evidence of the identity of the builders. We'll look at that evidence in this section.

12. ACTON STONE CHAMBER, ACTON, MASSACHUSETTS

13. UPTON STONE CHAMBER, UPTON, MASSACHUSETTS

14. PEACH POND STONE CHAMBER, NORTH SALEM, NEW YORK

Archaeological perspectives

I am, as I write this, sixty-five years old. I mention that only to affirm to you that I am a full-fledged grown up. I do not believe in ghosts, spirits, demons, devils, evil elves, gremlins, jinn, goat-sucking chupacabras, werewolves, moth-men, death-eaters, ring wraiths, or Carrot-Top. Nevertheless, I must confess, despite my physical and emotional maturity, basements still totally give me the creeps. I'd say they give me the "willies" or the "heebie-jeebies" but who uses those terms anymore? But "willies": yup. "Heebie-jeebies": oh yeah. It is not my favorite thing when my wife says: "I think I heard something in the basement. Could you go down there and check it out?" I've seen way too many creepy movies to feel comfortable about going down there. Basements, especially dry-laid stone cellars in old houses (like my own), are dark and dank—I don't think I've ever used the word *dank* in any non-basementy context. They're just unpleasant and, to be entirely honest, weird, spooky, and skin-crawlingly creepy.

Now add claustrophobia into the mix in the case of diminutive versions of dry-laid stone basements, little cellars so small that even a not-tall person, like me, has to bend over and sort of duckwalk just to enter them. Dark: check. Dank: check. All spidery and wormy: check and check. Entering into one is sort of like entering into your own personal burial crypt. So yeah, not a fan.

Here's why I'm leading off the conversation in this entry by talking about creepy mini-basements. The northeastern corner of the United States, especially New England and Putnam County in the Hudson River Valley of New York State, is filled with structures similar to what I have just described, small buildings called, variously: root cellars, ice houses, stone chambers, monk's caves, beehive structures, potato caves, receiving vaults, Muggs holes, and more. They're fascinating, and there's not just a little controversy concerning who built them, when, and their purpose. Here I'll walk you through a handful of them, providing archaeological contexts and explanations. Then go visit some for yourself, I mean, if you like dark, dank, creepy, and spooky little stone chambers. And who doesn't?

Here's what we know

I'm focusing here on a few of the better known, better preserved, and most thoroughly analyzed of these stone features: the Acton and Upton stone chambers, both in Massachusetts, named for the town in which they are located, and the Peach Pond Stone Chamber in North Salem, New York. Despite my wife's Harry Potter joke, none of them are "chambers of secrets," but they are still very interesting and intriguing sites.

The Upton, Acton, and Peach Pond chambers reflect dry-laid stone masonry of a type that people have been using for literally thousands of years, including the very recent past. In other words, no mortar was used to bind the stones together. The structures were made by laying one fieldstone on top of another with little more than gravity and the shape of the stones to bind them together in the manner of a three-dimensional jigsaw puzzle.

The Acton Chamber (figure 4.1) consists of a short passageway lined by two more or less straight, parallel walls with larger stone slabs serving as roofing stones (figure 4.2), and then a sort of anteroom to the right at the rear (figure 4.3). In other words, the footprint of the Acton Chamber is in the shape of a backward, uppercase letter *L*. You enter through a straight passageway (that's

Figure 4.1.   The opening to the Acton Stone Chamber, in Acton, Massachusetts.

Figure 4.2. Inside the Acton Chamber looking out toward the entrance.

Figure 4.3. The interior of the Acton Chamber. All artifacts recovered during an excavation of the chamber indicated a construction and use date in the nineteenth century. The chamber was built for storage or, possibly, as an ice house.

the long leg of the *L*) to a chamber in the rear that then expands to the right (the small leg of a backward *L*).

The Upton Chamber (whose entrance reminds me of hobbit houses in *Lord of the Rings*; figure 4.4) has a long passageway entrance (about twelve feet long and five feet high), a straight run of more or less parallel walls (figure 4.5) leading to an impressive domed enclosure about seven feet high at its peak (figure 4.6). The Peach Pond Chamber consists of a single, rectangular room. The Acton and Upton chambers are open to the public in town parks. The Peach Pond Chamber is located on a public road and bears a plaque indicating it is a historic landmark. All three chambers certainly are testaments to the construction practices of the people who lived in Massachusetts, but who were those people, how long ago did they build them, and what purpose was served by the structures?

Why are archaeologists skeptical?

Here's where it gets weird. There are a host of explanations, a number of suggested ages for, and several cultural affiliations assigned to the chambers of New England and New York (and those found elsewhere in the Northeast). Some are pretty, well, speculative, like this hypothesis: they were built to mark portals to other dimensions, located at the juncture between our universe and reality and

Figure 4.4.   The opening to the Upton Chamber in Upton, Massachusetts. Yeah, I know. It looks like a place in which a hobbit might live.

Figure 4.5.   I took this photograph just inside the entrance to the Upton Chamber, looking toward the domed room.

Figure 4.6.   The Upton Chamber domed room. Although one interpretation of the chamber's date places it before the settlement of the region by Europeans in the nineteenth century, no diagnostic artifacts of potential previous builders have been found.

some other, far weirder place (Imbrogno and Horrigan 2000), sort of like the "upside-down," for all of you *Stranger Things* fans.

The majority of archaeologists and historians are skeptical of such esoteric and paranormal explanations for New England's and New York's stone chambers for two essential reasons:

1. There are eighteenth- and nineteenth-century eyewitness accounts recorded by the people who built them or saw them being built, describing precisely how they were made and for what purpose.
2. When archaeologists have excavated in and around the chambers, they have found artifacts that provide testimony to their use as utilitarian outbuildings in the eighteenth and nineteenth centuries.

For example, on the topic of eyewitness accounts, there's a wonderful resource concerning life in the Hudson Valley of New York in the mid-nineteenth through early twentieth centuries. Published as a book in 2013, *Life on a Rocky Farm: Rural Life Near New York City in the Late Nineteenth Century* presents the descriptions of that life written down by Lucas Barger, a resident of the Hudson Valley. There's a wealth of interesting information that Barger recorded about his life on the farm, including a description of the construction of a stone outbuilding. He describes its masonry and talks about the use of ropes and oxen to pull the large roofing stones up a soil ramp to the top of the chamber's walls. There's no great mystery or enigma about them; Barger tells us that farmers built such structures for the storage of root crops in winter (keeping them from freezing) as well as ice houses for storing ice in the warmer months. In the specific case of the Acton Chamber, researchers have found a reference to an "ice house" on the property in an inventory dating to 1876 (Chartier 2007: 16). The most reasonable explanation for this chamber, therefore, is for cold storage.

One more thing: Some claim that many of the stone chambers of New England and New York are oriented toward the summer or winter solstice sunrise or sunset and are, therefore, of astronomical, calendrical, and ceremonial significance. Like Stonehenge. That might sound convincing and not in keeping with a mundane, utilitarian outbuilding. Why would there be any pattern to the direction faced by the opening of a structure if it were solely intended for the storage of potatoes, turnips, carrots, or ice? Actually, however, there's a very good practical reason for specific alignments of such structures. For example, if the purpose of a chamber is to maintain a temperature that is warm enough in winter that your root crops won't freeze, and, at the same time, you require natural light to illuminate the interior, you need to position the opening in line with the location of the sun during most of its transit of the sky during the winter. So, the chamber seems aligned with the winter solstice, but that's entirely for practical, not ceremonial, reasons.

The Acton Stone Chamber

The Acton Chamber was the location of an archaeological excavation conducted as part of a reconstruction and stabilization project making it safe for public entry before incorporating it into the Nashoba Brook Conservation Area (Chartier 2007). Archaeologists excavated extensively both inside and outside of the chamber along with digging a number of smaller test pits. More than a thousand artifacts were recovered from these excavations, many from inside the chamber including nails; glazed ceramics; a bullet; pieces of brown, green, and clear bottle glass; bits of rusted iron; part of a rake; and lots of bits of charcoal. All of the items fit nicely in a nineteenth-century temporal provenience, and all of it is Euro-American. None of it is ancient Celtic or Phoenician, and beyond one possible spear point found outside of the chamber, none of it is Native American. Having spent some time in the chamber when I visited the quite wonderful Nashoba Brook Conservation Area (http://www.actontrails.org/nashoba-brook/), I can say with some certainty that the chamber isn't the entry to a Hell Mouth, a passageway to another dimension or reality, or the entry to the Upside Down. It would appear that the Acton Stone Chamber is nothing more—and nothing less—than a fascinating farm building dating to the nineteenth century. Is it possible that it actually was built by Native Americans or wayfaring Celts and that the historical objects found in its excavation reflect a much later reuse of the chamber? That is possible, but purely conjectural, and it's better to base conclusions on what is rather than what might have been. There is no evidence to support those other claims so, applying the scientific method, its identification as a nineteenth-century farm outbuilding is the most likely explanation.

The Upton Stone Chamber

Research has also been conducted at the Upton Chamber (Mahan et al. 2015). Here the investigation appears to have been focused primarily on dating soil samples of the surface upon and in which the chamber was constructed using an established technique called thermoluminescence (the same procedure used to date one of the ceramic objects in the **Michigan Relics** assemblage). The results were intriguing, and the researchers suggest that the chamber was built at least five hundred years ago, long before the area was occupied by known European colonists. However, no artifacts indicating the timing or cultural affiliation of the chamber were discovered and, ultimately, datable, traceable artifacts are the gold standard in archaeological reasoning. If the calculations used in the determination of age were off even by a little, as the authors recognize, the determined dates can be off as well. So yes, the Upton Chamber dates are interesting but do not conclusively prove the age and cannot be used to identify the builders.

The Peach Pond Stone Chamber

We had been examining the Peach Pond Stone Chamber in North Salem, New York, for only a couple of minutes when a local property owner wandered over to my wife and me, very politely asking about our interest in the chamber (figure 4.7). I told her that I was fascinated by these kinds of structures, which resulted in her telling me that this one had been built a very long time ago and how thrilling it was to stand within it and watch the sun rise at the summer solstice. She admitted to not knowing who built the chamber or when, but clearly it was a wonderful feature, surrounded by mystery, having something to do with an ancient calendar.

I thanked the woman for her information, took some photos, and wondered at how mystery and legend can be inspired by a structure that had been most likely used for an obvious, if macabre, purpose and likely was built only between one hundred and two hundred years ago. In fact, it was pretty obvious that the Peach Pond Chamber wasn't particularly ancient, and it wasn't used as part of an ancient astronomically based calendar. The not-so-secret truth about the Peach Pond Stone Chamber (located, not on Peach Pond Road but on Peach Lake Road; go figure) can be determined by the configuration of the structure and its very clear context (figure 4.8)

Figure 4.7. The Peach Pond Chamber located in North Salem, New York. Look above the chamber and to the left in the photograph. Between the trees you'll see a handful of gravestones from the Peach Pond Cemetery. That fact represents strong evidence of what the Peach Pond Chamber actually is.

Figure 4.8.   The interior of the Peach Pond Chamber, a "receiving vault" in which bodies were stored in winter when the ground was too frozen to dig graves in the Peach Pond Cemetery.

Archaeological analysis relies on the examination of context—where something is located and what other things are spatially associated with it—and one needed only to expand one's perspective a little—both figuratively considering local history and also literally simply by taking an actual step back from the chamber and looking at its surroundings—to have the actual purpose of the Peach Pond Chamber revealed. The chamber in question rests at the bottom of a hill, and here's what's key; above it and immediately to the north is the Peach Pond Cemetery, in use between 1815 and 1905. In that fact rests a definitive explanation for the purpose of the chamber. Look again at figure 4.7. Did you catch it the first time you looked at the photograph? There in the upper left you can see them through the trees—old, white gravestones.

Before there were backhoes and other mechanized ways to dig graves, if someone died in the middle of the winter here in the Northeast, relatives were often faced with an enormous challenge. The ground here becomes as hard as stone, and it is virtually impossible for grave diggers to dig a grave with shovels. That presented a real problem—if the deceased couldn't be buried until the spring thaw, what in the world were you going to do with the body until then? It certainly was cold enough in winter to keep the body frozen outside, but that would invite animals to pick at the flesh, a rather awful thought if that were your beloved grandparent in cold storage on a table behind the house.

A solution prevalent during the nineteenth and early twentieth centuries—precisely the period during which Peach Pond Cemetery was in use—involved the construction of buildings called "receiving vaults," often dry-laid, semisubterranean stone chambers built into the side of a hill near a cemetery. Receiving vaults were cold enough to keep a dead body frozen, and a sturdy door kept out curious and hungry animals like bears, wolves, and coyotes.

The Peach Pond Stone Chamber checks off all of those boxes. It was built into the side of a hill and, though the door is gone now, there is a clear door frame at its entrance. Most revealing of all, as noted, it is located immediately adjacent to the Peach Pond Cemetery. Search "receiving vaults" and then look at the images link. You'll find all manner of such structures, reflecting an admittedly unpleasant but absolutely necessary practice of people living here in the Northeastern region of the United States, a region beset with long, cold winters and their attendant hard freezes. Some receiving vaults are elaborate and impressive temporary houses of the dead. Some are simple, purely utilitarian structures, much like the Peach Pond Chamber.

As is so often the case, modern confusion arises over the meaning and purpose of historical artifacts and features because our lives are so different even from those who lived only a couple of centuries before us. We don't need to build root cellars, ice houses, and receiving vaults and, as a result, many of us are unaware that they were a common part of the landscape throughout the 1800s and into the early 1900s. The Acton, Upton, and Peach Pond stone chambers have nothing to do with archaeoastronomy or ancient, Pre-Columbian visitors to the New World. Most such structures probably have nothing to do with Native Americans. Instead, these chambers are a fascinating reminder of a way of life lived not so long ago but quite different from our own.

Whodunit?

I think Jack Hitt (1998) hit the nail on the head in his article, "How the Gungywampers Saved Civilization." Stone cellars and places like **Gungywamp** and **Mystery Hill** are viewed by some as not interesting or important enough as they have been interpreted in traditional history and archaeology. The bias appears to be that the temples of Druids, Celts, or Phoenicians are so much more historically momentous than the outbuildings built and used by eighteenth- and nineteenth-century farmers. As Hitt points out, many of the supporters of such claims are themselves of Celtic lineage, and it is easy to understand their desire to place their ancestors on the landscape of the American Northeast in deep time, dating to nearly as long ago as the Native People. The bottom line in all this, however, is data, the "material culture"—the artifacts—which, of archaeological necessity, would have been lost or discarded in the soils in and around those chambers. When archaeologists have had the opportunity to look, that material culture shows an eighteenth- and nineteenth-century age and a Euro-American affiliation of the chambers. But, as is almost always the case in archaeology, more research can certainly contribute to a final answer to questions regarding the stone chambers of New York and New England.

Why?

The Acton, Upton, and Peach Pond stone chambers are extremely cool and absolutely worth a visit. Removed from their most likely historical contexts as farm or mortuary outbuildings, it is not surprising that to many people—me included—they seem like pretty spooky places. Their functions in historical farming communities as utilitarian features intended for a mundane use in the storage of potatoes, turnips, carrots, ice, or dead bodies are so far removed from our modern world, it shouldn't surprise anyone that more esoteric and romantic explanations—as ancient Druid worship sites, portals to other dimensions, or as cosmic beacons for extraterrestrial travelers—have become popular. Some Native Americans and non-native researchers (Hoffman 2019) now lean toward the identification of at least some of the chambers as ceremonial structures built within the context of what they call an indigenous "Ceremonial Stone Landscape," or CSL. The CSL includes a broad pattern of the construction of stone cairns to mark sacred places, astronomically aligned stone walls, effigies (in the shape of animals) of piled stone, and chambers for religious ceremonies.

I perceive the CSL interpretation as part of a completely reasonable effort on the part of Native Americans to reclaim the ancient landscape and to reject its appropriation by the modern descendants of European colonists of New York and New England who claim that, in particular, the stone chambers of the region are the sacred structures of their ancient (not recent) European ancestors who, they believe, beat Columbus to the New World by a few thousand years. Whether all or some of the stone features of the Northeast were constructed by Native People in antiquity must be, as is the case for any other hypothesis concerning their origin, assessed though evidence.

As just briefly shown, at least so far all of the current evidence recovered in the chambers points to their eighteenth- and nineteenth-century construction intended for the mundane uses just enumerated. The facts suggest that their construction is relatively recent—two or three centuries at most—and that their purpose was strictly utilitarian. This in no way implies that these chambers aren't fascinating, historically significant, worthy of protection and preservation, and just plain fun places to visit. Kudos to the towns of Acton and Upton, both of which have incorporated their respective chambers into town parks. The Acton Stone Chamber is incorporated into the Nashoba Brook Conservation Area, which is both a nature and a history preserve. Along with the stone chamber, the trails in the preserve take the hiker through old farmlands and past the remnants of a pencil factory where, apparently for the first time, pencils were produced in hexagonal and octagonal form. And you have to love the fact that the founder of the pencil company's name was Ebenezer Wood. Get it? "Wood."

The Upton Chamber is incorporated into a town park (the Upton Heritage Park) with its own sign and parking lot. As noted, the Peach Pond Chamber has been formally identified as a historical landmark by the town of North Salem, New York. Whatever your opinion about the specific function, age, origin, and meaning of the Acton, Upton, and Peach Pond stone chambers, it's wonderful that the towns in which they are located celebrate their presence and historical importance.

Fake-o-meter

The Acton, Upton, and Peach Pond stone chambers aren't fake; there merely are various interpretations of them. Five for claims that they are somehow related to the paranormal. Four for claims that they are ancient Celtic, Phoenician, or built by Native Americans.

Getting there

Punch in Wheeler Lane in Acton, Massachusetts, into your GPS. You'll drive by some private residences and then the road dead ends at a small parking area adjacent to a historic foundation. The clearly marked trail leads off to the right. Follow that trail past a pond and in about a mile you'll see the opening of the Acton Chamber up a little hill and to the right (http://www.actontrails.org/nashoba-brook/).

The Upton Chamber is located in Upton Heritage Park on Elm Street in Upton, Massachusetts. There is a large sign along the road at the park's entrance on the west side of Elm Street (there's even a depiction of the chamber on the sign). Pull in at the sign; there is a small car park ahead on the left. The chamber is located to the north (right) of the car park and down a little hill (https://www.uptonma.gov/sites/uptonma/files/uploads/stite_plan_of_heri tage_park_pdf.pdf).

The Peach Pond Chamber is located on the east side of Peach Lake Road (Route 121), just north of the intersection with Vail Boulevard (on the west side of Peach Lake Road) in North Salem, New York. By the way, the Peach Pond Stone Chamber is only 2.4 miles from **Balanced Rock**, also in North Salem, New York. You may have noticed that North Salem, New York, has two locations highlighted in this book, and that it is the same name as the town in New Hampshire where **America's Stonehenge/Mystery Hill** is located. That is purely coincidental, unless you have a penchant for conspiracies, in which case a "coincidence" is just what I'd like for you to believe.

15. DRUID HILL, LOWELL, MASSACHUSETTS

Archaeological perspectives

Though I might be highly skeptical concerning many of the popular interpretations of or claims made about the sites highlighted in this book, in virtually every instance I have still been able to appreciate and enjoy those places. They're all interesting, engaging, even aesthetically interesting sites. My issue with some of their interpretations doesn't change the fact that they are interesting places, worthy of a visit. I can even, at least in most instances and perhaps grudgingly, understand the confusion that might result from those popular interpretations and claims.

The Druid Hill site, located in Lowell, Massachusetts, is an unfortunate exception. I am including the site in this book because the claims made about it are extraordinary and pretty strange, but the site itself isn't particularly impressive. Oh well.

Here's what we know

Built more than 4,500 years ago in the Salisbury Plain of southern England, Stonehenge is an enormously impressive "megalithic" monument (figure 4.9).

Figure 4.9. The deservedly famous 4,600-year-old Stonehenge located in the south of England. Though Stonehenge is the most impressive and elaborate, there are more than 1,000 stone circles built by the ancient people of Western Europe.

Almost certainly you've heard of Stonehenge, seen photographs, and likely marveled at its great beauty. You might not know, however, that though it is the most complex of the stone monuments of ancient western Europe, it isn't anywhere close to having the largest footprint or the construction project that included the greatest number of large (mega) stones (liths). In fact, the culture responsible for the construction of Stonehenge built hundreds of stone circles and linear alignments in England, Scotland, Ireland, Wales, France, Italy, Spain, and Portugal. There's even a tourist atlas for them that includes information on over three hundred sites (Burl 2005).

Many of these monuments are enormously impressive. They're all fascinating, the product of the communal labor of ancient farming people who seem to have been rather obsessive about erecting heavy stones generally, but not always, in circular patterns. Take a look at figure 4.10, my photograph of the Swinside circle located in Cumbria in the west of England. Swinside consists of about 60 stones positioned in a circle roughly ninety feet in diameter. Though each stone is only a few feet tall, they are each quite heavy and must have taken quite a bit of muscle power to move them into position.

Like Stonehenge, many stone circles appear to have served as calendars marking important celestial events, including the rise and set points of the sun at the solstices (June 21 and December 21, marking the first days of summer and winter) as well as the equinoxes (March 21 and October 21, marking the

Figure 4.10.   Located in the Lakes District in the west of England, the Swinside stone circle is a truly beautiful ancient monument, a 98-foot-diameter circle consisting of about 60 stones, each a few feet in height.

beginning of spring and fall). The ability to keep track of the seasons was important for an agricultural people, and many megalithic monuments seem to have been aligned in such a way as to mark key points of the sun's yearly dance across the horizon and, therefore, served a calendrical purpose.

Why are archaeologists skeptical?

I think that one need only compare my photograph of the Swinside stone circle with my image of the Druid Hill stone circle to understand my skepticism about claims that right here in Lowell, Massachusetts, there is a megalithic monument the equivalent of those located in Western Europe (figure 4.11). There are a handful of upright stones located on the top of a hill that is now a playground in a park adjacent to a school. But the stones certainly aren't positioned in a circle, or any particular geometrical shape for that matter. You know the term *circle* is inappropriate when the layout of stones measures about 114 feet by 62 feet. That's a pretty squished circle and, therefore, isn't a circle at all.

However, and perhaps as a result of the geographical name—Druid Hill—there has long been speculation about the meaning of the site, so archaeological and documentary research was conducted in 1985 (Gorman et al. 1986). The results of this research are pretty clear:

1. Though the area is well documented from as early as the seventeenth century, there is absolutely no reference to a stone feature at the site, circular or otherwise.
2. An excavation in and around the stones revealed nineteenth- and twentieth-century artifacts, some related to an isolation hospital (as the

Figure 4.11. It's pitiful, I know, but this is what passes for a "stone circle" in Massachusetts in the minds of folks who cannot possibly have ever seen real stone circles in Western Europe. The Druid Hill Stone Circle isn't ancient, and it isn't even a circle.

name implies, a place where people with a very contagious disease, often tuberculosis, were kept in isolation from people without the disease) located on the hill.

3. *Beneath* one of the upright stones—and, therefore, predating the erection of that stone—the excavators found a stone pavement that dated the beginning of the twentieth century.

Clearly, the Druid Hill Stone Squished Circle (my new name for the feature) was constructed, for whatever reason, in the early twentieth century.

Whodunit?

The Druid Hill Stone Squished Circle was, as nearly as I can figure, brought to the world's attention by James Whittall. Whittall was an interesting character— I actually met him at a conference in the early 1980s—with a firm belief that ancient Celts had discovered, explored, and settled in North America thousands of years before the Columbus and Norse voyages to the New World. As I have stated previously in this book, there's nothing intrinsically wrong with a hypothesis that proposes such voyages of exploration and attempts at colonization, but any such hypothesis requires testing with archaeological data that simply have never been found. Needless to say, Whittall did not agree with that. Upon first seeing the place in Lowell, Whittall recorded these thoughts:

> There I saw a sight I had not seen since my travels in the British Isles. Situated on a mound were weathered megalithic stones. I was filled with disbelief—it just couldn't be—western Europe, yes, but here in Massachusetts—no. The reality of the scene was astonishing. (Whittall 1984)

Wow. That's some pretty hyperventilated writing. Remember in the introduction to this book I quoted the John Adams aphorism: "Facts are stubborn things." Despite Whittall's assertion that the Druid Hill Stone Squished Circle is an eerily precise match for ancient megalithic sites, the facts of archaeology and history—ever stubborn—clearly show that the stones were erected just a little more than one hundred years ago and, again, compare the photographs in figure 4.9 (Stonehenge) and figure 4.10 (Swinside). The Druid Hill Squished Circle (figure 4.11) isn't a particularly good match for those genuine megalithic monuments.

Why?

Whittall was firmly committed to his belief that ancient Celts inhabited North America. His embrace of Druid Hill was, I think, a product of that commitment. And hey, what's not to like about the possibility of ancient Druids in Lowell, Massachusetts?

Fake-o-meter

Five.

Getting there

The Druid Hill Stone Circle (that isn't a circle) is located in LeBlanc Park in Lowell, Massachusetts. The access road for the park is located at the intersection of West Meadow Road and Gumpus Road. Follow the park access road; the boulders that make up the site are on the left (south), opposite the baseball field. If you're asking yourself, "Huh, those rocks; you can't be serious?" you're at the right place. There's a parking lot a little past the stones.

16. BALANCED ROCK, NORTH SALEM, NEW YORK

Archaeological perspectives

I knew I was in for an interesting conversation when, immediately after giving a public lecture about a famous archaeological fraud (the **Cardiff Giant**), a friendly gentleman approached me bearing two fat binders that, it turned out, were filled with 3 × 5 photographs.

> "Dr. Feder; I wonder if you might look at these photos? I'm sure *these* aren't archaeological frauds!" he said with a bit of a twinkle in this eye.

I smiled back at the man and placed one of the binders down on a nearby table, whereupon I began to skim through photographs of what appeared to be isolated boulders in forests, on mountain tops, and in cleared pastures.

> "So," he continued. "How do you explain *these*? *These* can't be frauds, right?"

No, they weren't frauds. In fact, it was pretty easy to come up with a reasonable hypothesis for what the photographed features likely were. Sure, the photos had no scale, so it was a bit of a challenge in many cases to figure out how large the boulders actually were. Some of the photographs were poorly focused, and the lighting was positively awful in many. But all things considered, it seemed apparent that this man had obsessively tracked down and photographed dozens of examples of a well-known category of entirely natural, glacial features. These boulders are called *erratics* and resulted from the movement of giant sheets of ice during the Pleistocene or Ice Age, that I talked a bit about in chapter 3, dating to between 1.8 million right up until about ten thousand years ago. In fact, the presence of large, often isolated boulders of raw materials different from all the surrounding rocks and underlying bedrock, often found many miles from and sometimes at a much higher elevation than their source—and even balanced upon other, smaller rocks as if placed there by a whimsical giant—was one of the key clues cited by geologists in the eighteenth and nineteenth centuries when they first suggested the existence of an ancient Ice Age. Only large bodies of slowly flowing ice would have been powerful enough to have moved large rocks so far from their sources—*and* sometimes uphill—and setting them down, sometimes on other clusters of smaller boulders. My region, New England, is loaded with glacial erratics, so that seemed the most logical explanation.

My new friend was not convinced by my diagnosis.

"Well, Dr. Feder, I don't know anything about geology, but I know these are not glacial erratics."

I'll let you think about that for a bit. A person prefaces a statement by admitting that he doesn't have any knowledge of the field of science most directly related to his question, and then makes a definitive statement about that question. How can anyone rationally do that? "Hey, I don't know anything about neurology, but I going to recommend you cut back on gluten to address your terrible headaches, insomnia, and dizziness." Please don't listen to me! I don't know what I'm talking about. Consult a physician immediately.

He went on to suggest that the boulders had not gotten there naturally but, instead, were placed at their locations in deep time by some highly advanced ancient society whose people had, apparently, a mania about strewing large rocks across the landscape. Of course. We agreed to disagree, parted on friendly terms, and he handed me his card. That business card contained his name and contact information and proclaimed, in all uppercase letters, his profession: ARCHELOGIST. My spell check keeps trying to fix that but that is precisely how he spelled ARCHAEOLOGIST (ARCHEOLOGIST would also have been acceptable) on his card. Sigh.

Here's what we know

Balanced Rock (figure 4.12) in North Salem, New York, is, almost certainly, one of those rare and wonderful instances in which a glacial erratic was serendipitously perched on smaller rocks as glacial ice flowed southward through eastern New York State, probably toward the end of the Pleistocene. It is a very large granite boulder, about sixteen feet long, fourteen feet wide, and ten feet tall.

Figure 4.12. The truly beautiful and extraordinarily impressive Balanced Rock located in North Salem, New York (just a few miles away from the Peach Pond Stone Chamber). Geologists identify Balanced Rock as an erratic, an entirely natural feature, produced during the Pleistocene or Ice Age, when large boulders were pushed miles from their sources by glacial ice, occasionally resulting in their being plopped on top of other, smaller boulders.

The signage at the boulder proposes a weight of about sixty tons, but it may be much more than that.

Sure, it's fun to speculate about an ancient culture in the area, capable of moving giant rocks and perching them on smaller ones—and you will see lots of such speculating on the internet—but there's simply no evidence for a human agency involved in creating Balanced Rock (figure 4.13).

We know the area experienced glaciation. There are other erratics scattered across the nearby landscape of New York State. Beyond this, Balanced Rock consists of a pink granite that is unlike the underlying bedrock of its present location. In fact, pink granite bedrock is found to the north, exactly what you'd expect for an erratic; the glaciers came from the north and deposited boulders both large and small as they expanded to the south. Further, the underside of Balanced Rock exhibits another glacial feature, striations. Striations are scratch marks created when small bits of rock embedded in the base of the glacier rode over other rocks, scratching them and leaving marks of that scratching. Don't get me wrong. Balanced Rock is a fascinating geological feature. But it was made by nature. It simply wasn't made by people.

Figure 4.13.   A closeup of the stones that underly the large boulder that is Balanced Rock. There is no indication whatsoever that the juxtaposition of the stones was the intentional work of human beings.

Why are archaeologists skeptical?

Archaeologists—and geologists: http://hudsonvalleygeologist.blogspot.com/2013/07/north-salem-balanced-rock.html—are skeptical that Balanced Rock is a cultural feature, the equivalent of the features called *dolmens*, *quoits*, or *cromlechs* in Great Britain, for two essential reasons:

1. Balanced Rock doesn't look like those genuine, archaeological features. By whatever name is applied, these genuine features ordinarily consist of three or four upright stones with a flat roof stone placed on top creating a chamber. Within that chamber archaeologists usually find evidence of a human burial or burials (although, at this point, most of those have been looted long ago). A wonderful example of this is Lanyon Quoit (figure 4.14) in Cornwall, in the southwest corner of England (also see Chun Quoit, figure P.1). Yes, Lanyon Quoit and Chun Quoit consist of a large rock balanced on some smaller ones, but Balanced Rock in North Salem, New York, certainly looks nothing like this beautiful example in England.
2. Suppose ancient Celts from Western Europe had sailed across the Atlantic deep in antiquity—during their megalithic age when they constructed sites like Stonehenge and built burial chambers like Lanyon Quoit—as much as five thousand years ago. You've heard this before;

Figure 4.14.   Lanyon Quoit and Chun Quoit (see figure P.1) are two very impressive, more than 4,000-year-old tombs located in Cornwall in the southwestern corner of England. Though some compare Balanced Rock to genuine cultural features like these, there certainly is no comparison or connection between them.

had they settled in New York State and lived there long enough to make a rather poor replica of one of their burial chambers, then they must have been around long enough to have settled in a village where the archaeological remains of their unique material culture would be found by archaeologists. Archaeologists certainly find the remains of Native American settlements in New York State, recovering ancient stone implements and ceramics. Archaeologists similarly find the remains of European colonial settlements there, recovering bits and pieces of a wide range of seventeenth-, eighteenth-, and nineteenth-century artifacts including glazed crockery, nails, coins, gun flints, lead shot, window glass, and lots more. Allow me to repeat my mantra: the material culture—the physical evidence—left behind by those Native and colonial people are recognizable, they are as diagnostic as the fossil of an animal. And just as we can identify the species of an animal from its bones, we can identify a culture from the artifacts its people left behind. No ancient European artifacts dating to the time period in Europe when stone burial chambers were being built have ever been found in North America. That lack of evidence is pretty convincing that those Europeans weren't here, and this alone is sufficient grounds for skepticism.

Whodunit?

Well, who made Balanced Rock? A glacier did. Who wants to believe that ancient Celts (or whoever) made Balanced Rock? I guess it's people who would rather believe that in Balanced Rock there resides a great historical mystery—one that will make us rewrite the history books to include a chapter about the wayfaring builders of monuments like Stonehenge who landed on the shores of North America in antiquity, leaving behind not evidence of their habitations, but only the occasional megalithic monument. However, it's not only the history books that would need rewriting if this were true, it's also the archaeology methods textbooks. Hey, I wrote one of those books, so I take that personally (Feder 2010). Kidding. Nevertheless, our current understanding of how archaeological sites come into existence simply doesn't allow for people living in an area long enough to leave behind a large stone monument but no evidence of their daily lives.

Why?

This one puzzles me. The balanced rock feature is quite real and fascinating, and the result of some very interesting natural, geological processes. Why folks want to deny that those processes produced Balanced Rock and prefer the notion that ancient European migrants built it is the real mystery.

Fake-o-meter

Five.

Getting there

Balanced Rock is located in North Salem, New York, 4.2 miles south of Route 6 in Brewster, on the east side of Route 116, just south of its intersection with Keeler Lane. There's a small parking lot there. It's very cool.

17. NEWPORT TOWER, NEWPORT, RHODE ISLAND

Archaeological perspectives

There is no argument: the Newport Tower, located in Newport, Rhode Island, is a beautiful and fascinating stone structure, definitely worth checking out (figure 4.15). It is a twenty-four-foot-high cylindrical building made of large, roughly hewn pieces of mortared stone. The base of the tower is circular, with an

Figure 4.15. The famous Newport Tower of Newport, Rhode Island. Though some claim that the tower was built by ancient Norse—or maybe it was ancient Chinese—visitors to the New World, the tower was almost certainly built by Benedict Arnold, the great-grandfather of the infamous traitor to America during the Revolution.

exterior diameter of between twenty-two and twenty-three feet. There are eight stone columns at its base, which are separated by eight open archways. The archways are a bit more than seven feet in height. Three wood-framed windows were built into the tower a little more than halfway up; these windows would have served the main floor, whose wooden joists and planking are long gone. There are four additional very small openings closer to the top of the stone structure, likely intended to increase air circulation.

Though beautiful, the tower appears to be old, is an obvious ruin, and as such has generated a raft of speculation about both its purpose and the identification of the builder. History and archaeology, however, dismiss that speculation and clear up three mysteries: who built it, when was it built, and what was its purpose.

Here's what we know

The tower actually has a clear connection—at least an indirect one—to one of the most famous men in American history. You've all heard the name "Benedict Arnold." He is known, after all, and will be known for all time, as an iconic traitor to the American cause.

Commissioned as a general in the Continental Army during the Revolutionary War, Arnold was actually a mole, clandestinely working for the British defeat of the revolution. During the war, Arnold, a member of a powerful, wealthy, and respected family, was given command of the colonial army fortifications at West Point in New York State. From this powerful position, instead of working for the colonial cause against the British, he actively plotted to hand over the base to those British overlords. When his traitorous plan was exposed, Arnold defected to the British invasion force, where they made him a brigadier general. Imagine if George Washington, while ostensibly leading the colonists, was actually working undercover for the British. That was Benedict Arnold.

I provided that brief summary of the treachery of Benedict Arnold because that name is intimately associated with Newport Tower, though indirectly. The tower is not associated with the traitor Benedict Arnold; it is associated with his great-grandfather who bore the same name.

That Benedict Arnold was born in AD 1615 in England, specifically in Ilchester, Somerset. In 1635, when he was nineteen, he immigrated to America with his parents and siblings, all settling in the Massachusetts Bay colony. About a year later, the family moved to the shores of Narragansett Bay, helping establish the English settlement called Providence Plantation, which would become Rhode Island. This elder Arnold became a well-respected and powerful man and ultimately became the governor of the colony. He appears to have won the trust of local Native Americans and became proficient in the languages of two tribes, the Narragansett and the Wampanoag.

This Benedict Arnold died in 1678, and here is where we see his clear and obvious connection to what is now called the Newport Tower: he owned the property where the tower is located, and the structure is twice mentioned in his last will and testament (you can find copies of his will online)! First, he describes where he wants to be buried: "*near ye line or path from my dwelling house leading to my stone built windmill in ye town of Newport abovementioned.*" Elsewhere in his will he bequeathed to his wife: "*ye other and greater parcel of ye tract of land aforesaid upon which standeth my dwelling or mansion house and other building thereto adjoining or belonging, as also my stone built Wind Mill.*" In terms of location and timing, this is clearly a reference to what is now called the Newport Tower.

There's one more thing; there is no historical reference to the structure already being there when Arnold obtained the land. There is no mention of or speculation about a stone tower on the land before it shows up in the will. That would seem to be pretty good evidence that there wasn't any great mystery about the tower in the seventeenth century. Nobody wondered about its origins because everybody knew who built it. This leads to the conclusion that Arnold had the structure built during his tenure there.

Why are archaeologists skeptical?

Archaeologists are extremely skeptical of the claim that the Newport Tower is far older than Benedict Arnold's ownership of the property for a number of reasons, including the fact that, as mentioned, it's in his will. Another major piece of evidence of a seventeenth-century AD temporal provenience for the tower is the fact that the tower is a dead ringer for another seventeenth-century building, this one located not in Rhode Island or even in America, but in England. It's probably not a coincidence that the English tower is located only a hundred miles from where the elder Benedict Arnold grew up. That structure, the Chesterton Windmill (figure 4.16), built in the seventeenth century and was well known, being located along a main road past town. Another colonist in Providence Plantation, George Lawton, grew up less than twenty miles from Chesterton, and he became a builder and is known to have built a number of mills in America. There's even a reference in a document dating to 1668, mentioning that Mill Street in Newport was "a way leading to George Lawton's Mill" (Hertz 1997). And Mill Street does, indeed, lead right to the Newport Tower. In all likelihood, Arnold was at least passingly familiar with the Chesterton Windmill, and perhaps with Lawton's assistance, he had a similar one built on his property.

Even so, and to be consistent in my archaeological approach, while a written document and a historical coincidence can supply important information, archaeologists live and die on the basis of material, physical evidence. No archaeologist is going to be completely content with documentary evidence alone. The gold standard for determining the age and origins of an old structure is material, archaeological evidence, especially recognizable, datable objects that are diagnostic of a particular time period and culture. And there is plenty of that to add to the historical documentation.

There was an archaeological excavation conducted at the base of the tower in 1948 and 1949. Directed by archaeologists from Harvard University, the results of the dig were clear and indisputable; artifacts including pieces of glazed pottery, fragment of white clay (kaolin) smoking pipes, a gun flint, and rusted nails were found in the remnants of a trench that had been dug *under* the tower by its builders (Godfrey 1951). A colonial boot print was actually found in a clay deposit lying between two of the tower's columns. The artifacts and the boot print could only have been made *before* the tower was built.

So, can we date the artifacts recovered in the excavation of the builders' trench? In fact, several of the objects excavated in the original builder's trench were temporally diagnostic and datable to a narrow period of time. The oldest of these were typical colonial artifacts all dating to the middle of the seventeenth

Figure 4.16.   Looking very similar to the Newport Tower, the Chesterton Windmill is located just outside of the village of Chesterton, in England which is only about 100 miles from where Benedict Arnold grew up before immigrating to America. The Chesterton Windmill may have served as Arnold's model for the windmill we now call the Newport Tower.

century. As the director of the excavations, William S. Godfrey, concluded, this means that tower cannot have been built before the seventeenth century.

More recently, Scandinavian scientists who were applying radiocarbon dating to the carbon in the limestone used in mortar in medieval churches in Europe were invited to try the technique on the Newport Tower (Ringborn et al. 2003). The result; the mortar found deep in the tower's structure bonding the stone blocks together and, therefore, dating to the tower's construction, produced a radiocarbon date of AD 1680. Case closed.

The point is, archaeological and historical evidence converges on the conclusion that the mill was built sometime in the mid-seventeenth century and that the great-grandfather of the famous American traitor was responsible for its construction.

Whodunit?

Undeniably, the tower, as a beautiful ruin, raised questions in the nineteenth century, a period of rampant speculation about American antiquity. One of the best known of the speculators was Carl Christian Rafn, who devoted his life to investigating what he perceived to be great historical mysteries, especially relating to those places where he believed there was evidence of ancient migration to and settlement of America. Rafn believed that the Vinland landfall and settlement dating to about AD 1000 and described in the Norse sagas was, in fact, located in Rhode Island. Rafn thought **Dighton Rock** bore an ancient Norse inscription, so it's no surprise that he embraced the notion that the stone tower in Newport was a Norse building.

More than anything else, the popular idea that the tower was Norse can be traced to a romantic poem written by Henry Wadsworth Longfellow in 1841 and titled "The Skeleton in Armor" (the "skeleton in armor" is supposed to be the remains of an ancient Viking found in New England). The poem is a fantasy, a purely fictional account about a wayfaring Viking and the great love he had for his wife. His wife dies during a rough passage across the sea, and in his grief he builds a monument to her upon making landfall in a new land. The new land is America, almost certainly Rhode Island, and the monument is a stone tower:

> Three weeks we westward bore,
> And when the storm was o'er,
> Cloud-like we saw the shore
> Stretching to leeward;
> There for my lady's bower
> Built I the lofty tower,
> Which, to this very hour,
> Stands looking seaward.

It's a sad story. And there sure is a lot of rhyming. But the poem is only fiction.

Why?

I guess the claim that there is an ancient Norse tower located in the middle of Rhode Island just has a lot of romantic appeal. Okay, the Norse didn't build anything like the Newport Tower anywhere else, including back home in Scandinavia, but whatever. The Vikings are cool and fun to speculate about. How about an ancient Chinese origin? Again, an interesting, actual speculation about the Newport Tower and, oh yeah, let's rewrite those history books, even though the tower doesn't look anything at all like Chinese architecture. Certainly it would be fascinating if, instead of a beautiful but otherwise mundane windmill, the tower was an astronomical observatory because, hey, you can see the sun rising from the windows. Okay, you can see the sun rising from the windows of my house, built in 1840 and, as far as I know, it was never used as an observatory. But why be a party pooper? Perhaps Portuguese sailors built it, you know, the ones who left their signature on Dighton Rock.

Sure, any of these are possible. The problem is, however, that there is absolutely no evidence to support any of these speculations. The evidence points to the seventeenth century and its ownership by Benedict Arnold.

Fake-o-meter

Five. The abundance of independent and converging streams of evidence for the colonial hypothesis—documents, archaeology, radiocarbon dating—shows that the Newport Tower isn't Norse, Chinese, Portuguese, or anything other than a colonial period windmill.

Getting there

The Newport Tower is located in Touro Park, on Mill Street, in Newport, Rhode Island. Set your GPS to Touro Park and you'll get there. It sits in the middle of a residential area, and it is surrounded by an iron gate, in the middle of a field of cut grass. It's a very beautiful setting and the tower really is fascinating, even if, horrors, it's just the remnants of Benedict Arnold's windmill.

Category 3 Ancient Visitors: Villages

𝒯here are at least a couple of sites in our odyssey that have been claimed to be, not just a written message or an isolated stone monument, but the remnants of entire villages of ancient European settlers to the New World. The very same problem I've addressed in reference to written messages and stone monuments is magnified further here. Ancient Celts or Phoenicians or Romans or Jews or whoever cannot possibly have built and then lived in a village and never dropped or lost or discarded or put away for safe keeping something that an archaeologist could find, identify, and then trace its cultural and geographic source. However, as we'll see, at neither **Gungywamp** in Connecticut (Hitt 1998) or **America's Stonehenge/Mystery Hill** in New Hampshire (Vescelius 1956) is there a single artifact—much less an entire assemblage of artifacts—that would be out of place at an eighteenth- or nineteenth-century New England farm or community. Without any thousand-year-old bronze tools traceable to Western Europe at these New England sites, lacking European ceramics or burials—in essence, without an archaeological context for these places—archaeologists will be highly skeptical.

There is an exception to this. There actually is an entire archaeological site in the New World left behind by settlers five centuries before the Columbus expeditions in the late fifteenth century. Archaeologists found the remnants of cooking features, trash pits, house remains, and tool-making areas that are not associated with Native People and representing a time and material culture not associated with nineteenth-century settlers. The **L'anse aux Meadows** site in Newfoundland provides exactly what an archaeologist would expect at an eleventh-century AD Norse colony, wherever it was found, including North America (Ingstad 1977). The other sites included in this category of archaeological oddities simply don't. L'anse aux Meadows is, in a sense, a model or template for what an archaeological site should look like when it represents the remains of a colony of people bearing a culture markedly different from that of local, Indigenous People; this is where the other two sites discussed in this section come up woefully short. Let's take a look at these places and examine what archaeological research can tell us about their origin.

18. GUNGYWAMP, GROTON, CONNECTICUT

Archaeological perspectives

Take a walk deep into the woods just about anywhere in southern New England and you might be surprised by what you'll see. Despite its current appearance as an uninhabited wilderness, all around you'll find abundant evidence of past human occupation. Sometimes along a hiking trail, but just as likely far off that beaten path, you will almost certainly encounter some of our seemingly ubiquitous, often finely made stone walls. But why would anyone construct all those walls in the middle of the woods? Within a complex grid of walls you might also see stone-lined cellar holes—the foundations of old houses—the footings for small outbuildings, and sometimes even isolated clusters of gravestones (figure 5.1). What are those signs of human activity doing deep in the forest? To the uninitiated, it might sound strange. After all, why are there signs of a human population effectively in the middle of nowhere?

Figure 5.1. The modern woodlands of New England are sprinkled with the remnants of abandoned nineteenth-century communities. House foundations, wells, roads, and cemeteries provide mute testimony to those once thriving villages.

Don't be fooled by the current appearance of our southern New England forests. Today, about 60 percent of Connecticut is wooded. Massachusetts is about the same. But that number actually represents a substantial rebound from what it was at the beginning of the nineteenth century when it is estimated that only about 25 percent of Connecticut was wooded (https://www.fs.fed.us/ne/ newtown_square/publications/resource_bulletins/pdfs/2004/ne_rb160.pdf). In fact, much of Connecticut's woodlands had at one time been cleared for farming, for pasture lands, and for raw materials needed for construction and fuel. Areas that today are deep in our state forests were, in the past, cleared, settled, and heavily utilized. Those stone walls were built to mark property boundaries, keep cattle in their pastures, or just to clear glacial boulders from agricultural fields. House, barn, and other outbuilding foundations represent the archaeological evidence of often intensive previous human use.

Outside our river floodplains, Connecticut's soil is rough, rocky, and acidic. Though people made a valiant effort to make agriculture economically viable, many farmsteads and even entire communities in our uplands were abandoned by the early twentieth century. The houses were burned or left to fall in on themselves, the barn boards were taken for reuse, and all that remains are the stone foundations and walls you can see during a walk in the woods. Those material remnants of cleared fields, houses, barns, and other outbuildings are the equivalent of ghost towns, with only their "bones" remaining to reflect what were once active and vibrant communities. Though deep in the woods today, they were not during their heyday.

One such place is Gungywamp located in the town of Groton in south-eastern Connecticut. Much of the perceived strangeness associated with Gungy-wamp stems from that misunderstanding. It can't just be a farmstead; why would a farmstead be located deep in the woods? The simple answer is, it wasn't.

Here's what we know

At least some of the stonework at Gungywamp, including walls, foundations, and stone-lined root cellars, may date back to the earliest European settlement of Connecticut. In AD 1654, colonist Thomas Pynchon wrote a letter to John Winthrop of New Haven mentioning stone walls and a fort (it's impossible to determine what he meant precisely by that term) in the "Gungywamp range." (I've left all of the original spellings, punctuation, and capitalization intact.)

> Honored Sir;
> Sir I heare a report of a stonewall and strong fort in it, made all of Stone, which is newly discovered at or neere Pequet, (presently known as the Gungy-wamp Range), I should be glad to know the truth of it from your selfe, here being many strange reports about it.

Remember, Pynchon isn't saying that he himself witnessed the stone wall or fort; he's merely inquiring about a report that he had heard. We don't have Winthrop's response, if he ever made one, and no one has ever found anything even vaguely resembling an actual fort, as we would define it anyway, anywhere in the area. But it is intriguing and suggests that perhaps some of the Gungywamp features may date to at least as far back as the mid-seventeenth century. That's fascinating, but it lends no support to the claim made by some that Gungywamp is Pre-Columbian, and it doesn't mean the site was built by ancient Druids or Celts, and it doesn't mean the stonework is somehow related to an ancient solar calendar. Finally, it certainly doesn't mean that Gungywamp is a freaky and paranormal place, as some claim.

Why are archaeologists skeptical?

Several years ago, the Archaeological Society of Connecticut held its fall meeting at the wonderful Peqoutsepos Nature Center. Following lunch, we carpooled to a parking area and then all hiked to the Gungywamp site. Among the attendees were a handful of people who genuinely believe that Gungywamp is weird, consisting of a series of out-of-place buildings that perhaps represents a ceremonial center of ancient European settlers who, apparently, worshipped the sun. Some of those same people—and you can't make this up—also believe that Gungywamp is located at the confluence of a series of inexplicable paranormal streams. Seriously. They claim that some people become dizzy, lightheaded, and even nauseated when they walk through the site which, in actuality, is simply an old farmstead. Near the farmstead is a cliff, and apparently, some people spontaneously burst into tears (they even call the cliff the "Cliff of Tears") when they get to the top. Others begin to bleed from their eyes, from their ears, or from their wherever (thank you Donald Trump; http://www.messagetoeagle.com/mysterious-ancient-gungywamp-could-be-a-gateway-to-a-parallel-reality/). The only reaction I've had to walking the trail to the top is an increased heart and respiration rate. I'm going to go out on a limb here and assume this happens, not as a result of anything supernatural, but because it's a pretty steep ascent and I don't get enough exercise. But what do you expect from a skeptic?

Anyway, I was, in a sense, a tour guide during the aforementioned hike, and we had just walked by what was rather obviously the foundations of a dwelling and a barn (figure 5.2). Nothing weird about that. We continued on and, honestly, not more than about thirty seconds past those foundations, we came upon a fascinating feature, a double circle of shaped stones on the ground (figure 5.3). As cool as that was, there wasn't anything particularly strange about it. In all likelihood those stones were the base of a bark mill, like the one pictured here (figure 5.4). Where water power wasn't available—or where building an elaborate water-driven mill would have been overkill—a solid stone mill wheel could be placed upright within

Figure 5.2. Gungywamp is one of the abandoned communities mentioned in the introduction to this section. Here are the remnants of the stone foundation of a house and the adjacent barn in what is now an abandoned farmstead.

Figure 5.3. Though looking quite mysterious to the modern observer, this double ring of stones isn't an ancient Celtic ceremonial monument. It's a bark mill used in the production of tannin which, in turn, was used in hide working.

Figure 5.4. The remnants of a nineteenth-century bark mill with a double row of stones and the attendant vertical mill wheel still in place.

a concentric double circle of stones. A horizontal axle passed through the center of the mill wheel and connected to a vertical axle set into the ground in the center of the double circle. The outside of the horizontal axle was harnessed to a horse, mule, or oxen. When the animal(s) were induced to walk in a circle, the mill wheel would turn within the double stone circle, and anything placed therein—for example, bark to remove the chemical tannin for leather working or even apples for cider—would be crushed. It's a pretty clever, decidedly low-tech way of crushing stuff. Nothing particularly paranormal about it.

So, the double stone circle isn't an oddity at all. What was odd for me as a tour guide was the fact that someone in the group questioned my interpretation, saying: "But why would a mill be placed here, in the middle of the woods, far away from anything else?" The implication was that the feature must really be something ceremonial, sacred, and strange and not just an ordinary bit of farm equipment because it was located in isolation, a lonely cluster of stones deep in the piney woods.

Wait, what? We encountered the double circle of stones literally thirty seconds after we walked by the foundations of the farmhouse and the barn (see figure 5.2). Had the questioner not been paying attention? I think the existence of the house and barn foundations might provide a tiny hint that, at one time, the location was not in the middle of nowhere. It was in the middle of a farm where a farmer might want to extract tannin or make cider.

Nearby the bark mill are two small chambers made of field stones (figure 5.5). Stone chambers like the ones at Gungywamp are interesting, of course, but

Figure 5.5. A storage chamber that was part of the farmstead at Gungywamp. Look at the chambers shown in figures 4.1, 4.4, and 4.7 for a comparison. Once again, no artifacts have been found in the chamber that would suggest a particularly ancient or alien (Celtic or Phoenician, for example) origin for the feature. It's part of a farmstead and, therefore, likely was built and used in farming operations.

as we've already seen in the example of the Acton, Upton, and Peach Pond stone chambers, they aren't particularly mysterious to historians or archaeologists. Colonists built chambers like them for the cold storage of root crops and as ice houses. In fact, they're often called "root cellars." And as discussed previously, their orientations have to do with temperature control, not sun worship.

Finally, there simply are no artifacts, no bits and pieces of material culture, recovered at Gungywamp that can be traced to or associated with ancient Europeans. The only artifacts recovered at Gungywamp are of nineteenth-century European origin (Jackson, Jackson, and Linke 1981).

Whodunit?

We can't always call out a single individual and bestow credit (or maybe blame) for an interpretation of a site that doesn't match that of archaeologists or historians. Here we can. I met the gentleman in question, David Barron, more than thirty years ago. I didn't spend very much time with him, but he certainly was an intelligent, interesting, energetic, and well-meaning guy. He believed that the structures at Gungywamp were built by Irish monks who had traveled to and settled in the New World about a thousand years before the Columbus voyages of exploration. To be sure, Barron wasn't an archaeologist or historian, but he was a passionate believer in his interpretation of the site, and in 1979 he founded the Gungywamp Society whose purpose it was to further that view. In a fundamental way, Barron inspired many followers who were animated by his desire to paint what they perceived to be a more romantic history of their own southern New England backyards, a history that included ancient Irishmen coming here in their quest for a quiet place to worship God.

Why?

Writer Jack Hitt (1998) interviewed a bunch of "Gungywampers" some years ago for an article, participating in one of their hikes to the site. Hitt reports that among the believers there was a tremendous amount of resentment aimed at anyone with a degree in archaeology who questioned their interpretation. They expressed, according to Hitt, a special vitriol for people with degrees and training from Ivy League schools. Hitt also noted that the ethnicity of many of the Gungywampers matched that of the ancient Celts who they wanted very much to believe inhabited Connecticut in the distant past. Hitt noted the fact that at least the folks he encountered while writing the article were largely men of Irish descent intent on proving that Irishmen in antiquity were already living in Connecticut long before Columbus voyaged to the New World and also before those bloodthirsty Norsemen and Norsewomen explored and briefly settled in northeastern Canada.

I have no stomach for long-distance psychoanalysis, but we've already seen a strong current of ethnic pride running through the issue of which European group arrived in the New World first (for example, the Norse affection for the **Kensington Runestone**). I actually received a rather nasty letter from an Italian American woman in response to a mild op-ed piece I wrote pointing out that Columbus could not, in the true sense of the word, "discover" a land in which there were already millions of people living. A few years ago I met a very enthusiastic Jewish woman who was a passionate searcher for evidence that might support her strong belief that Jewish mariners had, in antiquity, plied the Atlantic and had landed upon the shores of America. So, if there is a component of ethnic pride here among the believers that yet another ethnic group beat Columbus to America, well, it wouldn't be the first time.

Fake-o-meter

Five.

Getting there

The Gungywamp site is currently located on private land and not open to the general public, but it is in the process of being transferred to the State of Connecticut. It's a fluid situation as I write this (in March 2018). Until that transfer is complete, the Denison Pequotsepos Nature Center (DPNC) serves as the steward of the property, and they provide guided tours of the site. To read their sensible interpretation of the site and to arrange a tour, see: http://dpnc.org/gungywamp-structures/. You can also call them at (860) 536-1216. I have taken a couple of their tours, and the people are simply terrific. The nature center is located, conveniently enough, on Pequotsepos Road, Mystic Connecticut.

19. AMERICA'S STONEHENGE/MYSTERY HILL, NORTH SALEM, MASSACHUSETTS

Archaeological perspectives

The original, historical name for the site that is the focus of this entry was Pattee's Cave, named for Jonathan Pattee, the nineteenth-century landowner of the property located in the southern New Hampshire town of North Salem. Not really caves, the site consists of a series of dry-laid stone walls, more than a dozen chambers made from the same fieldstone used in the walls (I guess those are the "caves"), stone wall enclosures (figures 5.6 and 5.7), a stone-lined passageway, and a large, flat, grooved stone that I'll discuss in detail.

Figure 5.6. America's Stonehenge consists of a jumble of stone walls and a warren of stone chambers. It is an interesting site, to be sure, but nothing there is even vaguely reminiscent of the morphology of Stonehenge.

Figure 5.7. An example of the dry-laid stonework at America's Stonehenge.

"Pattee's Cave," you will admit, isn't a particularly romantic, poetic, or even accurate name for the site, but that's how it started. The name applied to the place today by the current owners is America's Stonehenge which, in all honesty, is overblown and flat-out inaccurate. I've been to Stonehenge in England and I've been to America's Stonehenge in New Hampshire and, frankly, the latter is no Stonehenge (see figure 4.9).

Make no mistake, America's Stonehenge is a fascinating place, and I do encourage you to visit it, but "Stonehenge"? Really? There's no defining "henge" or stone circle at the New Hampshire site, which is kind of a deal killer. It can't be Stone*henge* without a henge. There are no impressive sarsen stones, each weighing in at about fifty thousand pounds. There are no precisely carved lintels connecting sarsens with mortice and tenon joints, the equivalent of giant stone Lego blocks. There are no looming trilithons in New Hampshire, features in which two upright stones, each more than twenty feet tall and weighing nearly twice as much as the sarsens, are connected, again in a stone version of mortise and tenon joinery, by bulky lintel stones. No one, truly no one, has ever walked into the middle of the place now called America's Stonehenge and thought, "Wow, this is a dead ringer for Stonehenge." Other than the fact that the original Stonehenge and America's Stonehenge are, well, crafted of stone, along with the claim that, like the real deal, the American knockoff was built to record celestial alignments, there's no comparison.

Which brings me to this: when I first encountered the place as a kid, it was called Mystery Hill. In fact, it was called that from the late 1930s or early 1940s right up until 1982 when the name was changed to America's Stonehenge. For what it's worth—not much, I agree—I think "Mystery Hill" was a more interesting and far more accurately descriptive name for the place, and I don't mean that ironically. The mysteries implicit in that name and to be discussed in this entry focus on the same questions long raised about this admittedly idiosyncratic site: Who built the place, when did they build it, and what was its purpose?

Here's what we know

Connecticut insurance executive William Goodwin thought he knew the answers to those questions after visiting the warren of stone chambers, walls, and other features that characterized Pattee's Cave and then purchasing the place in 1937. Goodwin was convinced it was one of the most important historical locations in North America, remains of a settlement of Irish Culdee monks who, fleeing from the Vikings as they spread across the North Atlantic in the sixth and seventh centuries AD, made it to the New World where they established a little colony in North Salem, New Hampshire (Goodwin 1946).

Now, the Norse were real, of course, and pretty much lived up to their reputation of badassery. Further, they did kick a bunch of monk butt more than a thousand years ago in their geographical expansion across the Atlantic, displacing them from Iceland, for example, at the end of the eighth century AD. Goodwin, essentially, ran with that and proposed that the place then called Pattee's Cave had been an important and ancient sanctuary for Irish monks who had been chased away by the Norse.

So sure, the Norse were expansionist and displaced people who were already living in territories they, the Norse, wanted. And sure, there were Irish monks living in places the Norse coveted, and certainly these monks had seafaring capabilities. To get to some of the islands they reached to establish monasteries where they could worship God unimpeded by the considerations of the mundane world, they had to be able to construct and sail boats. We also know that the preferred vessel in Ireland, the ox-hide *curragh*, was remarkably seaworthy. Modern experiments have successfully sailed replicas great distances (Severin 1977). So, could America's Stonehenge be a settlement of Irish monks? Well, yes, but there would need to be archaeological evidence of their presence there. And that evidence doesn't exist.

After Goodwin passed away, the site became the property of the highly appropriately named Robert Stone. Stone and many others interested in the site eventually abandoned the Irish monk hypothesis and began pushing the age of the site back to two thousand, three thousand, and even four thousand years ago, and changing its hypothesized cultural affiliation from that of medieval Irish monks to ancient Celts led by their Druids, the priestly class of ancient Celtic culture (Fell 1976). Oh, and more recently it has been proposed by some that the place was built by Indians, making it ground zero for an entirely Native American Ceremonial Stone Landscape discussed in the entry for the Acton, Upton, and Peach Pond stone chambers (see Gage and Gage 2008).

Irish monks? Druids? Native Americans? Whatever; let's not discriminate here. The only important questions, at least at this point, are, What is the *evidence* for who built the site, when, and for what purpose?

Why are archaeologists skeptical?

An immediate problem we run into concerning an interpretation of the meaning of America's Stonehenge results from the fact that there is clear photographic evidence that Goodwin, entirely well intentioned but unfortunately, reconstructed at least some of the features at the site. In doing that, Goodwin was following in the footsteps of similarly well-meaning but similarly wrongheaded reconstructions by professional archaeologists at sites all over the world. Goodwin had a template of what he thought the structures at Pattee's Cave should look like based on his belief that the site was the settlement of medieval Irish monks. That's a problem in interpreting the original form, use, and meaning of those structures.

Okay, but what if Goodwin hadn't changed any of the original structures? Are their shapes and construction methods enough to prove that the chambers, for example, date to more than a thousand years ago and were brought here by immigrants from Europe? Actually, the answer to that question is a big fat "no"! Dry-laid stone masonry of the sort seen at America's Stonehenge was employed by ancient Celts in their sacred architecture, but as already shown, it was also used in recent history in the construction of farm and pasture walls and outbuildings, including root cellars. Just because a structure looks old, mysterious, and weird to our twenty-first-century eyes doesn't make it old, mysterious, or weird.

You won't be surprised that, in my opinion, archaeological evidence is the gold standard for determining who built and used the structures at America's Stonehenge. And in fact, the site was excavated in the mid-1950s by a crew directed by Gary Vescelius, then a graduate student at Yale University (Vescelius 1956). The excavation yielded a rich and diverse assemblage of over seven thousand artifacts including pottery, nails, metal, and brick fragments, along with Native American artifacts that are common throughout New England. Here's the thing; Vescelius and his crew did not find a single artifact at the site that could be traced to Western Europe dating to the period either of the Culdee monks or the even older Druid-led Celts. Once advertised as a Bronze Age site, it is telling that the excavators did not find a single bronze artifact there. There simply are no artifacts—no crockery or metal, for example—traceable to the ancient Old World either in style or raw material found among the ruins of America's Stonehenge. That's a deal killer for an archaeologist for the hypothesis that America's Stonehenge was built by ancient European settlers of New Hampshire. That leaves open the question of what the site actually is. I'll get to that in a moment.

Whodunit?

We have, more than anyone else, William Goodwin to thank for popularizing the notion that the site was something other than an interesting nineteenth-century farmstead. We have the Stone family to thank for maintaining the site and having it open to the public. I do not use the term *thank* ironically here. We really do have these folks to thank for preserving the place. It deserves preservation, attention, and study. The Goodwin and Stone families were well meaning; I simply disagree with their claims about the site's age and cultural affiliation.

Why?

The place that began its life as Pattee's Cave, then morphed into Mystery Hill, and is now called America's Stonehenge is a genuine historical archaeological site. It's a nineteenth-century farmstead consisting of features that were common in the nineteenth century, though the specific combination and configuration of the place is fascinatingly idiosyncratic. The "why did they do it?" question here is about why different people interpret it in ways that are simply not supported by the historical or archaeological records. That's a more nuanced question than simply "Why did they do it?"

For example, I think that for those who like the idea that, just maybe, ancient Celts visited and even settled in the New World long ago, perhaps thousands of years before Columbus, America's Stonehenge is viewed as a key piece of proof for that hypothesis. For those who like the idea that, just maybe, ancient Native Americans living in eastern North America built substantial features in stone, perhaps thousands of years before Columbus, America's Stonehenge is viewed as a key piece of proof for that hypothesis.

Then there are those who view America's Stonehenge as not just ancient Celtic, but as an ancient pagan site where fascinating, weird, and creepy rituals took place, conducted by an ancient priesthood called the Druids. The Druids were an actual priestly class in ancient Europe and have, since the Victorian Era, been the focus of intense romantic speculation and even veneration, with the Druids being viewed as the carriers of ancient mystical and spiritual truths that have been lost in the dim recesses of time but that we can and should aspire to recapture in the modern world.

What does America's Stonehenge have to do with an ancient priestly class in Western Europe? It's all about human sacrifice. One of the less appealing practices of the Druids was, at least according to the claims made by the Romans who encountered them in Gaul (France) and in England, was that of human sacrifice. Most historians today take those descriptions by the Romans of the pervasiveness of this practice with a grain of salt, viewing it as largely "fake news" for consumption back home in Rome. Nevertheless, the canard has stuck, though among modern Druid-o-philes, it's viewed through a romantic lens. Sure, human sacrifice is terrible, but it's pretty cool to imagine white-robed priests who are the bearers of esoteric knowledge conducting blood-soaked rituals in a deep and spooky time (Card 2018). Creepy, sure, but kind of cool and romantic at the same time (well, as long as you're not on today's sacrifice menu).

Here's the connection: Visitors to America's Stonehenge are directed to a flat slab of stone by signage printed in appropriately red, bold lettering: "To the Sacrificial Table" (figure 5.8). So, one must assume, a band of ancient Celts, led by their priests, journeyed to New Hampshire in deep time, built a settlement, and continued their grisly practice of human sacrifice in the dark forests of New England. We have the sacrificial table, more than large enough to accommodate a human being, with the predictable grooved channel along its perimeter to collect the life blood of the victim as it oozed out of his or her body. There's even an exit channel, allowing the blood to be collected, likely for some grisly and unspeakable rite (figure 5.9).

Figure 5.8. The positioning of what the owners of America's Stonehenge have long labeled the "sacrificial table," a flat slab of stone resting on legs of stone.

Figure 5.9. The so-called sacrificial table at America's Stonehenge is a flat slab of local stone with a channel carved along the perimeter of the surface. Notice in the lower right, there is an exit channel for whatever liquid was being collected on the surface. As a "sacrificial table" (yeah, those are my scare quotes), the owners of America's Stonehenge believe the liquid was blood and the clear implication is that it was human.

Cool story. It might make a great movie. Well, not a great movie, but an okay movie. But no. In fact, nothing about the sacrificial table identification is supported by evidence. Those Roman descriptions of Gaul and England never describe anything that looks even vaguely like the table at America's Stonehenge. The archaeology of the homelands of the ancient Celts lends no support to the claim either; there are no artifacts in Europe that resemble the table at America's Stonehenge. In fact, rather ironically, if you perform an internet search on the terms *sacrificial table*, *Europe*, *Druid*, or *human sacrifice*, the images that commonly turn up are of the table at America's Stonehenge! In other words, if you look for an ancient model or template in Europe, where the Druids originated, for America's Stonehenge table, you come up with photographs of itself.

What could a flat slab of stone with a channel obviously meant to collect a liquid be intended for if not for collecting blood? Actually, that's easy, and the America's Stonehenge example is far from unique (figure 5.10). It's called a cider press bed stone. Such stones served as the platforms for human-powered screw presses that squeeze the juices out of crushed apples. How do we know this? Even into the 1980s there were working apple cider presses in the UK that used bed stones that look like the America's Stonehenge example (Quinion 2008). The presses were positioned upon, you guessed it, flat, channeled stones; that's why they are called cider press bed stones. The artifact at America's Stonehenge

Figure 5.10.   The sacrificial table at America's Stonehenge is not unique. I have seen several in museum collections in Southern New England where they are well known as cider press bed stones. This one is located at the Farm Museum in Hadley, Massachusetts. Serving as the base of a cider press, the press squeezes the juice from the apples and the bed stone collects the juice where it accumulates in the carved channels, finally flowing through the exit channel. Working cider presses with bed stones similar to this one and the one seen at America's Stonehenge can still be seen.

is a fascinating example. But it's for cider, not blood, and shouldn't be interpreted through the anachronistic lens of Victorian Era romanticism, though art work from that period depicting Druidical sacrifice are gruesomely interesting (figure 5.11). I will admit, however, that "This Way to the Cider Press Bed Stone," with lettering in the amber color of cider, would not be quite as spookily romantic as "To the Sacrificial Table."

Figure 5.11. This wonderfully macabre 1851 engraving by Felix Phillippoteaux is titled *Human Sacrifice by a Gaulish Druid*. With the victim splayed out on a stone table, his blood being collected in a chalice by a Druid priest, this image seems to be the perfect model for those who claim that the cider press bed stone at America's Stonehenge is, in reality, a sacrificial table. But the engraving is, itself, a fantasy.
Public domain.

Fake-o-meter

America's Stonehenge is a real, nineteenth-century site. But as far as being a medieval settlement of Irish monks or a Bronze Age village of immigrant Celts in the New World, there's just zero evidence, so I'm going to need to go the full five on that claim.

Getting there

Pattee's Cave, I mean Mystery Hill, no, actually America's Stonehenge is located in North Salem, New Hampshire. Punch in 105 Haverhill Road, Salem, New Hampshire, on your phone or GPS to get there. I highly recommend a visit. It is a very cool place. Maybe don't mention my name to anyone there. Just sayin'.

20. L'ANSE AUX MEADOWS, NEWFOUNDLAND, CANADA

Archaeological perspectives

The best answer to the question "Who discovered America?" seems manifestly obvious: The ancestors of today's Native Americans did. As we've already seen, archaeological, geological, and biological evidence proves conclusively that they were here more than fifteen thousand and probably closer to twenty thousand years ago. So, of course, they discovered America as they were the first people to arrive here and settle. That's not politically correct speech, it's just an accurate statement of fact.

So, it's peculiar that there sometimes is an implication that this doesn't really count as "discovery," and the question is intended to ask "When did the first, you know, 'people who count' get here?" Meaning Europeans. So Indians, well they're part of the natural world—like deer and buffalo—but Europeans are a part of history.

The truth is, Christopher Columbus did not "discover" America by any reasonable interpretation of that term. When he arrived, the New World consisted of two continents with tens of millions of people speaking hundreds of different languages and practicing at least that many distinct cultures. Imagine Christopher Columbus today, parking his boat—well, mooring it—on your street, walking onto your lawn, planting Spain's flag, and sonorously intoning, "I claim this land I have just discovered in the name of the king and queen of Spain." Your response likely would be: "Hell, no," and then you'd escort him off of your property and call the cops.

That doesn't mean that there aren't interesting questions that might be asked concerning who made it to North America *after* northeast Asians living in Siberia crossed over Beringia to become the first Americans and *before* Columbus. A bunch of sites in this book have been proposed as the ancient, Pre-Columbian settlements of any one of a number of different Old World peoples—Celts, Israelites, Phoenicians, Egyptians—here in North America. I've been skeptical about those interpretations. But how about this case?

Here's what we know

Bjarni Herjolfsson was just a guy hoping to meet up with his dad for the holidays. Of course, his dad was living in Iceland—at least that's where he believed his father was—and Bjarni was living in Scandinavia, which necessitated a perilous crossing of a bit more than nine hundred miles of the north Atlantic for the planned family reunion. Oh, and by the way, the trip took place more than a thousand years ago, in AD 986.

To make matters worse, Bjarni made it safely to Iceland only to find that his father had already left that island and had moved to a newly discovered country, Greenland, another 750 miles to the west. Bjarni must have been pretty frustrated, but his dad couldn't very well have alerted him to that piece of news with a text, email, or Facebook post. Nevertheless, Bjarni was a brave and hardy Viking. Persevering, after stopping over in Iceland he continued to sail west, looking for his father's new country.

Bjarni may have been a tough customer, but he wasn't the best navigator in the world and, whether through error, bad luck, bad weather, or a combination of the three he sailed too far south, missing Greenland entirely. However, by making that mistake he accidentally made one of the most momentous discoveries ever made by a European sailor—one not to be replicated until the voyage of an Italian navigator five hundred years later. Bjarni spied the shores of the New World (though it wasn't called that at the time; that title would have to wait until Amerigo Vespucci coined that term in 1503).

We know of Bjarni's exploits from two manuscripts written two hundred years after the fact: *The Greenlander's Saga* and *Eric the Red's Saga* (Magnusson and Paulsson 1965). In those narratives—which both told, essentially, the same story—after missing Greenland entirely by traveling too far south, Bjarni continued sailing westward, eventually spotting three lands not previously known even to the seafaring Norse.

Now, at least one reason that I am not writing today from my home in the United States of Bjarniland is the fact that Bjarni never made landfall on any of these newfound lands (which, as you'll soon see, is sort of a play on words). He wasn't an explorer, and he wasn't looking for new countries to invade or settle. He was just looking for his dad, who he did find when he turned his boat back around to the east and eventually made his way to Greenland.

After suitably greeting his father, Bjarni told the community of Vikings living there about his discoveries. That group included the infamous Eric the Red. Eric was living in Greenland because he had been exiled from Iceland for killing a man, but he had already been living in Iceland because he had been exiled from Norway for, you guessed it, killing a man. Eric had decided his days of exploring were done, but his son, Lief Ericson, wanted to know more about these new lands and attempted to convince Bjarni to take him there. Bjarni, however, had decided that his days of plying the Atlantic were done as well, so Lief did the next best thing; he bought Bjarni's boat, believing that the vessel would remember the way back, which is kind of a charming belief.

Well, that must have worked because, as is very clearly detailed in the aforementioned sagas, just a little before AD 1000, Lief and a crew of about thirty-five Norsemen launched an expedition of exploration, sailing west from Greenland and encountering the three lands Bjarni had described. Sailing from north to south, Lief called these lands Helluland (translation, "Flat Slab Land," for the rocks he spotted along the coast); Markland (translation, "Forest Land" for the abundance of trees growing along there); and Vinland (translation, "Wineland," for the grapevines he thought he saw growing there). We now understand that Helluland is the northern Canadian territory of Baffin Island; Markland is Labrador; and Vinland is Newfoundland.

Lief and his men are said to have built "booths," essentially houses, creating a small village, probably on Vinland, and then returned to Greenland. Their stories of the new lands inspired a number of Norse expeditions to Canada through the early years of the eleventh century culminating in a trip in AD 1022 led by Thorfinn Karlsefni—whose intention was to create a permanent settlement—and a group of sixty-five men and women and a small number of cattle (figure 5.12). We've already encountered Karlsefni; some have claimed that he left the markings on **Dighton Rock**. He didn't.

Helluland had already been deemed inhospitable, Markland seemed perhaps too big a challenge, but Vinland appeared to be just right. The sagas state clearly that a Norse colony was established and that it lasted for only a few years. The Norse abandoned the Vinland colony due to a combination of internal bickering and violence—some of it instigated by Lief's sister Freydis who, if the sagas are to be believed, appears to have been quite a badass—but also as a result of poor relations with the Native People, Native Americans who the Norse called *Skraelings*.

Why are archaeologists skeptical?

It must be said that by the latter years of the nineteenth century, most historians regarded the *Greenlander's* and *Eric the Red's* sagas to be reasonably historically accurate, presenting the largely true story of the brief and ultimately unsuccess-

Figure 5.12. A reconstruction of the Norse structure built in its archaeological footprint at L'anse aux Meadows in Newfoundland. Radiocarbon dating indicates that the Norse settlement there dates to about 1,000 years ago, making it a European settlement in the New World predating the Columbus expeditions by about 500 years.
iStock ID: 503176269; Credit:GeorgeBurba

ful Norse attempt at colonizing the New World five hundred years before the voyages of Christopher Columbus. Archaeologists were, perhaps, a bit more skeptical, as is often the case, of making a definitive identification of Vinland based primarily on written documents. As I have relentlessly asserted in this book, archaeology is all about material evidence, diagnostic remnants of culture left behind by people that can be definitively associated with them and unlike that of any other group. A reliance on and even a reverence for material evidence is encoded in our professional DNA, and there was no such evidence for a short-lived Norse colony in Canada in the tenth and eleventh centuries. This all changed, however, in 1960 when a husband and wife team of researchers excavated the archaeological remnants of a village site located on a promontory of land in northwestern Newfoundland and found a definitively Norse settlement dating to about a thousand years ago.

Whodunit?

In 1960, archaeologist Anne Stine Ingstad (1977) and her husband, writer and explorer Helge Ingstad (1964), discovered the location of a Norse settlement at a place called L'anse aux Meadows in the Canadian province of Newfoundland

Figure 5.13.   This is precisely the kind of artifact archaeologists expect at a settlement of ancient visitors and colonists of the New World. A ring-headed bronze pin is not part of the native artifact assemblage but represents the material culture of the Norse in the tenth and eleventh centuries AD.

(Ingstad and Ingstad 2000). As the *Greenlander's* and *Eric the Red's* sagas indicate that the Greenland Norse had made a number of attempts to settle the New World, it's impossible to say with certainty that the L'anse aux Meadows site represents Lief's booths, his brother Thorvald's 1002 settlement, or the later village established by Karlsefni. It makes little difference here. What's key is that the excavation at L'anse aux Meadows produced clear evidence of a Norse presence in the New World. Among the diagnostically Norse features and artifacts recovered were the remains of typical Norse turf houses (see figure 5.12 for a reconstruction in the archaeological footprint of the actual structure), iron nails and rivets, an iron smithy (for smelting iron), a soapstone spindle whorl, and a ring-headed bronze pin (figure 5.13). None of this material culture bore any resemblance to that produced by Native People in the region. Charcoal was also recovered in the excavation, producing a radiocarbon date of AD 920–930, a little early by the reckoning of the sagas, but it is possible that the fires there were fueled with older driftwood. This date shows definitively that the L'anse aux Meadows site represents a Norse presence in the New World more than five hundred years before Columbus set sail.

Why?

If the "they" in this question is the Norse, then the answer is simple: The Norse explored and attempted to colonize the New World because that's what they did. Their culture was expansionist, always seeking out new territories to explore, exploit, dominate, and settle. Once Bjarni had told his story, there was little way the Norse were not going to try to retrace his nautical footsteps and settle the new territory.

If instead the "they" in this question relates to the Ingstads, the answer is that archaeologists, while clearly appreciating the value of written records like the sagas, aren't necessarily comfortable relying exclusively on that written record. In his *Devil's Dictionary*, satirist Ambrose Bierce defined history as: "An account, mostly false, of events, mostly unimportant, brought about by rulers mostly knaves, and soldiers mostly fools." The written record is filled with exaggerations, misrepresentations, half-truths, outright falsehoods, and maybe even "alternate facts." Further, the people who control the historical narrative have agendas that don't necessarily conform with those of professional historians or archaeologists. As I have stated too many times to count in this book, the gold standard for archaeologists is physical, tangible, material evidence, the actual stuff left behind by a people. What the Ingstads found at L'anse aux Meadows—and what archaeologist Patricia Sutherland (2000) has continued to find at sites located throughout northeastern Canada—is dead certain proof that the Norse were in America long before Columbus made landfall in the Caribbean. For archaeologists, the sagas prove the hypothesis of a Norse presence in America before Columbus. The lack of any such confirming archaeological evidence in Minnesota (**Kensington Runestone**) or Oklahoma (**Heavener Runestone**) is precisely why archaeologists are skeptical of those sites. The recovery of definitively Norse artifacts at a site in Newfoundland and an associated radiocarbon date of AD 920 is robust proof upholding the validity of that hypothesis.

Fake-o-meter

0. I've included the L'anse aux Meadows site in this book about archaeological oddities as what amounts to a ringer. In fact, there's nothing fake here or odd. The kind of evidence recovered at L'anse aux Meadows is a model for the kind of evidence archaeologists demand for other claims of visitors to the New World in antiquity, whether those visitors were from Europe or Alpha Centauri.

Getting there

L'anse aux Meadows is part of the Parks Canada system. If you fly into the province's largest city, St. John's, it's still an eleven-hour drive on Route 1! So you really have to want to see the site.

· *6* ·

Category 4 Ancient Visitors: Aliens

$\mathcal{O}$kay, if there's no convincing archaeological evidence for the existence of Celts, Phoenicians, Egyptians, or ancient Israelites in the New World in antiquity at the sites highlighted in sections 3, 4, and 5 of this guide, how about really "alien" aliens, you know, the extraterrestrial kind? What kinds of evidence have been presented in support of claims that residents of another planet, almost certainly from outside of our solar system, visited Earth in antiquity and had a dramatic impact on our human ancestors? The answer to that question is, well, not much. Claims about an extraterrestrial presence on Earth in the ancient past are almost always based on indirect evidence and almost always (I'm being kind) based on a low opinion of human intelligence or human capabilities. Humans could not have, on their own, so the argument goes, accomplished the truly and undeniably remarkable things reflected in the archaeological record, things like pyramids, accurate calendars, or remarkable metallurgy.

The problem with such claims from an archaeological standpoint rests on the fact that if they were here, the ETs really did a bang-up job of not leaving behind any direct and definitive material evidence—the kind of stuff that resides at the heart of archaeological research and interpretation—of their presence on Earth in general or North America in particular. Archaeologists have not found bits of broken communicators or phasers (like in *Star Trek*), or fragments of crashed spaceships in ancient stratigraphic layers. As I've already claimed, too many times to count, it's reasonable to assume that if there are no artifacts, then there's no evidence that it happened. Those are the rules in archaeology. I don't make the rules, so please don't send me nasty emails about it.

Interestingly, scientists have not been close-minded on this issue and have seriously considered the *possibility* that artifacts reflecting extraterrestrial visitation to Earth *might* conceivably exist and could confirm the reality of such visits, which would be incredibly cool. For example, early in his career

142

astronomer, astrophysicist, cosmologist, and extraordinary science popularizer Carl Sagan (1963) actually proposed that geologists should investigate ancient strata in the search for material evidence left behind by extraterrestrial visitors to Earth in antiquity.

In that article, Sagan suggested that: (1) we are not alone; the universe is teeming with life; (2) some of that life likely has achieved great intelligence; (3) some of those intelligent beings probably developed spaceflight; (4) some of those aliens could have visited our planet as they explored the galaxy; and (5) those aliens may have dropped, discarded, or maybe even intentionally left objects on Earth for future humans to find. Sagan recognized that the odds against the scenario were pretty long, but those odds were not zero and the implications were stunning if such artifacts could be found.

It was an interesting hypothesis and certainly one worth exploring. However, there's an inconvenient but fundamental problem here for supporters of the ancient alien proposal—quite a lot of archaeological and geological research has been conducted since the 1963 publication of Sagan's article, and no such evidence has ever been found by archaeologists, geologists, or any other scientists in support of it. None. So, to repeat the mantra, archaeologists are skeptical because, artifacts or it didn't happen, and there are no artifacts. Hijacking an internet meme of a few years ago, "I'm not saying that it wasn't aliens, but it wasn't aliens."

As already noted, with no direct artifactual evidence of their visits, supporters of the ancient aliens hypothesis are forced to fall back on focusing, largely, on the great sophistication in the engineering, architecture, and science seen in the archaeological record. Their hypothesis is predicated on the assumption (and the libel) that ancient people weren't smart enough to have accomplished that stuff on their own. Basing a hypothesis purely on the assumption of a lack of intelligence, skill, sophistication, and abilities on the part of ancient people sufficient to have accomplished the many remarkable technological achievements clearly exhibited in the archaeological record is a losing argument, but supporters of ancient astronauts/ancient aliens have little else to go on (Feder 2018).

There is one category of physical evidence, artifacts alleged to support the hypothesis of the ancient alien visitation to Earth in the past: artistic depictions by ancient people of the aliens and/or their spacecraft. In this scenario, ancient people actually saw spacecraft or witnessed aliens walking around. Amazed, terrified, and confused, perhaps the ancient people thought these creatures were gods or spirits and felt compelled to make representations of those ETs on cave walls or rock faces, for example.

We will visit a number of sites here where material evidence has been proposed to support the ancient aliens hypothesis, both directly and indirectly. We'll examine the **Roswell Flying Saucer Crash Site** in New Mexico. Okay, the crash was supposed to have happened in 1947, so those aliens aren't exactly ancient, but it's worth a look. We'll also visit what are claimed to be artistic depictions of strange creatures, the aforementioned eyewitness representations of aliens (the pictographs in **Sego Canyon** and the **Head of Sinbad** in Utah). Finally, we'll take a look at **Serpent Mound** in Ohio, where aliens, apparently fueled up on the element iridium, and then marked the location with a giant coiled snake made of Earth. Yeah, that seems reasonable.

21. ROSWELL FLYING SAUCER CRASH SITE, ROSWELL, NEW MEXICO

Archaeological perspectives

We arrived in Roswell on a hot, quiet August morning in 2014. I was in the midst of an archaeological odyssey, collecting information for my book *Ancient America: Fifty Archaeological Sites to See for Yourself*. Roswell was not one of the planned stops for that project, but hey, I already was in southern New Mexico visiting a spectacular ancient rock art location, the Three Rivers Petroglyph Site near Tularosa. How could I not swing by Roswell and check out the International UFO Museum and Research Center, ground zero for the story of a purported flying saucer crash back in the 1940s?

The museum is housed in an old movie theater replete with one of those wonderful marquees that used to dominate American cityscapes (figure 6.1). The museum itself is decidedly low tech, low budget, and charmingly amateurish. Trust me; no one with an academic background in museology had anything to

Figure 6.1.   The converted movie theater in Roswell, New Mexico, that now is the International UFO Museum and Research Center.

Figure 6.2.　Exhibit showing the aliens exiting the spacecraft that crashed in Roswell. Um, am I mistaken, or are the aliens naked?

do with the exhibits. But the handmade feel to the place was part of its charm. The best analogy I can give for the vibe of the Roswell UFO Museum is this: It sort of looks like the local high school decided to have its senior prom in an old abandoned movie theater and, after ripping out the seats, decorated the place with this year's theme being "extraterrestrial aliens." I don't intend that to be in the least bit mean or disparaging. It's actually kind of cute. There's even a diorama showing the disabled spacecraft being exited by a group of extraterrestrial aliens. Who are naked (figure 6.2).

The museum wasn't particularly busy when we arrived; initially, at least, I was the only person in the ticket line. Curiously, the woman selling tickets, after greeting me warmly, appeared to be quite distracted, gazing past me and toward the entrance doors, as if she were looking for someone—or something. She soon returned her focus to me and apologized for the delay, explaining:

I'm so sorry. We're expecting a busload of visitors and I keep looking outside for their vehicle. They're about twenty minutes late and we're a bit concerned about them.

I can be an exceptionally silly person at times, and it just felt right to be silly at that moment waiting to purchase my ticket to the International UFO Museum. Leaning in toward the woman, and attempting to affect my most serious voice, I asked: "Oh my. You don't think they've been abducted, do you? You know, by extraterrestrials?"

Without the slightest hint of recognition of how intentionally silly my question was, she responded: "Oh, I don't think so. They're probably just stuck in traffic."

I responded in the only way possible: "Oh sure. That's what they want you to believe."

After a brief pause, she smiled broadly, patted my arm, and said, "Oh, you're just being silly!" Busted! I admitted I was being maximally silly and apologized. She assured me there was no need, and just bemusedly shook her head and took my admission fee.

Here's what we know

Entire books have been written about the "Roswell Incident," which is the focus of the museum in question. I have no reason—and no excuse here—to go into the story in great detail. Two terrific sources are Kal K. Korff's *The Roswell UFO Crash: What They Don't Want You to Know* (1997) and Karl T. Pflock's *Roswell: Inconvenient Facts and the Will to Believe* (2001).

Suffice it to say, something out of the ordinary definitely fell to Earth sometime in late June or early July 1947 just outside of Roswell, New Mexico, not too far from what was then called the Roswell Army Air Field (RAAF; this was before the air force was a separate branch of the military). Based on declassified military documents, the RAAF was the hub of Project Mogul, a secret program with the goal of spying on the nascent nuclear program of the Soviet Union. We know for certain that "balloon trains"—large, linear clusters of what were essentially helium-filled weather balloons, tethered together along with silver foil radar targets that looked like box kites—were launched from the RAAF during the summer of 1947. Project Mogul was intended to provide our military with, not an "eye in the sky," but an "ear." At the bottom of the balloon train was suspended a microphone and recording device. Though it may sound silly in hindsight, the hope was that the balloon train would rise high into the atmosphere, float toward the west and, if the Soviets happened at precisely the right moment to be conducting an above-ground nuclear test, the "boom" it made might be picked up by the microphone and recorded. Then, with close radar monitoring using the silver foil box-kite targets, the military would retrieve the recording device as it gently fell to Earth somewhere in the Pacific Ocean. Remember, this is long before spy satellites or even high-altitude spy planes, so this was about the best our military could do remotely to learn more about Soviet nuclear capabilities. Unfortunately, but in hindsight, not surprisingly Project Mogul was an abject failure and no booms were ever recorded by its microphones.

So, the thing that fell to Earth near Roswell can be explained most simply as a failed Project Mogul balloon train. In fact, all photographs and contemporary (1947) eyewitness testimony points in that direction (Pflock 2001). Nevertheless, the incident has become transformed into the story of the crash of an extraterrestrial spacecraft, sometimes even one with a surviving alien.

Why are archaeologists skeptical?

Before I explain my skepticism, you might ask, "Well, why is the Roswell incident in a book about archaeological oddities in the first place?" That's a good question. Here's the thing. I was informally talking to a group of students who had heard of the Roswell "crash" and wanted, for reasons not entirely clear to me, my opinion. I responded that, well, based on what I read it was abundantly clear that the thing that crashed was a Project Mogul balloon train. I then shot off my big mouth and bragged: "And, as an archaeologist, if someone gave me a bit of money, enough to bring a crew of a dozen or so of my field-trained archaeology students to New Mexico, set us up in tents, feed us, and provide us with trowels, shovels, tape measures, and sifters in a couple of months we would be able to find physical evidence to solve the 'mystery' once and for all. In other words, we'd find either: (1) pieces of radar targets and fragments of weather balloons, or (2) bits of an alien spaceship."

I was being just a bit sarcastic, but in truth, though the folklore claims that the military pored over the area collecting remnants of the crash (whatever might have crashed there), I bet they weren't as thorough as they wanted to be, and if there were fragments of either a Project Mogul balloon train or an extraterrestrial spacecraft at the crash site, we'd find bits of whatever it was. That's what archaeologists do, and we are very good at it. Just ask Richard Crafts, who is doing life in prison today at least in part because archaeologists using standard tools and methods found tiny pieces of his wife, Helle, even though he had run her body though a wood chipper in an attempt to eliminate any of the evidence of his crime (and this occurred long before the movie *Fargo*).

I was, after all, just bragging, and I never followed up on my interesting idea. You can imagine my surprise and, I admit a little regret, when while channel surfing in 2002 I encountered a show titled *The Roswell Crash: Startling New Evidence*. It turned out to be a documentary about, you guessed it, an archaeological excavation at the purported location of the crash of whatever it was at Roswell! Damn! I had blown my opportunity to star in a show about excavating for flying saucer parts. Oh well.

The excavation was directed by William Doleman, a real-deal archaeologist with training and lots of experience, the director of the Office of Contract

Archaeology at the University of New Mexico. He even coauthored a book about his experiences on the Roswell project (*Roswell Dig Diaries*, 2004). It's not exactly a page turner, but that isn't Doleman's fault; they simply didn't find anything in the dig, certainly nothing related either to Project Mogul or an extraterrestrial spacecraft.

So why are archaeologists skeptical that a spacecraft crashed outside of Roswell, New Mexico, in the summer of 1947 and skeptical that there's an archaeological site there containing the remains of that spacecraft? Easy. Archaeologists dug there and found no archaeological evidence that any such thing happened.

Whodunit?

When the news of a crash of some sort of craft spread in Roswell, the military, ever at the ready, came up with a cover story, one intended to deflect and distract reporters who were investigating. The goal of Jesse Marcel, the Intelligence Officer at the RAAF, was to hide the existence of the top-secret Project Mogul. So, he came up with what he thought would be a great distraction; he announced in a press release that the crash was of a flying saucer. That's right, the story of a crashed flying saucer was made up by the military to dampen interest in the story. The July 8, 1947, headline of the local newspaper, the *Roswell Daily Record*, blares out the remarkable story: **"RAAF Captures Flying Saucer on Ranch in Roswell Region."** The article credits Jesse Marcel with the information.

What was he thinking? Predictably, instead of dampening interest in what had crashed near Roswell, the cover story of a crashed flying saucer actually generated even more interest (duh!). So the military came up with a second cover story: weather balloons, which actually was accurate since Project Mogul made use of standard weather balloons to send their sound recording devices into the atmosphere. Eventually the public lost interest, and Roswell was forgotten about by most until an explosion of interest was reignited in the 1970s. This continuing interest ultimately led to the archaeological dig in 2002. And trust me; the lack of any archaeological evidence for the saucer crash has done little to dampen the enthusiasm of the people who want very much to believe that it happened

Why?

I would maintain that many archaeologists would be interested in the exercise of using archaeological methods in an attempt to investigate a modern controversy or mystery (even if a skeptical scientist would maintain that there's no real controversy or mystery in the first place). I would also maintain that any television station would be interested in broadcasting a show about archaeologists searching for the remains of a crashed flying saucer because, well, archaeology. And flying saucers. It's a television twofer nearly guaranteed to produce high ratings.

Figure 6.3. The good people of Roswell, New Mexico, may or may not believe the story of the alien spacecraft crash, but they have a good sense of humor about it. Here, just outside of town, a friendly denizen of Roswell offers a jump to the broken-down spaceship.

Fake-o-meter

Five.

Getting there

There's nothing to see at this point out in the desert of New Mexico north of Roswell. The International UFO Museum is great fun and, in fact, the entire town of Roswell is happy with the tourism the story generates and they don't seem to take it all that seriously (figure 6.3). The museum is located at 114 North Main Street in Roswell, New Mexico. Whatever you do, don't tell them you're coming and then delay your arrival. They might get worried.

22. SERPENT MOUND, PEEBLES, OHIO

Archaeological perspectives

When human beings consider the homes of their gods and spirits, they really have only a very few options concerning where to put them in a physical sense. For example, they can place them right here on Earth, but that's problematic since nobody ever sees the gods just walking among us. Then there's the option of placing them below ground. Some people, especially those who live in areas where deep, dark, and mysterious underground worlds are found in caverns, do just that. If you've ever visited one of the spectacular caverns in the United States open to the public, for example, Luray in Virginia or Carlsbad in New Mexico, you have experienced that strange and alien universe of phantasmagorically shaped stalactites and stalagmites. The extreme otherworldliness of those places explains why people might view them as being home to powerful spiritual entities.

Perhaps the most obvious place to put gods and spirits is in the sky. The sky above our heads—and we don't call them the "heavens" for nothing—is expansive, inaccessible (at least to mere humans), and populated by an astonishing array of mysterious lights that illuminate our world during the day, that change shape during the course of a month, and that shine and twinkle at night; some even streak flaming across the sky. It's not terribly surprising that many people position their gods and spirits in that vast sky, viewing those glowing lights as the material manifestations of powerful entities playing out their mysterious dramas.

Recognizing that the sky is an obvious location to place gods and spirits, it's no wonder that all over the world people have constructed enormous monuments honoring them and that would be fully visible only from their perch on high. Even in modern times, some churches have been built in the shape of a giant cross, one not visible from the ground upon which we human beings walk, but certainly visible and pleasing to a God residing in Heaven. More anciently, the gigantically scaled Nazca ground drawings—called geoglyphs—were made by the Native People of South America. Though lesser known, we have geoglyphs right here in the United States in the form of the Blythe Intaglios in southern California (figure 6.4). We also have the so-called effigy mounds in the American Midwest, monumentally scaled designs, often of animals, made of mounded earth. Like the other examples, they cannot be appreciated in their entirety by the people who made them—or by the modern visitors who come to admire their beauty—but would have been entirely visible only to the spirits who dwell in the sky. There is, in fact, an entire national monument in Iowa—Effigy Mounds National Monument—that was drawn up expressly to preserve a substantial cluster of such effigy mounds in the shapes of bears and eagles (https://www.nps.gov/efmo/index.htm).

Here's what we know

The best known of the American effigy mounds is in Ohio. It is in the form of a giant snake and is appropriately called Serpent Mound (figure 6.5). It's wonderful, and its vital statistics are quite impressive. Located on the relatively flat top of a narrow bluff overlooking Bush Creek in southern Ohio, the three-foot-tall earthen body of a sinuous snake coils along for more than 1,300 feet from tip

Figure 6.4. People all over the world have constructed large-scale monuments best appreciated from the air, the abode, not of aliens, but the gods for whom those monuments were produced. Here, in southern California, you can visit a giant ground drawing 120 feet across and about 180 feet tall. This image is one of several of the so-called Blythe Intaglios.
Courtesy of Desi Ekstein, On The Go Video.

to tip. The tail is tightly wound and opens up to the main part of the snake's body consisting of seven large and one small curved segment terminating at a head with jaws open wide. The object of the serpent's attention is an egg-shaped mound, perhaps meant as a meal for the snake.

It's clear that the configuration of the snake's body on the plateau wasn't random. The head and each of the loops or curves in the snake appear to be celestially aligned, pointing to important points on the horizon where the sun rises and sets on the solstices (the first day of summer and the first day of winter) and

Figure 6.5.   In Ohio, the ancient people produced the image of a gigantic snake by mounding up soil. Built at least 1,000 years ago, the 1,350-foot-long snake sinuously slithers across the top of a bluff. It is a beautiful work of art, a sculpture of Earth, made by Native Americans. It has nothing whatsoever to do with extraterrestrial alien iridium fill-up stations, the snake that tempted Eve in the Bible, or the coming of a new age.

the equinoxes (the first day of spring and the first day of fall). In other words, Serpent Mound may have been designed as a solar calendar. Other alignments of the mound suggest positioning of the moon was another factor in its design.

Unfortunately, the precise age of Serpent Mound is still a matter of some controversy, but a recent detailed and persuasive argument suggest the feature is about one thousand years old (Lepper et al. 2018).

Why are archaeologists skeptical?

The standard archaeological interpretation of Serpent Mound assumes that Native Americans were smart, creative, capable of working together toward a common goal, and interested in the world around them, including the sun and the moon. With all that we know about Native American cultures, we can be very secure in those assumptions. So, we're not at all skeptical about Native Americans being the people who created Serpent Mound as a form of worship and as a calendar. It makes perfect sense, and the existing physical evidence provides robust support for that understanding (Lepper et al. 2018).

However, there are a few alternative explanations for Serpent Mound that make no sense at all and that I can fairly say archaeologists and historians are skeptical about—and that make Native Americans pretty damn angry. We are skeptical and angry for two fundamental reasons: (1) we that know Native

Americans lived in southern Ohio when Serpent Mound was built, and (2) we know Native Americans were fully capable of building mounds. So there simply is no need for any alternative explanations involving construction by someone other than Native Americans, especially since there is absolutely no evidence to warrant any of them.

Whodunit?

First, we have the Biblical Proof hypothesis proposed by some Creationists who insist on a literal interpretation of the Bible. For them, Serpent Mound wasn't built by people at all, but by biblical giants called the Nephilim. So, you know, before the **Cardiff Giant** became petrified, he and his crew hung out in Ohio for a while and created an earth sculpture of a giant snake. That's an interesting hypothesis, but there is absolutely no evidence for biblical giants and, equally important, there is no pressing need for their existence to explain a three-foot-tall effigy mound that people were perfectly capable of constructing on their own.

Second, we have the New Age hypothesis. In my entry about the cliff dwellings in Sedona, Arizona (**Palatki** and **Honanki**) later in the book, I note that, among a number of world locations, Serpent Mound was a place of pilgrimage for New Age folks during the Harmonic Convergence in 1987. Those people showed up in Sedona, Stonehenge, the Giza pyramids, and Serpent Mound, among other places, to usher in a new era of peace, love, and understanding. Please examine world history since 1987 to see how well that worked out. Ultimately, however, the Harmonic Convergence New Agers were harmless, and good for them for hoping that the world really would get better.

That's a far cry from the New Age idiots—there is no more appropriate a term—who vandalized this sacred Native American site by taking it upon themselves to fix what they believed to be an energy imbalance there by burying "orgonites" in the effigy. Orgonites are, essentially, pieces of garbage (metal filings, quartz crystals) embedded in resin. The goal of the self-proclaimed "light warriors" in burying the orgonites was to "lift the vibration of the earth so we can all rise together" (http://www.dispatch.com/content/stories/local/2012/11/02/vandals-admit-muffin-crystal-thingie-assault-at-serpent-mounds.html). So, yeah, idiots. I can think of a better place they should have "buried" their orgonites, but removal would have involved an uncomfortable medical procedure. Taking it upon yourself to dig holes in a national landmark because of some New Age perspective is both illegal and tremendously disrespectful of the Native People whose ancestors actually built Serpent Mound. Like the Nephilim crowd, this was just another attempt to appropriate a Native American site for the perpetrators' purposes.

Finally, we have the ancient-alien-visitors-to-Earth hypothesis spread by folks like Giorgio Tsoukalos of the cable show *Ancient Aliens*, in which it was claimed that Serpent Mound was built to somehow mark a fueling station for extraterrestrial spacecraft. Seriously.

Serpent Mound is actually located on the rim of an ancient meteor crater, though it is highly doubtful that ancient people recognized that fact. The location of the mound at the top of a bluff on a flat plateau simply was convenient and logical. Because of the ancient meteor strike, there is a very high level of iridium in the soil underlying the mound. That's typical of meteor impact sites, including the most famous one in North America, Barringer Crater near Winslow, Arizona. It's entirely natural.

This high level of iridium in the soil under Serpent Mound led a researcher (gag) interviewed on *Ancient Aliens* to suggest the following connection: maybe extraterrestrial visitors to Earth in antiquity fueled their spaceships with iridium and needed to collect the stuff wherever they landed. Think dilithium crystals if you're a Trekkie. There was a ton of iridium-rich soil in this spot in southern Ohio, and they found and mined it. Peebles, Ohio, in essence, was like a big self-service station for extraterrestrial fill ups. Maybe the extraterrestrials could grab a cup of coffee, buy a lottery ticket, and maybe pick up a packet of Slim Jims while they were fueling. But why the effigy mound? Simple; instead of a big, illuminated "Cheap Iridium Here" sign, they marked the spot by building a giant snake made of dirt. Yeah, that makes sense. Sure. You just can't make this stuff up.

Why?

I hate to have to put on my psychologist hat here again (and what would a psychologist hat look like anyway?), but here goes. First, it's a snake. For whatever reason snakes just don't get a lot of love from most people. Maybe it's because of the Garden of Eden story. Maybe it's the fact that they're cold-blooded. Maybe it's just their whole slithery vibe. But lots of folks see snakes as evil, gross, and otherworldly. So perhaps it's no surprise that some make a connection between evil biblical snakes with evil biblical giants.

Perhaps for others, snakes aren't so much evil as they are powerfully alien. As a result, a perfectly human explanation for a piece of what amounts to sculptural art is rejected in favor of something more mystical or paranormal. Ultimately, all of these alternative explanations represent a denial of the capabilities of Native Americans. They lived here. They were fully capable of constructing mounds. They constructed mounds. They constructed Serpent Mound. End of story.

Fake-o-meter

Serpent Mound is a genuine and genuinely fascinating site built by ancient Native Americans. That part of the story deserves no stars. Nephilim, orgonites, and ancient aliens each deserve five stars of fakeness each for a total of fifteen!

Getting there

Serpent Mound is located at 3850 State Route 73, Peebles, Ohio 45660. Punch that into your GPS or cell phone mapping app and you're all set. That takes you to the access road, and then the parking lot for Serpent Mound State Memorial.

23. THE HEAD OF SINBAD, SAN RAFAEL SWELL, UTAH

24. SEGO CANYON, THOMPSON SPRINGS, UTAH

Archaeological perspectives

The strange interpretation of the two sites highlighted in this entry reflects the belief that ancient rock art may include depictions of actual extraterrestrial alien visitors to Earth in antiquity. This scenario—aliens land, ancient primitive people are awestruck whereupon they produce artistic images representing what they saw—has become a trope that shows up in popular culture. It even ends up being used in one of the Star Trek movie reboots. In *Star Trek: Into Darkness*, after completing a clandestine and completely unauthorized mission to save a planet from an imminent and catastrophic volcanic eruption, the *Starship Enterprise* makes a hasty escape and, unfortunately for sticklers about the "prime directive," is seen taking off by local primitives. Looking up in awe, one of the Natives takes a stick and draws an image of the *Enterprise* in the dirt. That's the equivalent of what is sometimes claimed regarding the kinds of ancient Native American art featured in this entry; local Natives saw actual extraterrestrials and more permanently etched or painted their images on rock walls.

Here's what we know

While the Head of Sinbad didn't make my final cut of fifty in *Ancient America*, it is nonetheless a beautiful rock art site made up of two main panels of astonishing and imaginative pictographs spread across a vertical rock face. Rendered in a deep, brick-red pigment, the panel on the left shows two anthropomorphs (figure 6.6). One has big, googly eyes, the other has no eyes at all but is holding a snake and is wearing some sort of head gear. Seven little birdlike critters stand between them; there's a flying bird, another snake, and some odd circles with lines emanating from them.

The panel on the right has another googly-eyed anthropomorph (figure 6.7). Next to him or her is a critter with humanlike hands, a broad tail, and horns; like the ancient Greek chimera, it appears to be an amalgam of different animals. There's also a snake and a circle above the anthropomorph's

Figure 6.6. One cluster of pictographs at the Head of Sinbad location in the San Rafael Swell region of southern Utah. Almost certainly depicting Native American spirit beings, one holding a snake, assertions that these are, in reality, paintings of extraterrestrial visitors to Utah (where it can be difficult to find a good cup of coffee) are pretty lame.

Figure 6.7. A second cluster of pictographs at the Head of Sinbad location. Beautiful, yes. Intriguing, yes. Worth a visit, yes. Mysterious depictions of ETs, nope.

head, and he's flanked by a couple of strange, linear images that almost look like elongated jellyfish.

The multiple panels of rock art that I visited in Sego Canyon represent one of the fifty sites I did highlight in my *Ancient America* time-travel guide. There are multiple and spatially distinct clusters of art at the site: (1) a group of fairly recent pictographs in red and white, including images of a horse and a shield, produced by the local Paiute Indians; (2) a cluster of "Fremont"-style petroglyphs etched into the dark patina of the rock surface featuring a couple of trapezoidal-bodied anthropomorphs—humanlike figures—dating to as much as three thousand years ago; (3) a series of seven (or maybe eight) large-scaled painted anthropomorphs, one even sporting a feathered headdress; and (4) some incredibly beautiful and admittedly spooky pictographs of anthropomorphs (figure 6.8), each one unique, some with googly eyes and some wearing head gear with what appear to be antennae or antlers (figure 6.9). This panel also has depictions of snakes. This is the panel in particular that has inspired rampant speculation about the message the artists were intending to convey. Those anthropomorphs are, you guessed it: extraterrestrial aliens. In spacesuits.

The art style seen at both the Head of Sinbad and Sego Canyon—with its abundance of red pigment and elongated anthropomorphs, some with googly eyes—is called "Barrier Canyon" and is found at a number of sites scat-

Figure 6.8.   Pictographs in Sego Canyon, just north of Thompson Springs, Utah. With their elongated bodies, googly eyes, and yes, antenna-like rays coming from their heads, these are wonderful examples of Barrier Canyon art, dating to as much as 2,000 years ago.

Figure 6.9. More examples of the Barrier Canyon-style pictographs at Sego Canyon. If these guys are supposed to be depictions of space-suited aliens, why is it that each one is wearing an entirely different space suit? Were they just "stylin"?

tered throughout southern Utah. Barrier Canyon itself (now called Horseshoe Canyon) is where the style was first recognized and defined and where today you can find a dense concentration of the most amazing examples of the style. Where dating has been possible, art of the Barrier Canyon style appears to be between about one thousand and two thousand years old. It's beautiful, imaginative, creative, and phantasmagoric. But why anyone would presume to suggest that instead of imaginative, the art is representational—in other words actual and accurate depictions of beings that Native American artists saw in the real world—is a mystery to me.

Why are archaeologists skeptical?

Let me begin to explain archaeological skepticism here, not at either of the rock art sites featured here but, instead, back at the International UFO Museum in Roswell, New Mexico, highlighted earlier. Walking through the museum with its host of low-tech exhibits and recycled display cases, there was a display highlighting photographs of ancient Native American rock art. Why in the world, you might ask, are photos of rock art prominently displayed at the International UFO Museum in Roswell? It's simple. According to the signs in the display, the creatures shown in the rock art photos taken at the previously described sites, the

Head of Sinbad and Sego Canyon, may represent ancient eyewitness depictions of extraterrestrial aliens! One of the captions encapsulates this claim perfectly; about the images, the caption quoted researcher Ron Regher: "Some seem to suggest flight or extraterrestrial alien influence." The caption continues, quoting an unnamed Hopi Indian leader who believes that rock art suggests that there is a "connection between the Indians and visitors from space."

Archaeologists are skeptical of this. Big surprise. The belief that ancient art must be interpreted as representational, depictions of creatures the artists actually saw, originates in a fundamental misapprehension of art in the first place. Look at artists like Picasso, Magritte, or Dali. Consider Picasso's Cubist style with people depicted as flat, all angled and without curves. Or Magritte's bizarre floating men with apples suspended in front of their faces. And of course, Dali's melting time pieces. Does anyone today look at the works of these creative geniuses and wonder: "Did Picasso actually see extraterrestrial aliens walking about with their eyes on just one side of their weirdly flat, square faces? Was Magritte taken to a planet where gravity doesn't apply to apples and men in suits? Did Dali visit a world where clocks are all melty?" Of course not. Love or hate their art, we all recognize that the imagery in their paintings are the result of creativity, imagination, some might say their genius. Apply the same perspective to ancient artists and the anthropomorphs become imaginative depictions of spirit beings, not strange renderings of ET.

Why?

I think this interpretation of ancient art stems from a lack of understanding both of art and of its place in ancient—and modern—cultures. We generally accept the fact that modern artists have thoughts, dreams, and visions that they download to a canvas in the case of a painting or wood, stone, or metal in sculpture. Their art doesn't have to be realistic or naturalistic or representational. It can be weird, inexplicable, annoying, perplexing, moving, whimsical, hallucinatory, or photo-realistic depending on the artist and depending on his or her mood. I sort of doubt that all of those medieval and Renaissance paintings showing fat little cherubim with wings or people sporting haloes are depictions of things the artists actually saw. We recognize that they were devout Christians who believed that such things existed. Doesn't it make sense—well, it does to me—to afford ancient artists the same degree of creative leeway we give more recent artists?

Further, it's important to remember that these ancient artists were ensconced in their own cultural traditions of art and spirituality that don't necessarily match those of the modern viewer. They saw in their dreams and trances manifestations of the spirits they believed inhabited their world and resided in their reality. Finally, they had the skill and the desire to artfully depict those spirits and gods and ghosts by etching into or applying pigment onto rock panels in places they deemed sacred. We simply shouldn't impose our modern, twenty-first-century sensibilities or perspectives on these ancient artists.

If, however, you insist on the notion that ancient art is representational, that ancient artists were necessarily depicting things or beings they actually saw—things that to you look like flying saucers and spacemen—then you need to be consistent and apply that perspective across the board. For example, look at figure 6.10, a photograph I took at the Sand Island Petroglyph panel in Bluff, Utah. At least a thousand years old, it's a petroglyph of a bighorn sheep. Standing on its hind legs. And playing a flute. If you insist that, yup, the artist must have seen a big horn standing up and playing a flute (holding it, by the way, in its front hooves), well, that's great. If, instead, you more sensibly accept the fact that an artist, including an ancient one, could be imaginative, creative, and even whimsical in this instance, you have to admit the same possibility for all other ancient artists and all of their art, including depictions of long-bodied, googly-eyed, headdress-wearing anthropomorphs. The art is amazing and fascinating and remarkable precisely for how it reflects human creativity and artistic diversity. It has nothing whatsoever to do with ancient extraterrestrial visitors to Earth. And the Head of Sinbad and Sego Canyon are there for you to see that for yourself.

Figure 6.10. Ancient artists were no different from modern ones, at least in terms of creativity and imagination. Don't assume that ancient art is representational, realistic depictions of things the artist actually saw—like extraterrestrial aliens. Trust me, this upright, flute-playing sheep I saw at Sand Island Campground in Bluff, Utah, wasn't something the artist actually encountered.

Fake-o-meter

Five.

Getting there

I hope you are able to see most or maybe even all of the sites and artifacts I highlight in this guide. If you can't and you have only a few to choose from and you happen to be in Utah, whatever you do, try to visit these two sites. The art is breathtaking and beautiful.

The Head of Sinbad   Traveling west of the town of Green River, Utah, take Exit 131 on I-70. Take the exit ramp south, pass under the highway, and follow the graded dirt road (west) signed U24/Goblin Valley/Temple Mountain. In 3.9 miles, take the right (west) fork for 1.0 mile to a tee. Turn right (west) and travel 1.7 miles to a fork. Take the right (north) fork for 2.3 miles to the concrete underpass and drive back under I-70. On the north side of I-70 the dirt road forks. Take the right fork to reach the Head of Sinbad pictographs. Follow that right fork for .25 mile until you reach a tee. Turn right (east) at the tee and follow the main road (don't head off to the right when the road forks again). You'll reach the Head of Sinbad in a little less than 1.2 miles. Toward the end, the road gets very sandy. I made the trip without 4WD, but a vehicle with high clearance, like an SUV, is a must.

Sego Canyon   Heading east or west on the interstate, I-70, take exit number 187 and get on State Highway 94 north (which becomes BLM-159 and then Sego Canyon Road), through Thompson Springs. There are not a lot of roads in Thompson Springs, so this is one of those instances where you really can't miss it; it's the only paved (sort of) road heading north out of town. You'll see an old, weathered sign along the way saying something like "Indian Writing." In about three miles from town you'll see a dirt parking area and pit toilets on the left. You'll already be able to see the art as you approach the lot. Park there. The Paiute art will be in front of you when you pull into the lot (you'll be looking west). The Fremont art will be to your right (north) when you pull into the lot. The large anthropomorphs are on the other side of the road. The really cool Barrier Canyon–style art that, for real, does not represent ancient depictions of extraterrestrial aliens, is around the corner of the rock face with the Fremont art. There's not real hiking to do. Just walk around and you'll find it all.

· 7 ·

Category 5 Lost Civilizations

$\mathcal{T}$he image is straight out of the Victorian Era: the ruggedly handsome adventurer (me, of course) furiously hacks his way through the dense jungle with his machete, revealing the remarkable remains of an unknown city, the capital of a lost civilization previously believed by most to be little more than a legend, a bedtime story, or a cautionary tale. The Victorians had a particular knack for discovering lost civilizations by repurposing actual ruins that were well known to local people as part of their native traditions and cultures, transmuting them into the remains of lost or legendary European colonies or the far-flung outposts of biblical people. For example, the native, sub-Saharan African civilization today known as Great Zimbabwe, long known to local people as the capital of an expansive and indigenous kingdom, became to many in Europe, instead, the city of the biblical Queen of Sheba (Connah 1987). In another instance, the earthen mounds of the American Midwest and Southeast became the remnants of the settlements and monuments built by members of the Lost Tribes of Israel (Silverberg 1989). While such rebranding isn't as common today, the theme of the white archaeologists discovering hidden, forgotten, and lost civilizations—now using sophisticated technologies like Lidar instead of machetes—has become a part of romantic discussions about archaeological research. Just such a misrepresentation has recently occurred in the case of the Ciudad Blanca in Honduras (Begley 2016).

Two converging channels underlie the lost civilization trope: (1) the western scientist discovers a great and previously unknown or merely legendary civilization, lost, apparently, even to the local people who live adjacent to it and (2) the lost civilization is not the product of local people but represents foreigners with a far more sophisticated culture than that of the Natives of the region. That latter trope is precisely what lies at the heart of the examples focused on in this guide under the heading Lost Civilizations: the forgotten Roman Jewish colony reflected in the **Tucson Artifacts**; the **Grand Canyon Secret Cave** in Arizona; **Burrows Cave** in Illinois; and the underground city of **Moberly, Missouri**.

25. TUCSON ARTIFACTS, TUCSON, ARIZONA

Archaeological perspectives

There's an important lesson here for all of you aspiring archaeological hoaxers; don't aim too high. Maybe just be satisfied with a one-off artifact. Though experts usually can diagnose a fake—wrong materials, wrong style, wrong language, or simply an impossible assortment of anachronisms—you might get away with a one-off for at least long enough to get your fifteen minutes of fame or a little spending money. However, once you start finding a bunch of stuff and then claim that the artifacts you have found represent the remnants of an entire, previously lost colony of ancient people, you are going inevitably to fail.

You need to understand that archaeologists are adept at recognizing the remains of a human settlement. That's what we do. As discussed throughout this book, people together in one place (a camp, village, town, or city) extract resources from the environment, they make tools from those resources, and with those tools they hunt (leaving behind the butchered bones of the animals they hunted), plant crops (leaving behind seeds, nut fragments, and pollen), and they prepare that food for eating (in ceramic pots or stone bowls). Most important from an archaeological perspective, people break, use up, lose, and throw stuff away, and that stuff is culturally diagnostic. As I have mentioned incessantly in this book, every culture's stuff is different and unique, and cultural stuff is precisely what we find at settlements that we now call archaeological sites. There simply is no culture in the history of the world where people left behind nothing more than about thirty crosses, swords, and assorted other tchotchkes—almost all of them in lead, by the way—and not a single other indicator that they had been there. Yet this is exactly the evidence presented for the existence of a lost colony of Roman Jews in Arizona more than a thousand years ago. You read that right.

Here's what we know

The richly detailed story of the Tucson artifacts has been wonderfully told by Don Burgess (2009). It all begins on September 13, 1924, when Charles Manier and his family stopped at an old lime kiln located on Silverbell Road in Tucson, Arizona. Lime kilns are found all over the world. Their purpose is to produce quicklime from the calcium carbonate contained in a natural deposit called *caliche*, a kind of natural cement. Quicklime in Arizona was long used in the production of plaster and mortar needed in adobe construction. The Silverbell Road lime kilns had been abandoned in 1910. Poking around the remnants of the old kiln, Manier saw a piece of metal firmly embedded in the dense calcium carbonate. He needed a pick to remove it and was amazed at what he found it to be: a more than sixty-pound lead cross bearing a detailed inscription that he could not read (figure 7.1).

He was stunned, of course, and realized that he didn't know nearly enough about history, linguistics, or archaeology to explain the object, so he brought it to

Figure 7.1. This lead cross inscribed in Latin was found at an abandoned lime kiln outside of Tucson, Arizona, in 1924. Some interpreted it as proving the existence of a Roman Jewish colony in Arizona dating to between AD 775 and 900.

Courtesy of Don Burgess

the Arizona State Museum on the campus of the University of Arizona. Scientists at the museum—including A. E. Douglass, who would go on to become an icon in archaeology for developing the very accurate and precise technique tree ring dating—examined the cross and, it is fair to say, were intrigued. Thinking he had stumbled onto something of great monetary value, Manier brought the object to a local man, Thomas Bent, and offered him a financial partnership in their own dig at the site on land that, as it turns out, was not owned by anyone at the time of the initial discovery. Bent agreed, and thus began a period of a few years during which thirty-one more objects—thirty made of lead and one actually made from a piece of the local caliche—were excavated from the abandoned lime kiln. Most were crosses, many were swords, and there was a lance head and a fan-shaped object as well. Some noted the obvious at the time; lead would seem to be an especially poor choice for a sword. It doesn't keep a sharp edge, and it is monstrously heavy.

Then there was the story told in the Latin (!) inscriptions on the objects. Together, they identify the place as a colony called Calalus, a settlement of Roman Jews that existed between AD 775 and 900. The inscription claimed that the colonists arrived from across the sea and that they had contacts with the Toltecs to the south. Toltec is the name given to a Mexican civilization that predated the Aztecs, who were encountered by the Spanish conquistadores in 1519.

If the thirty-two artifacts were genuine and if the inscription could be verified, the implications certainly were mind blowing. More than a thousand years before the discovery of those objects, a group of European Jews had established a colony near modern Tucson! Remarkable indeed. But are the Tucson artifacts legitimate? People began arguing that point almost immediately upon their discovery.

Why are archaeologists skeptical?

Seriously? Dull-bladed, impossibly heavy lead swords? A colony of Roman Jews lasting 175 years in the desert of southern Arizona that left no material traces behind—including no burials—other than a bunch of lead crosses (um, Jews with crosses?), swords, and a caliche plaque? How did anyone take the discovery seriously?

Much of the argument on the part of those who strongly supported authenticity along with those who simply weren't sure concerns the fact that the objects were found embedded in the caliche deposit. The caliche was ancient, so the artifacts must been even older than the caliche.

There was a serious problem with that argument. Sure, the caliche deposit in which the artifacts were found was ancient, but, in fact, it was far too ancient. Tucson geologist James Quinlan identified the caliche deposit on Silverbell Road as being Pleistocene in age and origin. In other words, the deposit in which the artifacts were found was, at a minimum, ten thousand years old! If the Tucson artifacts were legitimately encased in ten-thousand-year-old caliche, then they must be at least that old and possibly as much as 1.8 million years of age. Which is nonsensical, if you hold onto the one-thousand-year age as indicated in the translation.

A careful examination of the context of discovery of at least one of the artifacts showed pretty clearly that a hole had been etched into the caliche and the object jammed in; the gap in the caliche in which it was found was actually longer than the object, and that certainly aroused suspicion. It has also been suggested that once a gap was artificially made in the natural deposit and the object placed within, loose calcium carbonate was packed into the hole and around the object. With a bit of water added to the mix, a hard, dense, and of course, very modern caliche was produced, making the artifact appear to have been there since the natural deposit formed. However, whoever accomplished this task was unaware that, for that to be true, the artifacts would need to be at least ten thousand years old.

Clearly those who had the most to gain monetarily from the pieces were the most vociferous in their defense—Thomas Bent, the co-owner of the objects, wrote and self-published a 352-page report on the artifacts and their excavation. However, many (not all) trained archaeologists and language experts declared them to be poorly rendered fakes that made little sense.

For example, Frank Fowler of the Classics Department of the University of Arizona pored over the inscriptions. He not only declared them to be a poorly rendered fraud, he even found what appeared to be a source for the inscriptions. Apparently the hoaxer plagiarized bits and pieces of the inscriptions—word for word and in the same order—from three widely available books about Latin grammar (*Harkness's Latin Grammar*, the *Latin Grammar of Allen and Greenough*, and *Rouf's Standard Dictionary of Facts*).

When experts at the British Museum were shown photographs of the large lead cross, the consensus as reported to A. E. Douglas was:

> We all find it difficult to believe that the cross can be anything but the work of a person living not very long ago, and desirous of mystifying persons. In our opinion it cannot have any historical value. (as cited in Burgess 2009: 14)

As reported in the *New York Times* on December 13, 1925, when shown the lead objects including the swords, the curator of arms at the Metropolitan Museum of Art in New York City labeled them "crude and childish forgeries."

Beyond this, chemical analyses conducted on the lead indicated that the swords, crosses, lance head, and fanlike object had been made from a modern metal, similar, in fact, to the lead used to make the anodes of lead batteries! Shocking (sorry for the pun).

There was—and still is—the broader archaeological puzzle faced by supporters of the authenticity of the Tucson artifacts: Where are all of the other mundane objects that would be expected at an archaeological site that ostensibly represented a long-lived colony of Roman Jews in the eighth and ninth centuries? Where are the remains of their houses, their kitchens, their workshops, and, ultimately, where are their burials? Authenticity supporters like Byron Cummings, whose official title at the University of Arizona was Dean of the Archaeological Department and Director of the State Museum, recognized this very problem and, in December 14, 1925, in the *New York Times* admitted:

> "It is strange," he said, "that nothing, no human bones, were found with these articles. What must be done is what we are planning to do. I have promised to make further excavations in a systematic manner after the holidays. I will try to find the camp site of the people who had these articles. Apparently their weapons and crosses were washed down a slope in times of flood, and I think a camp site will be found near-by where they were washed from."

Search as they might, subsequent excavations revealed no evidence of the actual colony, and Cummings himself, one of the few experienced archaeologists who initially supported authenticity, changed his mind. The artifacts were isolated; there was no archaeological context for them, and they simply could not have been actual elements of an ancient colony of immigrants from Rome in the eighth century.

Finally, it didn't exactly help supporters of the artifacts' authenticity when, on April 5, 1925, another lead sword was found and on its blade one could very clearly see the image of an animal etched into its surface. The identification of the animal was, well, either perplexing or hilarious, and maybe both. The animal on the blade of the sword was a dinosaur, apparently a brontosaurus or apatosaurus, to be precise (figure 7.2). At this point I think it appropriate to raise the

Figure 7.2. This impossible lead sword is another of the Tucson Artifacts. Why is it impossible? Well, to begin, it weighs over forty pounds, which would be interesting in actual combat. Oh, and there's an engraving of what appears to be a dinosaur on its blade.
Courtesy of Don Burgess.

question: Had the hoaxer, whoever he or she was, tiring of the game, planted an absurdity, a sword bearing an image certain to signal that the entire thing had been a bad joke? Unfortunately, none of the believers in authenticity seem to have been bothered by the dinosaur, even when a drawing that appears to have been the source of the image on the sword was located in a book titled *The First Story Ever Told*. That book was in the collections of the University of Arizona Library. No surprise there.

Whodunit?

There are no deathbed confessions, no smoking guns, and no DNA recovered from any of the objects, so answering the "whodunit" question is a challenge. Don Burgess (2009) has enumerated the possible perpetrators, including: local Freemasons; Mormons; Daniel Soper (the individual responsible for the **Michigan Relics**); and an elderly Mexican man, Timotio Oldohui, who lived nearby, was familiar with metal fabrication, and apparently had hoped to inspire his son to go into the priesthood. As Burgess points out, most of these scenarios constitute little more than conjecture. He suggests that the most probable perpetrators were the individuals who revealed the existence of the site. Admittedly, the evidence is circumstantial, but Manier and Bent had primary access to the location where the objects were found and are the most likely perpetrators. But the truth is, we may never know.

Why?

If Charles Manier and Thomas Bent were the creators of the Tucson Artifacts, the motive is pretty clear: money. Manier and Bent hoped to sell the set of artifacts and digging rights to the University of Arizona. The deal was that the university would pay out $16,000 (the equivalent of $150,000 today), but this was "contingent on the artifacts being authenticated as pre-Columbian" (Burgess 2009: 36). The deal fell through when it became clear that the artifacts were frauds.

Fake-o-meter

Five.

Getting there

The lime kiln where the artifacts were "found" is long gone now. But the artifacts are stored at the Arizona Historical Society. Unfortunately, they are not on display as I write this, but it is hoped that one day, with a bit of funding, this fascinating saga in Arizona history and the history of archaeological oddities will take its rightful place, in public view.

26. GRAND CANYON SECRET CAVE, GRAND CANYON, ARIZONA

27. MOBERLY SUBTERRANEAN CITY, MOBERLY, MISSOURI

Archaeological perspectives

Fake news. As I write this in early June 2018, it's impossible to open a newspaper, turn on a cable news station, or read your online news feeds without encountering discussions about *fake* news. It's ironic, right? There's a lot of *real* news right now about *fake* news, stories that are either gross exaggerations of fact or entirely fabricated, simply made up out of nothing. American soldiers in Afghanistan have captured a biblical giant. Of course they have. It has been grotesquely claimed that the mass murder of children and their teachers at the Sandy Hook Elementary School in Newtown, Connecticut, in 2012 was a staged event, a so-called false flag engineered to take away people's constitutional right to own firearms—and no one actually died in the incident. Tell that to the still grieving parents. Hillary Clinton runs a child sex ring out of a pizza parlor in Washington, D.C. OMG. Just OMG.

As troubling and shocking as these false stories may be—and while it's getting a lot of press right now—fake news is nothing new. Elevating the assumed entertainment value of a story above its veracity, popular media has, for decades, printed or broadcast stories despite warning signs that they were fake. Even more troubling, popular media has, again for decades, reported stories they knew were false but whose implications supported the political views of the media outlet's ownership or that were simply viewed as harmless entertainment, the kinds of stories that sell newspapers. Fake news was so common at the turn of the twentieth century there was even a name given to it: yellow journalism. The supermarket tabloids so popular in the period before internet fake news took over were the ignoble descendants of the yellow journals of the last century. Think *The Onion*, only they sort of expected you to believe the nonsense.

Some fake news—both today and in the past—exploited people's fascination with human antiquity. Two examples—one from the late nineteenth and one from the early twentieth century—of archaeological oddities that involve entirely fabricated stories about the discovery of astounding ancient remains in the United States are: (1) the secret cave in the Grand Canyon, in Arizona and (2) the "lost" subterranean city of Moberly, Missouri. Let's look at them both.

Here's what we know: Grand Canyon Secret Cave

You will clearly notice many similarities between the story of the subterranean city of Moberly and that of a lost city hidden in the deep recesses of a cave in the Grand Canyon.

Figure 7.3. The Grand Canyon is emblematic of both the beauty of the American landscape and the tremendous success of our National Park system. I can't show you a photograph of the secret cave hidden here, and I can't show you a photograph of the remarkable bounty of Egyptian or Tibetan artifacts found within the case for one simple reason. They don't exist.

iStock ID: 511191448; Credit: Yue734

The Grand Canyon story begins with a newspaper account published in the *Arizona Gazette* on April 5, 1909 (you can read the text of the newspaper article at Jason Colavito's web page at: http://www.jasoncolavito.com/the-1909-grand-canyon-hoax.html, where he also provides a wonderful dissection of the hoax). That article concerns the discovery by Mr. G. E. Kincaid, an Idaho native, of the hidden entrance of a secret cave located high up on a vast rock wall, 1,486 feet from the top and about 2,000 feet above the Colorado River as it snakes its way through the Grand Canyon in Arizona (figure 7.3).

According to that article, Kincaid spied evidence of the hidden entrance to the cave while navigating the river, whereupon he scaled the immense rock wall, found the cave, and then entered it, discovering the lost world of a forgotten civilization.

Kincaid reported that the interior of the cave was gigantic and clearly artificially engineered with finely made, rectangular rooms and oval doorways. The walls over the doorways, along with urns and tablets, were covered in mysterious hieroglyphs that, the article admits, had not yet been translated. In those rooms, Kincaid discovered fabulous treasures, all indicating the presence of an advanced and populous "oriental" civilization in Arizona deep in antiquity.

Artifacts of gold and copper were strewn about in the cave. Some of the walls appeared to be overlain with thin sheets of platinum. One cavernous room was littered with cooking utensils; Kincaid concluded that it had been a dining hall for the residents of the colony who, based on the enormous size of the cave, he numbered at as many as fifty thousand. That's fifty thousand people living in a cave in the middle of a cliff. In Arizona. A long, long time ago. Secretly.

In the center of another room, Kincaid found the most impressive artifact of all, a monumental idol of what appeared to be a cross-legged Buddha holding a lotus or lily in each hand. The Buddha was surrounded by other statues; Kincaid likened them to those seen in ancient Tibet.

According to the article, Kincaid had already contacted and shared his discovery with Professor S. A. Jordan of the famed "Smithsonian Institute," which was now funding the research. Scientists at the Smithsonian were leaning toward the hypothesis that the residents of the cave were from Egypt—though how Tibetan statuary and a Buddha fit that hypothesis is unexplained—and may date to the period of the fabled pharaoh Ramses. As there are eleven pharaohs who bore the Ramses name, it's difficult to date the site based on an Egyptian king list, but I presume the article's author was referring to Ramses I, who ruled about three thousand years ago. The article further suggests that through study of the material in the cave: "the mystery of the prehistoric peoples of North America, their ancient arts, who they were and whence they came, will be solved."

We are compelled to ask the very same questions to be posed of the Moberly lost city: Who were the people who left their mummified remains in the lost Grand Canyon colony? Where did they come from? When did they get to Arizona? Where are their artifacts and mummies housed today? Where are the archaeologists who excavated the place, and where can we read their journal articles and PhD dissertations about the fabulous lost cave city of the Grand Canyon? All reasonable questions, but, as we will see in the case of the Moberly lost city, there are no answers.

Why are archaeologists skeptical? Grand Canyon Secret Cave

Though unlike the newspaper article about the subterranean city of Moberly, there never was a retraction of the *Arizona Gazette* article about the lost city of the Grand Canyon, there are many, many clues that it was a practical joke.

To begin, no one has ever been able to track down, either at the time or after the fact, G. E. Kincaid. As far as anyone can tell, he wasn't a real person. A story like one involving a lost city in a cave in the Grand Canyon would certainly have generated follow-up media coverage. Ambitious journalists would have made every attempt to track down Kincaid to get more information, to get an exclusive interview, to ask to be brought into the cave, and to photograph the fabulous treasures he had encountered there. But there's nothing. No interviews. No follow-up articles. No photographs. Kincaid said explicitly that he photographed one of the mummies, illuminating it with a flashlight. Where's the photograph? It doesn't exist, nor are there any museum exhibits. There's nothing.

How about the Smithsonian Institute's Professor S. A. Jordan? He should be easy to trace. What did he have to say about the lost city of the Grand Canyon? Well, he didn't say anything because he couldn't. He couldn't because he doesn't exist either. There was no S. A. Jordan, or anyone with a similar name at the Smithsonian. Ever. The Smithsonian has been queried about this story by curious researchers almost since the initial publication of the article. They have always maintained that there was no S. A. Jordan and, even more significantly, that they have absolutely no record of anyone contacting them about a lost city in a cave in the Grand Canyon. If you're going to now accuse the Smithsonian of being part of a grand coverup about the site (so of course they deny any knowledge of it), please provide some evidence for that claim. And even if they could cover it up, why, exactly, would they want to?

There is another little problem. There is no such thing as the "Smithsonian Institute." The national museum of the United States is called the Smithsonian *Institution*. (The same mistake was made by the discoverer of the **Heavener Runestone**.) Wouldn't a real journalist writing a real article about a real discovery by a real explorer whose discoveries were being examined by a real professor know the name of the national museum of the United States where that professor worked? One would hope.

Ultimately, it's abundantly clear that there is no hidden cave filled with the treasures of a lost civilization in the Grand Canyon any more than there is a lost city filled with treasures underlying the city of Moberly, Missouri. There aren't even any ostensible artifacts from Moberly or the Grand Canyon cave to argue about.

Though you won't find too many people who will still argue that the underground city of Moberly was the real deal, the internet is filled with claims that the secret Grand Canyon cave is genuine and that it has been found! I hate to be the party-pooping skeptic here—who am I kidding, I love being the party-pooping skeptic—but without any artifacts, no archaeologist is going to take such claims at all seriously. All the folks who claim to have found the cave need to do is bring in some skeptical archaeologists and a film crew from National Geographic or, better yet, the Smithsonian (Institution, not Institute), and show those skeptics the artificially carved cave, the shelves filled with mummies, and the lotus-holding statue of the Buddha, and we'll change our tune. Until then, well, I'll wait here.

Here's what we know: Moberly Subterranean City

On April 8, 1885, the *St. Louis Evening Chronicle* published a hyperventilated article about the accidental discovery of fabulous treasures seen in the ruins of an abandoned city deep beneath the surface of the town of Moberly, Missouri, to-day about a two-and-a-half-hour drive from St. Louis. You can read the original 1885 article on Jason Colavito's web page here: http://www.jasoncolavito.com/the-1885-moberly-lost-city-hoax.html.

The story claimed that while operating his coal mine, and at a depth of more than 360 feet, Tim Collins broke into a voluminous cavern beneath the coal seam where he and his crew discovered a (and all caps are in the original) "LITERAL WORLD OF WONDERS." The miners could readily see that the cavern was not natural, but artificial, with smooth stone benches, vertical walls, and polished floors clearly carved by ancient stone masons. Scattered throughout the cavern were the metal tools those masons had used in their work, though the wooden handles had turned to dust.

As the explorers traveled more deeply into the cavern along the remarkable, wide avenues of the subterranean city, they came upon a series of rooms, each filled with an array of spectacular artifacts. In one hall there were grotesque statues made of stone and bronze. In an adjoining courtyard they found a stone-carved fountain, and near it the skeleton of a truly giant human being. His femur (thigh bone) alone was about 4.5 feet (fifty-four inches) long. By way of comparison, the average adult male femur is about nineteen inches in length. Using a little math, a man with a 4.5-foot-long thigh bone must have been more than fourteen feet tall. It all sounds a bit like the author Jules Verne's story *Journey to the Center of the Earth*, published only about twenty years before the Moberly story hit the newspapers.

Who were these subterranean giants of Moberly, Missouri? Where did they come from? When did they get to Missouri? Where are the artifacts and bones recovered in the lost city housed today? Who were the archaeologists who excavated the place, and where can we read their journal articles and PhD dissertations about the fabulous lost city? Those are all very good questions. With no answers. That's because, like the Grand Canyon lost civilization, the entire thing was fake.

Why are archaeologists skeptical? Moberly Subterranean City

Certainly this was an amazing discovery, and interest was sparked all over the world. Can you imagine, with today's penchant for such stories and with the lubrication supplied by social media, the hundreds of websites and YouTube videos it would have generated? And maybe even a cable series?

There's just one problem. The story was entirely made up, and Col. John G. Provines, the newspaper's editor, admitted that it was a late April Fools' Day prank. Though he later claimed that he had been duped by his reporter, J. W. Estes, many at the time thought that, though the idea may have been the young reporter's, the details of the story were concocted by Provines.

The man who owned the mine, Tim Collins, was a real person, and the mine was a real place, but the story of the lost city was entirely fake news. The newspaper retracted the story just three days later, on April 11. The *Rockingham Register*, one of the papers that picked up and ran with the story, concluded, "The only truth connected with it being that there is a hole in the ground." Displaying his annoyance about the unwanted publicity the story had generated about his coal mine, Collins posted a sign with this poorly spelled message at its entrance: "No burryied sity lunaticks aloud on these premises." The lost city of Moberly was a blatant fabrication whose dual purpose was to entertain and sell papers, which, apparently, it did.

Whodunit?

Though we don't have a smoking gun in the case of the Grand Canyon hoax, it likely was the anonymous author of the article. We know the responsible party in the case of the lost city of Moberly, Missouri. It was Johnnie Estes, an ambitious young journalist who came up with a cool idea for an April Fools' Day story who then had his editor, Colonel Provines, fill in the details.

Why?

I began this double entry talking about fake news and the fact that fake news often supports a particular set of preexisting beliefs—sometimes not just bordering on the paranoid but full-bore pathological paranoia. In other cases, the intent isn't malevolent but simply to entertain by making up something that readers might find interesting. In the Grand Canyon story, there is the claim that Native American cultures will be explained as resulting from contact with those illegal aliens from Tibet (or is it Egypt?). This is a common theme among those who denigrate American Indians by ascribing all of their achievements to ancient visitors who taught them how to farm, how to build monumental structures, and how to make calendars. Nevertheless, I suspect that the intent of the Grand Canyon hoax was primarily to sell newspapers. Please note that, as we saw in the Moberly hoax, the Grand Canyon lost city article was published in early April, perhaps as an April Fools' prank.

Fake-o-meter

Ten. That's five for each.

Getting there

When I submitted my proposal for this book to the publisher, I requested that I be given sufficient time to visit at least the great majority of the sites or museums in my listing of archaeological oddities. Unfortunately, dear reader, I was not able to fulfill this goal for the two sites discussed in this entry. But you need to cut me some slack. I couldn't visit the Moberly underground city or the lost cave of the Grand Canyon because neither are real places. But I plan to visit them. In my imagination.

28. BURROWS CAVE, SOMEWHERE, ILLINOIS(?)

Archaeological perspectives

It may be Gertrude Stein's most quoted quip. In her 1937 autobiography, Stein indicated that she didn't have any desire to visit Oakland, the city where she was born and raised, simply because "there's no there there." She meant that very narrowly, that her childhood home was no longer standing so there was nothing to draw her back, but people have applied the phrase ever since much more broadly and metaphorically to places that don't seem to have any strong personality, individuality, or unique sense of place. I will now take further liberties with Stein's phrasing and apply it to an archaeological site. Though thousands of strange and unique ancient artifacts are alleged to have been recovered from Burrows Cave, ostensibly in Illinois, the fact is, no one other than the individual claiming to have discovered the artifacts has been there, and he hasn't taken anyone there to see it. Further, his story about its location and disposition have changed dramatically through time. Though the artifacts are here for us to marvel at, it has never been proven that they were recovered from Burrows Cave and, in fact, there's no evidence that Burrows Cave exists in the first place. It would appear, in my application of the Stein quote, there literally is no there there.

To characterize the story behind Burrows Cave as a hot mess would be a vast understatement. It's more a molten shitstorm. This is largely because there is no single "story" but a bunch of differing and contradictory tales, none of which make any sense. Oh, and there is no evidence to confirm any of the myriad versions of the story concerning the cave's discovery or location.

Burrows Cave is yet another example of an ostensibly spectacular archaeological site in North America that contradicts the standard histories of our continent. It is supposed to be a secret cave chock-a-block with remarkable ancient artifacts traceable to the Old World—a combination of the **Grand Canyon Secret Cave** (also of no known location) and the **Moberly Subterranean City** (lots of artifacts said to have been witnessed but never produced), but with a plethora of actual objects, however fake they may be. So where is Burrows Cave, and what do the artifacts allegedly recovered there imply about the history of North America?

Here's what we know

The story of the discovery of Burrows Cave—actually, the two different and contradictory stories—originates with one man, the ostensible discoverer, Russell Burrows: and yes, the cave is named for him. There is absolutely no way to verify his story as there were no eyewitnesses to any of it. According to that story, Burrows was walking around somewhere—the exact where has never been revealed—in Illinois in April 1982 (as described in Wilson 2012; Wilson's article is a fantastic and detailed summary of the Burrows Cave tale). Burrows states that he was looking for artifacts, maybe with a metal detector, when either he simply found the entrance to a cave or nearly fell into a trap designed to kill whoever dared disturb the sanctity of the site. Wilson notes the similarity between that version and the original *Indiana Jones* movie. Anyway, after either falling or walking in, he noted a staircase hewn into the stone and, upon descending that staircase, he breathlessly encountered the presence of hundreds upon hundreds of artifacts strewn about. As he entered a series of chambers, he encountered numerous crypts, life-size statues of Egyptian deities made entirely of gold, gold coins, suits of armor, and lots more.

Most of the objects Burrows said he found in the cave were stones with inscriptions that have later turned out to represent messages in various ancient Old World scripts, including Egyptian, Etruscan, Greek, and Sumerian (note that these languages date to wildly different periods in the Old World, so their presence together in one place, no matter where, represents a series of extraordinary anachronisms). Also among the inscriptions were drawings of oared boats, helmeted warriors, profiles of individuals who appear to be wearing Egyptian headgear, Egyptian gods and goddesses, people with Nubian (south of Egypt) hair types, and lots of other images, none of which would appear to belong in an authentically ancient site in Illinois. If genuine, a heretofore entirely unknown chapter of the history of North America is revealed and all of us archaeologists and historians are going to need to obey the cliché, tear up our archaeology and history books—and it might not be a bad idea to tear up our PhDs while we're at it—and start them afresh, leaving plenty of room for the cosmopolitan, multicultural lost civilization of Illinois.

Why are archaeologists skeptical?

It is fair to say the scientists are skeptical about claims that turn our knowledge of any particular subject on its head. And it is reasonable to be skeptical. Skepticism is not cynicism, and doubt isn't denial. After all of the work archaeologists have done excavating at thousands of places in North America, we have a pretty good idea of what happened here and when. Not perfect, of course, not complete, certainly, but pretty good. Of course, we're willing to revise our consensus, tweak our reconstructions, and yes, even throw out what we thought we knew and start from scratch. But we need—I should even say we demand—definitive and convincing proof. In the case of Burrows Cave, that proof has been neither definitive nor convincing.

Here, our understanding of the history of human movement into and through the New World would certainly need to be reevaluated and completely revised if the artifacts claimed to have been found in Burrows Cave—including evidence that ancient Egyptians, Etruscans, Greeks, Nubians, and Sumerians were all living together as one happy family in a cave in Illinois—were genuine. It is important to add, however, that scientists are also intrigued by game-changing discoveries, and many want to investigate them more deeply. And following the discovery and revelation of those discoveries of Russell Burrows, there certainly was an interest on the part of researchers, some sympathetic to the possibility that ancient Europeans, Africans, or Asians traveled to the New World in antiquity and left behind artifacts confirming their presence here. Unfortunately, however, none of these interested researchers have ever been shown the cave. Burrows has steadfastly refused to take anyone to the site or reveal its location. Ostensibly it is located near the Embarras River (write your own joke) somewhere in Richland County, Illinois, but that's all we know. And we don't even know that. By the way, the existence of an actual cave in Richland County, Illinois, would be mind boggling to geologists; there are no known caves there, and local geology simply isn't conducive to the creation of actual caves or caverns. I won't waste time here going into the personality of Russell Burrows, but if you're interested, check out the late Rick Flavin's detailed description of his personal experiences with Burrows and the, um, interesting cast of characters involved with Burrows Cave (Flavin 2012).

Now back to the archaeology, such as it is. Burrows was approached by the Early Sites Research Society, a group dedicated to the idea that there's lots of evidence of the presence of Old World people in North America in antiquity. Members of that society can in no way be characterized as mainstream, skeptical naysayers, so Burrows couldn't claim that they were a group of unfair skeptics predisposed to reject his discoveries. Yet Burrows turned them down flat simply because they wanted to document the discoveries made in the cave, something that scientists and historians might be able to assess for themselves (Joltes 2003). Burrows has explained his reluctance to show anyone the cave as resulting from his fears that once its location becomes widely known, it will be looted. As a working archaeologist I sympathize with that perspective, but I also know that there are ways of protecting the site, so Burrows's explanation simply doesn't ring true. Burrows has gone further to suggest that he won't take anyone into the cave because there's $60 million worth of gold artifacts hidden there. Of course there is.

If you need to ask why scientists are skeptical of the claims made about Burrows Cave, you haven't been paying attention and need to go back and read the opening chapters of this book. You might end up failing the course and will have to attend summer school to repeat it.

When trained scientists have had the opportunity to examine artifacts allegedly extracted from Burrows Cave, the verdict has been unanimous: they aren't ancient, the drawings are absurd and childish, and the writing is nonsensical.

And there's this: several of the Burrows Cave–inscribed stones are made of marble. On one side of those marble artifacts is a carving of a woman squatting on one knee. Above her head, with her hair done up in a very ancient Egyptian look, is a circular image of what almost certainly is intended to represent the sun with a series of lines representing rays descending from it. It has been proposed that the woman in the carving is a representation of the Egyptian goddess Isis, the mother of the falcon-headed god Horus.

Of course, an image of Isis or, for that matter, any other Egyptian deity, is completely out of place in an Illinois cave, at least in terms of an existing archaeological consensus about the history and prehistory of the American Midwest. However, it fits nicely within the assemblage supposedly found in Burrows Cave. But this artifact can easily be shown to be a fake, and an obvious one at that. The person who used the particular piece of marble to craft the Burrows Cave artifact made a very big mistake.

That mistake was first noted by Dorothy Hayden (1993) and later confirmed by Scott Wolter (2010), whose cable show *America Unearthed* was not exactly a model of skeptical inquiry. Wolter is a geologist, but you really don't need a degree in geology or anything else to prove the fakery here. All you need is a working pair of eyes. Or even one working eye. As Hayden noted, one of the Burrows Cave–inscribed artifacts was actually made on a fragment of a marble, historical gravestone! Wolter confirmed this, finding on the reverse side of the stone with a carving of Isis cursive letters spelling out the word *there*. Anyone even passingly familiar with eighteenth- or nineteenth-century cemeteries will recognize that the Isis carving was made on the back side of a gravestone, in all likelihood one not more than about 250 years old. Looking at a photo of the back face of the stone, it appears that someone attempted to remove the text carved there by striking the surface, perhaps with a rock hammer, but they weren't entirely successful. Wolter goes on to conclude that ten more marble objects found in the cave bear properties that similarly suggest that they were made from the same gravestone material. He suggests that all of these artifacts were frauds made after the discovery of the cave in 1982.

Now, in fairness I should add that Wolter continues to at least entertain the possibility that Burrows Cave and many of the artifacts said to have been found there are authentic and ancient. For him, evidence that eleven of the Burrows Cave artifacts aren't genuine but twentieth-century fakes manufactured from a repurposed gravestone does not reflect on the authenticity of the rest of the assemblage. Okay, but this clear evidence of fakery seems pretty damning. In the article, Wolter pleads with Burrows to actually take people to the cave to clear up these issues. Yeah, Wolter's never been to the cave either.

The only rational conclusion to reach concerning Burrows Cave is that it is a big fat fake. The archaeology and history books are safe.

Whodunit?

Let's see: Russell Burrows discovered the cave; Russell Burrows is the only person who has ever entered the cave; Russell Burrows is the only person who has actually seen artifacts in place in the cave; Russell Burrows is the only person to have recovered artifacts from the cave. Whodunit? Hmm. Not sure.

Why?

The motive behind the Burrows Cave fake artifacts—I can't bring myself to call it "the Burrows Cave Site" because there simply does not appear to be a cave or an actual site—is pretty simple, a combination of money and attention. There are people who admit to having purchased artifacts either directly or indirectly from Burrows. And Burrows and his followers certainly have garnered quite a bit of attention from the place; a cursory glance at issues of the magazine *Ancient American* shows quite a bit of coverage concerning Burrows Cave and, with the exception of the piece by Scott Wolter, it's all been credulous as hell. Ultimately, as Rick Flavin (2012) succinctly put it, the Burrows Cave humbug is: "Talk-radio silliness, financially motivated fraud, outrageous religious agendas, and amateur historical revisionism is what this is all about. It's never been about history or science."

Fake-o-meter

One hundred.

Getting there

This one is easy. To get to Burrows Cave first, think happy thoughts. Then, fly off to the second star on the right and straight on till morning. Be careful though. The cave might be guarded by pirates. Sorry for the snark, but it's easy to wipe that snark right off my face; reveal the location of the cave, bring in a film crew from *National Geographic*, photograph the fabulous array of artifacts in situ. Done. Until then, scientists are going to figure that the cave is located in Neverland, as the directions indicate.

Category 6 Biblical Proof?

$\mathcal{A}$s you already know, events described in the Judeo-Christian Bible happened a long time ago. As a field that focuses on the past, archaeology, not surprisingly, has been used, and has been useful, in the search for evidence of the historicity—just a fancy word for historical validity—of stories and places mentioned in the Old and New Testaments of the Bible. While historical and archaeological research hasn't confirmed any of the miracles mentioned in the Old and New Testaments—as alluded to in the preface, archaeological research has not provided evidence for the Garden of Eden, nor has it confirmed the existence of Goliath, the Tower of Babel, or the flood of Noah—it has confirmed some biblical details, including the actual existence of some ancient cities, palaces, and temples mentioned in the Bible (Cline 2007). For example, the Old Testament city of Jericho really did exist and has been excavated by archaeologists, though there is no evidence that the walls fell as the result of Joshua playing a trumpet. So, while science can't confirm the miracles and supernatural occurrences highlighted in the Bible, it has, to an extent, confirmed some elements of the physical and cultural landscape in which those miracles are claimed to have taken place.

Here in North America, we are pretty far removed from the locations in which biblical events transpired, so nobody is looking for the archaeological remains of Noah's Ark here (as some have in Turkey, on the top of Mount Ararat).

Nevertheless, there are people who subscribe to a literal interpretation of the Bible and describe themselves as "Young Earth creationists" (YECs). At least some YECs believe there is general archaeological evidence here in America that supports a literal interpretation of biblical chronology. Following seventeenth-century Bishop Ussher of Ireland, YECs believe that the entire universe was created by God in six literal, twenty-four-hour days just a little more than six thousand and likely less than ten thousand years ago. Compare this to the scientific consensus that the universe is about 13.5 billion years old and Earth is about 4.5 billion years old. To YECs, 4.5 billion years of Earth history as calculated by scientists actually can be shoehorned into just a few thousand years, including the tenure of all of those extinct animals whose fossilized bones are found by paleontologists. That includes the dinosaurs, who are believed by scientists to have thrived between about three hundred million years ago until their extinction about sixty-five million years ago. YECs instead believe that dinosaurs lived less than six thousand years ago and were brought on board the ark by Noah to save them from the flood. There even is a YEC museum—built, by the way, in the shape of Noah's Ark as detailed in the Bible—dedicated to their belief that a universal flood actually happened (Ark Encounter: https://arkencounter.com).

As believers in the literal truth of the Bible, YECs also tend to accept the existence of giant humanlike beings, like the Nephilim; as stated in Genesis 6:4, "There were giants in the Earth in those days." YECs don't interpret that as a metaphor. They believe there really were giant, humanlike beings during the days of the Old Testament. And hey, archaeologists might be able to find their remains.

Obviously, if the world is only six thousand years old and, therefore, people and dinosaurs have overlapped in time, then perhaps people encountered dinosaurs and left footprints in the same mud flows that through time became stone. Perhaps people hunted dinosaurs—I imagine that even a young brontosaurus would have kept a tribe fed for months. If that happened, we might be able to find butchered, gnawed on, and charred dinosaur bones in the hearths or roasting pits of ancient people. Or maybe instead of eating dinosaurs, human beings were on the menu—though we would have likely been not much more than a snack for a hungry tyrannosaur. Human bones might be found in dinosaur coprolites, the fossilized remnants of their feces. Admittedly this would not have been a particularly romantic end for a human ancestor, but it would mark definitive proof of the coexistence of human beings and dinosaurs. Finally, ancient humans who shared a world with dinosaurs and were mightily impressed by the massive size and even grace of those great beasts may have painted or etched images of them onto stone, just as they depicted deer, bighorn sheep, bison, elk, and antelope (Nelson 2012).

These scenarios are pretty extreme and contradict the scientific consensus about the universe, the planet, biological evolution, as well as human prehistory and history. It should surprise no one, not even YECs, that such claims are going to generate quite a bit of skepticism on the part of scientists. The most significant question for us here is, is there any physical evidence in North America for any of the mentioned scenarios? Let's visit a few places located in North America that some YECs claim provide convincing evidence in their attempt to overturn that understanding: the **Cardiff Giant** in New York State; the **Paluxy River Footprints** in Texas; and the **Black Dragon Pictograph** and the **Kachina Bridge Pictograph**, both in Utah.

29. THE CARDIFF GIANT, COOPERSTOWN, NEW YORK

Archaeological perspectives

I couldn't have been much more than nine or ten when I first met the big dude. It must have been sometime in the early 1960s. My parents, sister, and I were on one of our patented, two-week, car-trip summer vacations, leaving ridiculously early in the morning from our house in Syosset, Long Island, New York. In those wonderful, truly intellectually formative trips for my sister and me— thanks Mom and Dad!—we visited various and sundry educational attractions scattered across the Northeast: Old Sturbridge Village in Massachusetts; Ausable Chasm in New York State; the Amish country in Pennsylvania; the monuments and museums of Washington, D.C. In one of these trips, we stopped off at the Baseball Hall of Fame in Cooperstown, New York (for me and my dad) and took a side trip to the Farmers' Museum, a truly wonderful outdoor museum comprised of a cluster of old houses, a farm, and outbuildings dating to the nineteenth century.

On the side of one of the buildings, a barn, maybe, protected under a wooden lean-to, was what appeared to be the remains of a giant man, a man whose body, it seemed, had turned completely to stone (figure 8.1). I remember the giant being both a bit scary but also silly, lying in silent and naked repose on his back with his right hand resting on his stomach, his legs both bent a little at the knee, with an enigmatic look of contentment on his stony face.

There was a sign explaining that this was the infamous Cardiff Giant, a humbug that fooled thousands when it was "discovered" in 1869. As I remember it, this was my first personal encounter with an archaeological fraud and, in hindsight, it may have served as the inspiration for a major part of my career, and counting what you are reading here, the focus of three of my books. So, Mr. Cardiff Giant, I guess I owe you a great debt of gratitude. But who was the Cardiff Giant; why were people fooled into thinking that a simple statue was actually the petrified remains of a genuine, ancient, giant man; and, of course, who did it and why?

Here's what we know

As the story unfolded immediately after its "discovery" (those scare quotes are well deserved) in late October 1869, farmer Stub Newell hired two men to dig a well on his farm in the tiny, rural community of Cardiff, New York. While doing so, they unexpectedly encountered something exceptionally hard at a depth of about three feet in the otherwise fine alluvial soil deposited by nearby Onondaga Creek. Stub was reported to be annoyed by the delay caused by this impediment to well digging, but he was amazed by what lay in the bottom of the

Figure 8.1. In silent repose, the Cardiff Giant rests eternally, bearing witness, not to the existence of biblical giants, but to the unbounded capacity of people to be fooled, if only temporarily.

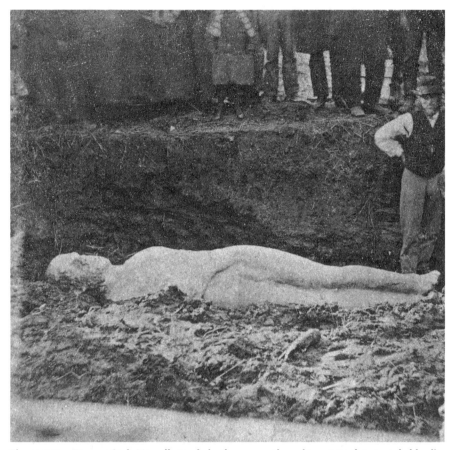

Figure 8.2. Farmer Stub Newell stands in the excavation pit next to the remarkable discovery (ahem, humbug) found by workers digging a well on his property in October 1869.
Fenimore Art Museum Library, Cooperstown, New York, Cardiff Giant Collection Number 431 Box 1. NM72.69(3).

pit when the workmen expanded their excavation; it was the apparently petrified or fossilized body of a giant naked man, more than ten feet in height (figure 8.2).

Newell's neighbors immediately flocked to the farm to gaze in wonder at the amazing discovery that lay at the bottom of the pit. As a local newspaper phrased it: "Men left work, women caught up their babies, and children in all numbers hurried to the scene where the interest of that little community centered" (The Lafayette Wonder, 1869). Recognizing the economic potential of such an amazing find, within a few days Newell had erected a circus tent over the giant, hired a carnival barker to serve as his docent, and began charging folks, first a quarter and later fifty cents, to have a peek at what people had begun to call the Goliath of Cardiff or just the Cardiff Giant. Calling it a "Goliath" was no mere metaphor or analogy. Many felt that the Cardiff Giant was, like Goliath, a representative of a population of giants mentioned in the Old Testament of the Bible, perhaps one of the Nephilim, the evil offspring that resulted from fallen angels mating with human women. Soon, ministers were including references in their sermons to what they perceived to be the physical proof of biblical stories of giants.

Whatever and whoever he was, the giant fascinated people, and newspapers ran with the story of the fabulous archaeological discovery made by a simple farmer in Upstate New York. These stories served as free advertising, and soon, on any given weekday, hundreds of curious visitors arrived on the Newell farm, and on weekends those numbers swelled to a couple of thousand (figure 8.3). Clearly, Newell was making more money exhibiting the giant than he ever made as a farmer, but local businessmen in Syracuse, the nearest large town, were also benefitting from the economic fallout of having a fascinating and enigmatic tourist destination nearby. Syracuse hotels and restaurants filled, and just about any other business that could supply the needs of visitors to town also saw their bottom lines increase, and they had the giant to thank for it. In fact, so impressed were local businessmen by the economic fallout of the giant—and also because of their concern that Newell might opt for a one-time big payday and sell the giant to an outsider—a consortium made him an offer he couldn't refuse: $30,000 for a three-quarter interest in the giant. This meant that, along with (in today's dollars) a payout of more than half-a-million bucks, Newell would continue to earn twenty-five

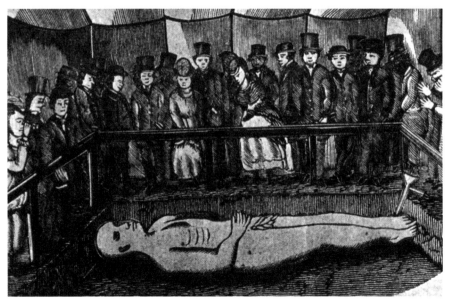

Figure 8.3.   Resting in his original find spot, this engraving shows the giant on display. Note the appropriately placed fig leaf. And no, I will not speculate what the woman with opera glasses on the left is looking at.
Public domain.

cents for every dollar the giant continued to generate. And considering the fact that Connecticut circus impresario P. T. Barnum actually attempted to purchase the giant, the concerns of those Syracuse businessmen were well founded. Their coffers swelled, Newell continued to make money, and thousands of people made a pilgrimage to see the giant from before Noah's flood.

Why are archaeologists skeptical?

Scientists and sculptors who examined the giant immediately and nearly unanimously declared it to be a crude fake, a chunk of rock only recently carved and even more recently set into the ground. Othniel C. Marsh of the Yale Peabody Museum and arguably one of the most famous American paleontologists of the nineteenth century, recognized that the giant was made of gypsum, a soft rock that was entirely unlike petrified or fossilized material. In a letter he wrote to the *Syracuse Daily Journal* and reprinted in the December 1869 *Proceedings of the Massachusetts Historical Society*, he diagnosed the Cardiff Giant: "It is of very recent origin and a most decided humbug" (1869: 161). He went on to question how any reasonably intelligent person could accept it as an authentically ancient, fossilized human body. A local geologist, J. F. Boynton, suggested, based on the rate of erosion, that the giant could not have been in the ground for much more than a year before its "discovery" (there are those scare quotes again). Eratus Palmer, a well-known sculptor, actually identified marks on the giant's face that could only have been produced by a sculptor carving the stone. The giant had obviously been a fraud, a sculpture planted in the ground as a prank, and a valuable one at that. For details of the story, Scott Tribble's 2009 book, *A Colossal Hoax*, is a terrific read.

Whodunit?

While Stub Newell obviously was intimately involved in the hoax, the brains behind it was his cousin, George Hull. Hull was by profession a cigar manufacturer and by inclination an atheist. He also was a bit of a scoundrel. In a confessional newspaper account published in the *Ithaca Daily Journal* in 1898, Hull recounted a confrontation he had with a minister in Iowa in which the two argued about the literal truth of the Bible. The minister, naturally enough, was a true believer. Hull was a skeptic. Hull reported that their discussion turned to biblical stories that he felt were ridiculous on their face—like stories of ten-, eleven-, or twelve-foot-tall giant human beings. According to Hull, the minister would not budge on his opinion that such biblical stories were literally true. On that insistence, Hull found his inspiration to take financial advantage of people he considered to be credulous and gullible. He would make a giant man from stone but pass it off as a genuine and ancient petrified giant man.

Hull purchased a large block of gypsum—exactly the raw material that paleontologist Marsh had diagnosed—from a local quarry in Iowa and shipped it to a sculptor in Chicago with instructions to carve it into the image of a giant, naked man lying on his back. Once that work had been completed, Hull had the sculpture shipped to his cousin's farm in Cardiff where, with additional help, they deposited the giant, naked man at a depth of three feet and left him there to season for, just as geologist Boynton had deduced, about a year. Once a year had passed, Hull gave Newell the high sign and Newell then hired his well diggers, instructing them to dig exactly where he knew they would find the humbug. The rest is ignoble history. By the way, Hull provided this detailed confession because Stub Newell had been bragging all along that he had personally pulled off the greatest American humbug. Once the Chicago sculptor was tracked down and confirmed Hull's story, the giant fell into obscurity. For a while.

Why?

The answer to this question is easy; after his discussion with the minister, Hull concocted a scheme to make money from unsuspecting believers in the literal truth of the Bible but also anyone else who just thought it would be fun to see a strange artifact. Newell provided the venue in which to plant the giant, and he got paid handsomely for his part in the conspiracy.

One more thing; P. T. Barnum never liked being rebuffed or one-upped. When his offer to purchase the giant was rejected, he responded in a particularly Barnumesque way; he had his own Cardiff Giant made. So his Cardiff Giant was, put bluntly, a fake version of what was already a fake artifact. Amazing. And of course, when he displayed his version, he advertised it as being the real thing! After his fake of the fake outdrew the real fake when both were on display in New York City, Mark Twain was inspired to write a very funny tale called "A Ghost Story." In Twain's telling, the ghost of the Cardiff Giant is in New York City haunting the venue in which his petrified body is being cruelly displayed. There's only one problem; the giant made a terrible mistake and actually is haunting the wrong version, Barnum's fake. Barnum had managed to fool even the Cardiff Giant!

By the way, you'll sometimes see people credit—or blame—P. T. Barnum for the phrase "There's a sucker born every minute." Barnum didn't say that but he is connected to that iconic phrase, and it involves the Cardiff Giant. When David Hannum, a member of the consortium of Syracuse businessmen that had purchased 75 percent of the giant from Newell, and, ostensibly, a believer in its legitimacy, heard that Barnum's fake was more popular than his "real" giant, he complained about that fact by poking fun at the folks who got taken in by the fake fake, explaining Barnum's success by saying, "There's a sucker born every minute." And I guess he was right.

Fake-o-meter

Five.

Getting there

After the giant fell from grace, it was sold to a newspaper editor back in Iowa where his journey began. He kept it in his basement for years. You will admit that a recumbent statue of a giant naked man makes for a unique conversation piece. Later on, the New York State Historical Association bought the giant and returned him to New York, and placed him on display pretty close to the "scene of the crime" at the already mentioned Farmers' Museum where, as I mentioned at the beginning of this entry, I was inspired by the silly hoax as a child. You can see the Cardiff Giant—the real fake—in the lobby of the main building of the museum located on 5775 State Highway 80, Cooperstown, New York (figure 8.4).

But wait, there's more; if you'd like to see Barnum's fake of the fake, it's on display at Marvin's Marvelous Mechanical Museum in Farmington Hills, Michigan (http://marvin3m.com). It's presented there as the real Cardiff Giant. P. T. Barnum would be so proud.

Figure 8.4. Today the Cardiff Giant is on display at the Farmers' Museum in Cooperstown, New York, not far from Stub Newell's farm where he was originally planted, discovered, and then displayed as proof of the existence of giants in biblical times.

30. PALUXY RIVER FOOTPRINTS, GLEN ROSE, TEXAS

Archaeological perspectives

Archaeology isn't paleontology. I do not dig up dinosaurs. Of course, I have always been fascinated by them. In fact, according to my mother, when I was about four years old I told her that when I grew up, I wanted to be a dinosaur. A Tyrannosaurus rex. But despite the questions people commonly ask me: "How do you find dinosaur bones? Where do you keep the bones you find? What's the most interesting dinosaur you've dug up?"—I am an archaeologist, not a paleontologist. Dinosaurs became extinct more than sixty million years before the evolution of even the earliest ancestors in the human line. It is interesting, however, that not everyone accepts that firmly supported scientific consensus. That brings us to the focus of this entry: the Paluxy River "man tracks" in Glen Rose, Texas. But first, a little context.

Here's what we know

We have a sharp-eyed bulldozer operator, Edward McCarthy, to thank for the 1966 discovery of an astonishing assemblage of dinosaur footprints, not in Texas, but in Rocky Hill, Connecticut (Carlson 1966). McCarthy was working on a construction job for a new state office building when he uncovered about fifty footprints—birdlike, but enormous—frozen in the ancient sandstone bedrock revealed by his bulldozer. McCarthy recognized the significance of his accidental discovery, ceased work, and informed his boss. As a result, the entire construction project came to a halt, and in 1968 those footprints along with hundreds more became the centerpiece of Dinosaur State Park. It took about ten additional years—and a closure and associated threats to simply rebury the footprints if they could not be adequately protected from the elements—but in 1978 the state finished construction of a permanent dome that both preserved the footprints and highlighted them in a dramatic setting.

I was relatively new to Connecticut when the dome was built and the park rededicated. I remember clearly our local newspaper, the *Hartford Courant*, publishing a series of informative articles about the footprints to commemorate the reopening. Some of those articles provided a bit of background about the dinosaurs who had left behind their tracks in the soft mud that had long ago turned to stone. There were footprints of the twenty-foot-long predator dilophosaurus; those of a small plant eater, anchisaurus; and the tracks of dimorphodon, a species of pterosaur, a flying reptile that also walked on the ground (figure 8.5). Those same articles noted that the sandstone (actually the state rock of Connecticut!) in which the footprints had been found was dated by geologists to the

Figure 8.5. A cluster of three-toed dinosaur footprints preserved at Dinosaur Park in Rocky Hill, Connecticut.

Triassic Period, a time between about 250 and 200 million years ago or right before the Jurassic (Lang 1978) (you know, like in *Jurassic Park*).

Interestingly, not everyone accepted the scientific consensus concerning the Connecticut dinosaur footprints. In fact, the *Courant* published the text of a peculiar letter to the editor, complaining about the misinformation being spread by the newspaper regarding the age of the dinosaurs (Jaworski 1977: 18). Had this occurred in more recent times, the angry letter writer might have labeled the *Courant* treatment of the dinosaur footprints as "fake news." The essence of the complaint lodged in the brief letter concerned specifically the age assigned by the *Courant* to the footprints in particular and dinosaurs in general—an age provided them by the state geologist. Implicit in the letter was the writer's belief that dinosaurs—and their footprints—were nothing like two hundred million years old. In fact, the letter writer went on, it had been clearly shown that dinosaurs and human beings were contemporaries, living at the same time—like in the cartoon the *Flintstones*, I guess. The proof of this, the letter writer maintained, had been collected along the Paluxy River in Texas where the footprints of not only dinosaurs but also human beings had been discovered, side by side, in the same geological stratum! This inspired images in my mind of a prehistoric human being doing walkies with his or her pet dinosaur. Can you imagine having to clean up after your T-rex does his business? You're going to need a hell of a big pooper-scooper. The place identified by the letter writer—the banks of the Paluxy River—where she asserted "the fossil footprints of both men and dinosaurs" had been discovered "in close proximity," is the focus of this entry.

What is the back story to that claim? It turns out that in the early twentieth century, George Adams, a kid living near Glen Rose, Texas, was playing hooky from school. While exploring the banks of the Paluxy River, he found the footprints of what appeared to be a three-toed creature, preserved in the sedimentary rock that bordered the river (Farlow et al. 2011). I guess, sometimes, you learn more cutting school than you do by attending class. Anyway, George informed his teacher of the existence of the footprints. Let's hope he didn't get in too much trouble when he fessed up. Further exploration revealed extensive and continuous trackways of the footprints of more of those three-toed (tridactyl) bipedal dinosaurs (believed to be carnivorous theropods). Later, even larger prints of quadrupedal sauropods like apatosaurus ("brontosaurus," if you grew up loving dinosaurs in the 1950s) were found along the river and in the bedrock in the stream bed. One fascinating and particularly well-preserved set of footprints near Glen Rose, sometimes interpreted as a chase sequence, shows a number of sauropod prints representing, perhaps, a herd of the beasts, all moving in the same direction and followed in apparent quick pursuit by the tracks of one of the three-toed carnivores (a theropod). Very cool—an ancient moment frozen in time.

In the meantime, researcher Roland Bird (1939), working for the American Museum of Natural History in New York City, visited the American Southwest in the 1930s to collect specimens for display and study. He found dinosaur footprints at a shop in Gallup, New Mexico, and was told that the footprints had come from the Paluxy River in Glen Rose, Texas. This led to his visit to Glen Rose in 1940; clearly it was better to collect the specimens at their source rather than indirectly at a shop in New Mexico. Bird's goal there was to extract slabs of rock exhibiting dinosaur footprints to send to the museum for study and display. I distinctly remember seeing replicas of those trackways—labeled as originating along the Paluxy River—on display outside one of the large dinosaur halls of the American Museum in New York City.

Here's where the weirdness starts. In that same New Mexico shop selling the dinosaur footprints, Bird saw a rock slab with what appeared to be a gigantic human footprint (figure 8.6). He recognized immediately that it was artificial, a crude attempt to carve a human footprint in rock. When he visited Glen Rose in search of dinosaur prints, he saw that there were more giant human footprints for sale there. In fact, he learned that at least one of those human prints had been carved by none other than George Adams, the same person who, when he was a kid, had alerted his teacher and, eventually, the world, to the existence of dinosaur footprints near Glen Rose. Adams crafted the false footprints to sell to tourists.

Figure 8.6. During the depression, some people in Glen Rose, Texas, manufactured fake "man tracks," very large-scaled and clearly humanlike footprints, for sale to tourists. This one was purchased by Roland Bird of the American Museum of Natural History in New York City. Bird was traveling in the West expressly to collect dinosaur footprints for the museum when he encountered this obvious fake.
Public domain.

When Bird visited Glen Rose, locals mentioned the existence of genuine "man tracks" mixed in among the dinosaur footprints. Of course, when he went searching for these purported gigantic human footprints, all he found were heavily eroded footprints of three-toed dinosaurs where the heel was elongated and the toe claw marks were indistinct enough to convince the gullible that the dinosaur heel was actually an entire giant human footprint without any of the toes showing (figure 8.7).

Why are archaeologists skeptical?

It should go without saying that when anyone makes a claim that contradicts virtually everything we know about the age of Earth, anthropology, biology, geology, and evolution—the existence of dinosaurs and humans, living side by side, in an Earth probably only a little more than six thousand years old certainly

Figure 8.7. Actual dinosaur footprints located along the Paluxy River in Glen Rose, Texas. Notice the similarity of some of these footprints to the Connecticut examples shown in figure 8.5. There are no gigantically scaled, authentic human footprints here, only obviously fake man tracks and misinterpreted, highly eroded dinosaur footprints.

qualifies here—scientists are going to be skeptical. "Skeptical" doesn't mean "close-minded," it means, well, skeptical, requiring a lot of evidence to discard a scientific consensus. Biostratigraphy, the positioning of the remains of plants and animals in soil layers, always shows separation between dinosaurs and even the oldest of human ancestors. Dinosaur remains are found in much lower strata than are the remains of human beings. You never find dinosaur bones in the remains of hearths built by people five thousand years ago. Paleontologists don't find the bones of a partially digested human being in fossilized dinosaur feces. Ever. So even based on our general understanding of the history of the world and of life on the planet, we are very skeptical of claims that dinosaurs and human beings were contemporaries and their footprints have been found together.

But there's more, specifically about the Glen Rose prints (see figure 8.7). Researcher Glen J. Kuban (1996–2016) has intensively researched the Paluxy River man tracks claims for more than two decades and has explained the prints as resulting from one of four processes:

1. the credulous acceptance of artificial, humanlike prints, fakes carved during the 1930s, similar to the one Bird found at the shop in New Mexico
2. the misidentification and misinterpretation of elongate impressions as giant human prints when they were, instead, produced by the central metatarsal (a foot bone) of three-toed dinosaurs. Those bones are elongate and, as is often the case, if the dinosaur was walking back on its heels (leaving no impression of its clawed toes), or if the claw impressions were shallow and subsequently infilled, they might look like the impressions left by giant human feet
3. erosional elements that, if you search through enough of them, are elongate and misidentified as footprints
4. other, random marks that can be made to look vaguely footlike if you try hard enough

Whodunit?

The scientific consensus is that Earth is about 4.5 billion years old. That number isn't drawn out of a hat, nor is it the result of mystical revelation or intuition. It's the result of physics and geology. Radiometric decay is a well-understood phenomenon, and the rates at which radioactive (unstable) isotopes (varieties) of elements like carbon, potassium, and uranium decay have been precisely measured. Those rates provide us with an atomic calendar of the history of our planet. The application of radiometric dating techniques has produced reliable dates for the age of Earth, the development of living organisms, the reign of the dinosaurs, their extinction, and the appearance of our first human ancestors. There's no room in those well-established chronologies for human beings chilling with dinosaurs.

As noted in the introduction to this section, YECs reject those chronologies and assert that Earth is only about six thousand years old. For YECs, galaxies, stars, the solar system, Earth, life on Earth, and the totality of human history—stone tools; the control of fire; copper, bronze, and iron tools; cave art; the human beings populating the world; the development of agriculture; the invention of writing; the urban revolution; and the introduction of the iPhone—have all occurred in a mere six thousand years. That is a breathtaking and breathtakingly absurd claim. In order to support the young Earth, YECs have to reject the collective wisdom of sciences like physics, biology, paleontology, paleoanthropology, geology, and archaeology, not to mention common sense. These Young Earth creationists, at least for a time in the 1980s and 1990s, used the ostensible footprints of human beings showing up side by side with those of dinosaurs along the Paluxy River as evidence of a young earth.

Why?

If your worldview is predicated on the belief that the world was recently created and that all of Earth history can be compressed into just a few thousand years, you simply are forced to accept and even embrace some extraordinarily weak evidence. But that's what it is. The good news is that Glen Kuban's analysis was so overwhelmingly definitive that most Young Earth creationists today no longer embrace or, at least, no longer like to highlight, the Paluxy River man tracks. But it's worth a visit to the real footprints that inspired this nonsense in the first place.

Fake-o-meter

We're talking a five here. I'd even give this a six for extra credit.

Getting there

You can actually see the real dinosaur footprints along the Paluxy River in person, depending on how high or low the river is flowing. The most impressive of the tracks are located in Dinosaur Valley State Park in Glen Rose, Texas. The address is 1629 Park Road 59, in Glen Rose. Take U.S. Highway 67 to FM 205 for four miles to Park Road 59; then go one mile to the headquarters.

Bonus: You can download the locations of footprint trails on the park's website: http://tpwd.texas.gov/state-parks/dinosaur-valley/dino-tracks.

31. BLACK DRAGON PICTOGRAPH, SAN RAFAEL SWELL, UTAH

32. KACHINA BRIDGE PICTOGRAPH, NATURAL BRIDGES NATIONAL MONUMENT, UTAH

Archaeological perspectives

Pareidolia is an ugly-looking word, and my spell check refuses even to acknowledge that it's real. But it is a genuine and useful term, identifying an interesting phenomenon: the ability and even the insistence of the human brain to perceive a recognizable and patterned image even when there isn't one there. Think about kids playfully seeing horses or dogs or boats in clouds. And do you remember the woman who saw the face of the Virgin Mary in the burned surface of her grilled cheese sandwich (Poole 2007)? She apparently sold it for $28,000 to the owners of an online casino. She missed having it so much, she had a likeness of the piece of grilled bread tattooed on her right breast, a supremely classy example of the combination of religious devotion and pareidolia. I guess.

Modern instances of pareidolia in America commonly have a religious theme, with people seeing the face of Jesus in a shower curtain stain, a dental x-ray, or in the grain of a piece of wood. Of greater interest here, pareidolia has also reared its ugly imaginary head in a number of instances of rock art interpretation. Random scratches and stains on the surface of a rock, often combined with actual art images, have been interpreted as representing something quite different from what was intended by the original artists. In some cases, those images have been interpreted as providing proof for the contemporaneity of Native Americans with animals presumed by science to have become extinct tens of millions of years ago. The claimed rock art depiction by Native Americans of a pterodactyl in the Black Dragon pictograph and the image of a sauropod (a dinosaurlike brontosaurus, apatosaurus, or maybe a diplodocus) at Kachina Bridge, both in Utah, are examples of pareidolia and wishful thinking on the part of YECs. In both instances a religious perspective underlies these claims; the YEC view that dinosaurs and people lived side by side at a time immediately preceding Noah's flood.

Here's what we know: Black Dragon Pterosaur

The image now known as the Black Dragon Pterosaur or the Black Dragon Pterodactyl (pterodactyls are the best-known species of pterosaurs) first came to the attention of non-Native People in 1928. It's located in Black Dragon Canyon, which is ensconced in the San Rafael Swell, a geologically stunning region in Utah characterized by an ancient "dome" of sandstone, shale, and limestone about seventy-five by forty miles across. There's been plenty of erosion in the relatively soft rock of the dome, and nature has etched a plethora of meandering canyons through it in the forty to sixty million years it has been in existence. When Native Americans entered the Swell several thousand years ago, they found an abundance of flat, vertical surfaces of rock along the walls of those canyons onto which they painted or etched truly beautiful images, some real or representational and some imaginary (the **Head of Sinbad** pictographs are located in the San Rafael Swell). In other words, some of the art is recognizable as depictions of real things, and some of it is phantasmagorical. The canyons that spider-leg through the San Rafael Swell are deservedly world famous for that amazing art. The Black Dragon pictograph panel is one impressive example (figure 8.8).

The art of the Black Dragon pictograph panel is categorized as an example of the Barrier Canyon style. There are a few other impressive Barrier Canyon pictographs nearby on the same rock face. That style includes elongated paintings (pictographs) of "anthropomorphs"—humanlike images—often with large eyes and lacking arms or legs. They are astonishingly beautiful, and admittedly, to modern eyes, even a little spooky looking. As noted previously, the **Sego Canyon** pictographs, misrepresented by some as depictions of ancient aliens, also reflect the Barrier Canyon style of art.

Figure 8.8. The Black Dragon pictograph is one of several located in Black Dragon Canyon in the San Rafael Swell in Utah. There has been significant weathering and an ill-advised attempt to "connect" some of the art; this is what it looks like today.

Figure 8.9. This image vaguely resembles a large bat or even, perhaps, a prehistoric pterodactyl—but one from the Island of Misfit Dinosaurs considering its right wing with all those humps and its skinny right wing. In any event, the outline is really not reflective of what the art looks like, but it suits the purposes of Young Earth creationists who think it represents proof that people and pterodactyls lived at the same time and, therefore, the Earth must be only several thousand years old.

Outline drawn by Jennifer Davis

A significant problem arose with the initial examination of the Black Dragon panel when well-meaning researchers chalked in lines that filled in the "gaps" they perceived in the faded and weathered image (figure 8.9). This "restoration" led to the initial identification of one of the elements of the Black Dragon pictographs as a large, winged creature identified as a "colossal bat, a dragon" (Barnes and Pendelton 1979), some sort of "weird bird," and even a pterodactyl (Simonson 1947: 24).

That was bad enough. Chalking in an ancient piece of rock art is today considered to be a variety of vandalism, an imposition of what the modern observer thinks is there, not necessarily what is actually present. In the 1990s and continuing to the present, YECs took quite seriously the offhand comment of author John Simonson about the art representing a pterodactyl and embraced the notion that the pictograph depicts a giant flying reptile thought by science to have become extinct more than sixty-five million years ago. Going even further, some maintain that historical references to or depictions of dragons in general are actually the reports and depictions by people who witnessed and even interacted with dinosaurs in the last few thousand years (Issacs 2010).

Wait, what? How could a Native American, alive sometime between a thousand and two thousand years ago—the time period of the Barrier Canyon art style—have known of the existence of pterodactyls and been familiar enough with the species to have painted one on a rock face in south-central Utah? The answer provided by YECs was that the Black Dragon Pterodactyl proves conclusively that humans and pterodactyls lived during the same recent period, a mere one or two thousand years ago. In their worldview, the Native People of the American Southwest saw pterodactyls flying through the piercingly blue skies of Utah just a couple of thousand years ago and then painted the image of one on the surface of a canyon wall located in the San Rafael Swell. That would be astonishing if true and, indeed, scientists including geologists, evolutionary biologists, archaeologists, historians, well, just about all scholars of all stripes, would need to rewrite all of their textbooks, cramming what we surmise to be 4.5 billion years of history into a mere six-thousand-year timeframe. But is the Black Dragon pictograph an actual, authentic, relatively recent depiction by a Native American of a living, breathing pterodactyl?

Here's what we know: Kachina Bridge Sauropod

Located within Natural Bridges National Monument in Utah, Kachina Bridge is a breathtaking natural feature, a beautiful sandstone arch sculpted by geological processes (figure 8.10). Ancient people certainly were no less impressed

Figure 8.10.   Kachina Bridge, a natural geological feature, is one of three such features located in Natural Bridges National Monument in Utah.
iStock ID: 640840506; Credit: kojihirano

Figure 8.11. Petroglyph that Young Earth creationists claim to represent the image of a long-necked, quadrupedal dinosaur, for example, a brontosaurus, at Kachina Bridge in Natural Bridges National Monument, Utah.
Courtesy of Phil Senter

by its beauty than are we in the present, and they left messages in a series of petroglyphs that adorn the legs of Kachina Bridge. Among those works of art is a panel that some YECs claim is a depiction of a gigantic, quadrupedal, herbivorous dinosaur with a long, narrow neck, a large torso, and then a long tail (figure 8.11). And if you look at enhanced versions of the image in various books, websites, and even the Creation Science Museum in Kentucky, it certainly looks like a sauropod, albeit a cartoonish version that would be at home in an episode of the *Flintstones* (figure 8.12) (Nelson 2012: 29). But is the representation of the petroglyph at Kachina Bridge accurate? Does that petroglyph constitute eyewitness evidence of the coexistence of human beings and dinosaurs just a couple of thousand years ago? How does it compare and relate to the pterosaur in Black Dragon Canyon?

Why are archaeologists skeptical? Black Dragon

The answer to the question "Why are archaeologists skeptical?" about the interpretation of the Black Dragon pictograph as well as the Kachina Bridge petroglyph as representing ancient animals is based on a version of the phenomenon of pareidolia defined at the beginning of this entry. In fact, the image of a "weird

Figure 8.12. The sauropod seen in this outline prepared by illustrator Jennifer Davis represents an image similar to what can be seen in Young Earth creationist websites and publications based on the petroglyph shown in figure 8.11.
Photo courtesy of Phil Senter

bird," winged monster, bat, or pterodactyl in Black Dragon Canyon resides in the mind of the beholder, not in the paint on the rock face. I mean, look at my photograph in figure 8.8. That's one funky-looking pterodactyl with all those weird humps on its right wing and the skinny little wing on its left side (I will forego tasteless references to the movie *Finding Nemo* here). The fact that the "pterodactyl" is, in actuality, a mistaken conjoining of several separate images into one was suggested by researchers in 1995, based only on their naked-eye observation (Warner and Warner 1995). More recently, through the application of imaging software, this artificial amalgamation was definitively debunked by researchers Jean-Loïc Le Quellec, Paul Bahn, and Marvin Rowe (2015). As noted by Warner and Warner, the Black Dragon Pterodactyl isn't a bird, or a plane, or, I might add, Superman, and it certainly isn't a pterodactyl. It's a forced combination of five separate and distinct images that have been indefensibly joined to artificially create a single, anachronistic winged reptile that has been extinct for sixty-five million years.

Using x-ray fluorescence, Le Quellec, Bahn, and Rowe were able to measure the iron content across the surface of the rock face and, in so doing, they were able to locate where paint had been applied. The red pigment used by Barrier Canyon artists was high in iron, so where x-ray fluorescence indicated that iron levels were

Figure 8.13. Applying image enhancement filters to photographs of the Black Dragon pterodactyl, the actual artwork produced in antiquity becomes clear. There is no pterosaur; instead there are five separate images including a couple of bighorn sheep, two humanlike individuals, and a wide-mouthed snake.

Courtesy of Jean-Loïc Le Quellec

high, even if the paint had substantially faded and could barely be discerned with the naked eye, they could identify where it had originally been applied to the rock. Then, employing the photo-enhancing software d-stretch, they were able to reproduce what the painting looked like when it was fresh (figure 8.13).

The application of x-ray fluorescence and d-stretch shows conclusively that there isn't just a single critter in the panel, and certainly no depiction of a flying creature, prehistoric or otherwise. Instead of a winged reptile: the supposed beak is, instead, merely the parallel arms in the image of a person; the left wing of the pterodactyl (the right side of the image from the viewer's perspective) is a horned snake (those exist in the Southwest) with a gaping mouth; the legs and part of the body of the critter belong to a bending, pretty typical Barrier Canyon anthropomorph, and the right wing (to the left when looking at figure 8.13) consists of the images of a couple of bighorn sheep. The entire panel, though weathered, is cool to see, but it certainly isn't the painting of a pterodactyl. The textbooks are safe, once again.

Why are archaeologists skeptical? Kachina Bridge

As mentioned, the Kachina Bridge sauropod image provided by sources to support a Young Earth creation model of the universe isn't what you see when you actually encounter the art. The images provided by those creationists have been enhanced, and there is a significant problem; those enhancements appear to have been determined entirely by eye. When scientists have examined the art in person, they have recognized that the creationists have, as was the case with the Black Dragon Pterodactyl, indefensibly filled in the blanks to transform the image into what looks like a brontosaurus, apatosaurus, or whatever (Senter and Cole 2011; see figure 8.12).

The Kachina Bridge image was produced by pecking; the artist repetitively pounded through the dark red, external layer of the sandstone near the bottom of the arch, creating an image by exposing the lighter rock beneath. In order to make the art resemble a dinosaur, areas devoid of this pecking along with sections of the rock that are a different color because of water staining have to be included in the body of the animal. Take a look at figures 8.11 and 8.12; there is a bunch of the brontosaurus outline that you essentially have to make up, especially in the legs, to make it work. If you look carefully, you can see that the large "tail" to the left isn't actually connected to the body of the supposed dinosaur. Once you eliminate those sections that don't show ancient human manipulation of the rock surface, the image looks nothing at all like a dinosaur (figure 8.14); it's an

Figure 8.14. If you want the image on Kachina Bridge to be a dinosaur, you can "fill in the blanks" and make it look like a dinosaur (figure 8.12). But that doesn't make it a depiction of a dinosaur. In this version of the photograph seen in figure 8.11, illustrator Jennifer Davis has outlined areas in the photograph supplied by Phil Senter, where distinct evidence of intentional pecking by an ancient artist is visible. This image is a reasonable outline of the actual art. There's no dinosaur there.

amalgam of a number of disconnected petroglyphs and natural staining on the rock. Some YECs have complained about this interpretation, essentially saying that their reconstruction is equally valid. Well, since the notion of dinosaurs and people living side by side is contradicted by geology, paleontology, and archaeology, the burden of proof is on those who interpret the Kachina Bridge rock art as representing a dinosaur alive when people lived in Utah and, at most, just a few thousand years ago. Some butchered dinosaur bones in the hearth of an ancient archaeological site or a spear point embedded in an apatosaurus bone would be pretty convincing. Until that sort of evidence is forthcoming, a highly weathered petroglyph is not going to be seen as convincing to any scientist.

Whodunit?

The Barrier Canyon artists who produced the Black Dragon panel and the artists who etched an image into the arch today called Kachina Bridge could have had no expectation that a couple of thousand years in the future, people would examine their art and conclude that it provided evidence for a literal interpretation of the origin story embraced by those future strangers. The misinterpretation of the Black Dragon pictograph panel and the Kachina Bridge apatosaurus is the work of YECs.

Why?

Some Young Earth creationists hope to find a piece of physical evidence—in this case in the form of an ancient painting—that at least indirectly might call into question the scientific consensus about the antiquity of Earth. If human beings and dinosaurs or extinct reptiles are not separated by tens of millions of years, if people and dinosaurs and pterodactyls lived at the same time, then maybe scientific notions of a 4.5-billion-year-old Earth are wrong and maybe Earth is only thousands of years old, just as some biblical literalists claimed in the seventeenth century. Maybe the seventeenth-century Bishop Ussher was right when he fixed the creation of Earth as having occurred in 4004 BC. Unfortunately for supporters of the accuracy of Bishop Ussher's assertion, the Black Dragon pictograph and the Kachina Bridge panel, as cool as they are, just don't provide them with that proof.

Fake-o-meter

Five.

Getting there

The Black Dragon pictograph is fairly easy to reach. Drive 12.5 miles west on I-70 from Green River, Utah, until you reach mile marker 147. A little past that there's a county road on the right. Just after you get on that dirt road there's an unlocked gate. You're on public property administered by the Bureau of Land Management, a federal agency. Stop your car, swing open the gate, drive through, and then make sure to close the gate. Remember to close the gate when you leave. Take that gravel road off the highway and drive .7 miles to an intersection and continue straight on for another .3 miles to a fork. Turn left at the fork. Drive a bit more than .5 miles to the Black Dragon pictographs. I found that after turning left, the road becomes filled with large rocks. Unless you have a high-clearance 4WD vehicle, you're better off pulling over at that point. From there, it's a short walk into a very spooky canyon with high, black-stained walls. You'll know you're there when you reach the BLM fencing on the right side of the canyon. There also are plenty of very beautiful pictographs of strange creatures with elongated bodies to the left of the "pterodactyl" (figure 8.15). To the right there's another panel with what looks like an armless person standing next to an animal (a dog?) standing on two legs. Further to the right there's an alcove with what appear to be tally marks and human hand prints. It's a very cool place.

Kachina Bridge is located in Natural Bridges National Monument in Utah. The Natural Bridges Visitors Center is located on Natural Bridges Road (Route 275), which can be reached from the Bicentennial Highway. Once you pass the center, drive on the paved road to Bridge View parking. From there, it's a relatively short hike (.75 mile) with lots of steps to Kachina Bridge.

Figure 8.15.   These stunning pictographs are located to the left of the misidentified pterodactyl in Black Dragon Canyon, Utah.

· 9 ·

Category 7 New Age Antiquity

$\mathscr{I}$ adore Sedona, Arizona. It is a jewel of a place with amazing geological formations painted by nature in every imaginable hue of red, orange, tan, and white. Ensconced among the sandstone cliffs and spires that characterize the area are small, ancient cliff dwellings and associated rock art including both pictographs (paintings) and petroglyphs (images carved into the rock). The geological formations and archaeological sites of Sedona are embraced by archaeologists, geologists, and historians for the insights they can provide concerning the evolution of our planet and the abilities of human beings to adapt to varying environmental conditions. At the same time, these places are viewed by many adherents to New Age beliefs as being more than simply impressive geologically, archaeologically, and historically but as imbued with powerful and mystical forces that create spiritual "vortexes." These vortexes, so the claim goes, represent doorways through which the acolyte can journey to other dimensions, levels of consciousness, or planes of reality. It's all good and science and philosophy or religion can live peacefully together side by side. However, as an archaeologist I think it is reasonable to check the specific claims made about archaeological sites by people who view them as something quite a bit more than simply places people once lived and died.

As a result of the New Age worldview, Sedona was a center of activity during the so-called Harmonic Convergence of August 16–17, 1987. Obscurely related to the ancient Maya of Mesoamerica and their calendar, Harmonic Convergence followers believed that the date was an inflection point in human history again having something to do with the Maya who were thought to be, not simply aboriginal people of the Americas, but a sort of ultraterrestrial power, "navigators or charters of the waters of galactic synchronization" (Argüelles 1987: 37). The Maya lived on Earth for a time, left long ago, and as of the summer of 1987, were embarked upon their return, not in pedestrian

Figure 9.1.   Sedona, Arizona, ranks among the most beautiful places I have ever visited. Pictured here is the stunning Bell Rock. Though it was the expectation of some New Agers, alas, the top did not pop off and flying saucers did not erupt from Bell Rock during the Harmonic Convergence in 1987.

spaceships but as pure DNA via "chromo-molecular transport" (Argüelles 1987: 258–59). I have no idea what that means, and I think that's the case because it actually is meaningless.

Along with Mt. Shasta (California), Giza (Egypt), Stonehenge (England), **Serpent Mound** (Ohio), and Mt. Fuji (Japan), Sedona was a Harmonic Convergence "power point," a gathering place for hordes of expectant people in the summer of 1987. One of the expectations was that the top of a beautiful and internationally known geological feature in Sedona, Bell Rock, would literally pop off during the Harmonic Convergence, and UFOs would fly out (figure 9.1). That didn't happen—you probably already knew that—but Sedona continues to be a place as wonderfully and polymorphously idiosyncratic as it is beautiful.

Archaeological sites in Sedona and elsewhere attract visitors at least in part as a result of their perceived connection to spirituality. Part of this perception appears to be predicated on the belief that Native American sites—even those that are simply the locations of their habitations, characterized archaeologically by adobe walls, potsherds, and food remains—are imbued with a deep and intrinsic spirituality that can be appropriated by non–Native American visitors in their quest for enlightenment. Needless to say, though, I am entirely sympathetic with the perspective that archaeological sites are beautiful, engaging, and often awe inspiring, but I am skeptical that the places where people once lived, worked, raised families, created art, and buried their dead are places where non–Native People can achieve spiritual enlightenment. Let's visit a number of sites in our archaeological oddities odyssey (try saying that ten times fast!) often embraced by those espousing a New Age philosophy: **Palatki** and **Honanki** in Arizona.

33. PALATKI CLIFF DWELLING, SEDONA, ARIZONA

34. HONANKI CLIFF DWELLING, SEDONA, ARIZONA

Archaeological perspectives

Let me begin with an admission: I sort of enjoy New Age people. I might think they're a bit looney, sure, but most of the New Age types with whom I have come into contact are incredibly sweet and well-meaning folks. I do, however, get a little uncomfortable when Native American lives, places, stories, traditions, histories, archaeological sites, and religions are appropriated by people who are not Native American in their quest for some new or syncretic sense of spirituality. And if you're thinking, "Hey, why is a white author lecturing me about the use of Native American wisdom?" Well, that's a fair point, but check out this article, written by a Native American, on this very issue (http://www.native-languages.org/religion.htm).

Here's an example of what I'm talking about. A few years ago I encountered a group of New Age truth seekers on a visit to the Palatki site in Sedona, Arizona, a lovely little cliff dwelling with an abundance of rock art. They had come to the place, as they freely shared with me, to have a mystical experience at the cliff dwelling and to commune with the ancient spirits who inhabit the place. Despite the protestations of the volunteer guide who was there that day to show visitors the cliff dwelling and rock art, the New Age visitors demanded to commune with the ancient ones in a depression some distance away from the actual site. It was only after they left that the guide confided in me that the spot they chose was actually the foundation of a building constructed in the 1930s by a white resident who was kind of a jerk. I'm not sure what kind of metaphysical connection to Native American spirituality those New Agers could have obtained there. Oh well.

Here's what we know

The archaeological sites of Palatki (figure 9.2) and Honanki (figure 9.3), two little jewel-box cliff dwellings, are located several miles outside of the center of

Figure 9.2. The Palatki cliff dwelling located in the Cononino National Forest in Sedona, Arizona. Palatki was a place where people were born, lived out their lives, raised kids, and then died about 1,000 years ago. In other words, it was a village. Some folks go there for spiritual enlightenment.

Figure 9.3. The Honanki cliff dwelling located in the Cononino National Forest in Sedona, Arizona. Like Palatki, Honanki was a place where people were born, lived out their lives, raised kids, and then died about 1,000 years ago. In other words, it was a village. Some folks go there for spiritual enlightenment.

Sedona, on land contained within the Coconino National Forest. Both are lovely examples of the architecture of the Sinagua people, one of a group of ancient, named cultures in the American Southwest (along with Mogollon, Hohokam, and Ancestral Puebloan). Those groups differed in their particular cultural practices but, by about a thousand years ago they shared a common form of architecture—adobe and stone buildings—and a similar agricultural base—you guessed it, corn, beans, and squash.

What is abundantly clear, based on actual, archaeological evidence, is this: Palatki and Honanki were each occupied by no more than a couple of families between AD 1100 and about 1400. They planted corn in the area around their villages, gathered wild plants, and hunted wild animals for their subsistence needs. They made pottery, stone tools and weapons, cooked their food, and also etched petroglyphs and painted pictographs onto the surfaces of the cliffs looming around the locations of their cliff dwellings (figure 9.4). Neither of these sites is in any way paranormal or mysterious. They were, simply, people's homes.

Figure 9.4.   Located in a rock alcove nearby to the Palatki cliff dwelling (figure 9.2), these pictographs at Woo Ranch are extraordinarily well-preserved examples of the art produced by the ancient residents of Sedona, Arizona.

Why are archaeologists skeptical?

Palatki and Honanki were places where people worked, loved, worshipped, raised crops, raised children, made tools and art, and mourned and buried their dead. In other words, they were places where people lived out their lives, not unlike the houses and neighborhoods in which you live. I'm all in if you call places like that "sacred"—after all, I'm an archaeologist. As an archaeologist, I hope to honor the lives of past people by studying what they left behind and allowing them to tell their own stories. I'm just the translator in this scenario, converting objects made of stone and clay into words. In a broad usage of the term, I view these places as sacred as well. As a visitor to modern Sedona, you can honor those ancient people by visiting the places where they lived, paying them the attention they so richly deserve.

Whodunit?

There isn't really a "who" here, but more a moment in history that "dunit": the Harmonic Convergence mentioned in the introduction to this section. Think of the Harmonic Convergence as Woodstock without the music. Or the mud. But some of the sex and drugs. That movement, perhaps more than anything else, inspired some to view archaeological sites as repositories of ancient wisdom. Okay, sort of like archaeologists do. They come, however, not with trowels and screens but just their vivid imaginations.

Why?

Look, any insights by me about the Harmonic Convergence and the ongoing pilgrimages to Sedona by people seeking spiritual enlightenment at amazing geological formations, impressive cliff dwellings, and breathtaking rock art would be little more than pop psychology. With that as a disclaimer, I'll give it a shot. New Agers appear to desire something from ancient people, a sense of enlightenment, harmony, balance, and connectivity that they crave but perhaps can't find in their materially rich, but spiritually impoverished, modern Western lives. Cell phones, laptops, tablets, and cars with bluetooth (and backup cameras!), as cool as those things are, leave them still feeling hollow. Of course it does.

But I fear that the promise of enlightenment from the mystical, spiritual Indians who inhabited the cliff dwellings of Sedona is based on little more than a modern version of the idealized "noble savage" myth of the seventeenth century. No longer noble savages, Indians now are noble mystics, and a visit to their ancient settlements is supposed to provide you with spiritual insights. Mystical or not, I encourage you all to visit Sedona and revel in the serene beauty of the place. While you're there, hike the trails, have yourself some blue corn pancakes and huevos rancheros, and visit Palatki and Honanki. They are splendid and beautiful places.

Fake-o-meter

I hate to give off a negative vibe here, but: Five. Palatki and Honanki are real sites, but the New Age interpretation of them is completely fake.

Getting there

From the I-17 interstate, Sedona is accessible from Route 179. Once you're in Sedona proper, to reach Palatki and Honanki (make it a double-header; both sites are cool, just a few miles apart on a well-maintained dirt road, and the rock art is beautiful), head west on 89A. In three miles, turn right (north) onto Dry Creek Road. That road ends in a bit more than two miles. When it does, turn left onto Boynton Pass. In another 1.6 miles, Boynton Pass ends. There, continue left onto East Boynton Pass Road. In 3.9 miles, turn right onto Red Canyon Road. In seven hundred feet, curve to the left onto Loy Butte Road (Forest 525 Road). At 1.2 miles, keep to the right. The parking lot for Palatki will be 2.7 miles from there. There's a small visitor center adjacent to the lot. Part of the trip is on a well-maintained, graded dirt road. The entire drive should take you about forty-five minutes from the center of town.

From Palatki, head back on the access road to its intersection with Loy Butte Road (Forest 525 Road) and make a sharp right. In about three miles you'll reach the parking lot for the Honanki site. Retrace your steps to return to 89A and Sedona proper.

Category 8 Unexpected Critter Depictions

Cryptozoology is a branch of the science of zoology, the study of animals. The *cryptpo* part of the term means "hidden," so the literal definition of cryptozoology is "the study of hidden animals." "Hidden" in this definition refers to animal species called *cryptids* that either: (1) are assumed to be extinct but perhaps that assumption is wrong and there are remnant populations still extant in some part or parts of the world; or (2) are not known to have existed ever and are usually thought to be merely the stuff of myth and legend, but maybe they exist after all.

In fact, there are multiple veritable examples of number 1. The most famous example is the coelacanth, a fish species initially known only from eighty-million-year-old fossils and assumed to have been extinct for about sixty-five million years. The coelacanths, apparently, hadn't gotten the memo announcing their extinction and, much to the surprise and delight of zoologists, especially ichthyologists, a living population was discovered in the western Indian Ocean near the east coast of Africa in 1938, and another population was discovered in 1998, six thousand miles away from the first, near the island of Sulawesi in Indonesia.

This selection isn't about zoology or cryptozoology. It's about an archaeological connection between those two disciplines in the form of ancient works of art; in other words, the depictions by ancient people of animals they encountered during their daily lives. If people encountered individuals within an animal species that orthodox zoology either rejects as real (unicorns, griffins, Sasquatch) or that orthodox zoology accepts as real but believes became extinct long before humans were around (dinosaurs, dinosaurs, and dinosaurs), and if those people then etched, painted, or sculpted images of those animals, then the zoologists need to go back to the drawing board and rewrite the textbooks about Earth chronology, evolution, and, well, zoology altogether.

The problem posed to scientists in such scenarios, and the reason they are skeptical, is that there really isn't much room in our well-supported animal taxonomies and Earth chronologies for remnant populations of dinosaurs walking around Utah barely a thousand years ago (**Black Dragon** and **Kachina Bridge**, catalogued in this book under Biblical Proof) or for gigantically proportioned, hairy bipeds ensconced in the deep woods of the American Northwest. Please note that since its 2011 premiere on Animal Planet, the show *Finding Bigfoot* has never produced anything close to definitive evidence that Bigfoot (Sasquatch) exists at all. No living Sasquatches, no bodies of dead Sasquatches, no bones of Sasquatches, no Sasquatch DNA. In other words, no definitive, indisputable, physical evidence. I hope this doesn't sound too mean—who am I kidding, I don't really care all that much if it sounds mean—but in the spirit of full disclosure, perhaps the name of the show should be changed to *Not Finding Bigfoot*, which they are far better at than actually finding the beast. In this book, we'll take a look at a site in North America where some have interpreted rock art as representing depictions based on eyewitness encounters of Bigfoot (**Painted Rock** in California).

35. PAINTED ROCK HAIRY MAN DEPICTIONS, TULE RIVER INDIAN RESERVATION, PORTERVILLE, CALIFORNIA

Archaeological perspectives

Virtually all human groups include in their mythologies spirit animals. The ancient Greeks had their minotaurs with the head of a bull perched on the upright body of a human being. And don't forget their winged stallion, Pegasus, and the half-horse, half-human centaur. The Hindu god Ganesha has the head of an elephant and the body of a human being. Many Native American cultures tell stories of the water panther, a supernatural catlike creature who lives in bodies of water and preys on women. In Great Britain, a gigantic, spectral spirit animal in the form of a black dog is said to prowl the moors in the dead of night. The paranormal black dog story contributed to Arthur Conan Doyle's Sherlock Holmes novel *The Hound of the Baskervilles*, where a phosphorescently glowing and supernatural giant dog terrorizes the Baskerville lineage.

None of these animals and the myriad others I could list from all over the world are intended to be biological creatures by the people who tell their stories and include them in their myths and in their religions. Not flesh and blood, these beings are spiritual entities, supernatural beings who play a role in their belief systems.

The same can be said for the large, hairy, upright creatures called Sasquatch by some, Bigfoot by others, and who inhabit the landscapes of myth and legend among some Native American tribes. For instance, among the Tule River

Indians of southern California, the creature they call *Mayak Datat*, commonly translated as "the Hairy Man," was involved in the creation of humanity along with Eagle who was in charge of the process, along with Fish, Turtle, Lizard, and Owl, among others (Moskowitz Strain 2012). These were not ordinary, run-of-the-mill representatives of known animal species. These were spirit beings with enormous intelligence and supernatural powers. It really is a lovely story as each animal confers upon the human race a feature that reflects that animal's characteristics. Naturally enough, Fish thought humans should be able to swim. Owl proposed that the people should be given knowledge and cunning. Lizard suggested fingers would be useful, enabling the people to make baskets and bows and arrows. Though Coyote thought humans should walk around on all fours, Mayak Datat convinced the creator spirits that people should instead be able, just like him, to walk on two feet.

The important point to reiterate here is that Mayak Datat is not an animal like a raccoon or a deer. He is a powerful spirit being. You can't shoot him, collect his scat, or recover DNA from his hair. Mayak Datat has very little to do with a bunch of white folks in camo, wandering the woods at night, decked out with night-vision glasses looking for a real-life critter they call Bigfoot.

Here's what we know

So how about Bigfoot? Is there a real, living, hairy, upright animal, perhaps serving as the inspiration for Sasquatch, the creature the Tule call Hairy Man? Short of an actual animal, is there other physical evidence that might convince even the most hardened of skeptics that Bigfoot exists, or at least has existed in the not-too-distant past? Well, among the evidence that has been presented, there are eyewitness accounts—*Finding Bigfoot* relies a lot on eyewitness accounts—some of which are suggestive but simply not definitive. Eyewitnesses are notoriously unreliable, and the testimony of someone seeing something scary, at a distance, in dark woods, is problematic. Hey, I once thought I saw a capybara crossing the road in front of me in broad daylight in the early morning in suburban West Hartford, Connecticut. Near the local Whole Foods. But capybaras are South American animals, sort of like gigantic guinea pigs. What on Earth was one doing wandering the streets of a city in Connecticut? When I got closer, I saw what the critter really was: a large, three-legged raccoon (Feder 2014). He must have been a pretty tough customer to survive the loss of one of his front legs, but he was not a capybara, though his injury made him walk like those denizens of South America.

Giant footprints in mud and snow are the most common kind of evidence for Bigfoot, but these can be too easily faked and non-Bigfoot prints can be misinterpreted, so those are not convincing either. We keep a compost pile about fifty feet from the house, and I regularly walk through snow to dump our organic refuse there. When the snow melts and compacts, it's fairly common for my footprints to metamorphose into something that seems decidedly nonhuman and a lot more Bigfoot like.

Grainy, poorly focused, and bouncy film or video are weak evidence as well. I often wonder why the equipment used by people to film Bigfoot, the Loch Ness Monster, and assorted UFOs perform so poorly. What in the world happens to autofocus on their equipment? And is the camera image so jerky because their hands are shaking as a result of being excited about capturing the thing on camera? Invest in a tripod, please! It certainly doesn't bode well for the science of Bigfoot that supporters keep returning to what's called the Patterson-Gimlin film, recorded more than fifty years ago, because that seems to be their best photographic evidence. It must be troubling even to them that, with all of the improvements in video recording since 1967 and with all of the people out there looking for Sasquatch, all of them holding cell phones with cameras that produce remarkably clear, high-resolution images, even under bad lighting conditions, there isn't anything better than those sixty seconds of footage.

There also is the occasional claim of the discovery of Bigfoot fur or hair. That's something we can sink our teeth into. Figuratively, not literally. I agree, short of an entire living Bigfoot or Bigfoot carcass, Sasquatch hair with recoverable DNA showing the existence of an unknown primate here in North America would represent important evidence. Geneticist Bryan Sykes and colleagues examined thirty hair samples of "anomalous primates," eighteen of which were found in North America. Sykes and his team recovered sufficient DNA from the hair to identify their sources, which turned out to be, specifically: raccoons, bears, sheep, horse, canids (wolf/coyote/dog), deer, cow, and human (Sykes et al. 2014). They found exactly zero Sasquatch (or, in the case of the European and Asian samples, zero Yeti) in the thirty samples from which they were able to recover DNA.

Why are archaeologists skeptical?

This entry is really not about the discovery of a live Bigfoot—or the body of a dead one—or eyewitness accounts, huge footprints, photographs, video, or hair. Instead this entry is about an ancient work of art, a truly beautiful pictograph—a painting on rock—located on the Tule River Indian Reservation in southern California.

Known to the outside world since at least the end of the nineteenth century—it's shown in a book written by the Federal Bureau of Ethnology researcher Garrick Mallery in 1894 titled *Picture Writing of the American Indians* (figure 10.1)—Painted Rock has a number of wonderfully artistic representations of animals including coyote (he's shown trying to eat the moon according to my wonderful Tule River Indian informant Zack), beaver, and a millipede. Among those animals there also is an impressively large painting of a more than eight-feet-tall, upright creature (figure 10.2). Nearby on the same rock canvas are a couple of similar but smaller images of upright critters that, it has been proposed, are depictions of "Mrs. Bigfoot" (she's about six feet tall) and Junior (about four feet tall).

Figure 10.1. This engraving of the rock art at Picture Rock on the Tule River Indian Reservation in California first appeared in print in 1894 in the book *Picture Writing of the American Indians* by Garrick Mallery. Mallery felt the entire scene depicted mourning with the large creature (who doesn't look particularly hairy) on the right weeping and the symbol for rain emanating from his fingers.
Public domain.

Figure 10.2. The Mayak Datat—the Hairy Man—of the Tule River Indians is depicted at Painted Rock on their reservation just east of Porterville in southern California. Mayak Datat is a spirit being who plays a role in the creation of humanity. Mayak Datat successfully proposes to the other creator beings that humans walk on two feet.

If you look at figures 10.1 and 10.2, I don't know about you, but I don't see the "hairy" aspect at all. The painting of "Mrs. Sasquatch" and the kid are not depicted with any hair, and even in the case of the largest figure, the actual "Hairy Man," he simply isn't "hairy." He has lines streaming from his eyes—Mallery interpreted these not as hair but as tears, which conforms to the Tule who say he's weeping—and there are a bunch of vertical lines intersecting with his arms. That's it.

Most important of all, in 2008 the Tule River tribe published a compendium of their stories that had been originally collected in 1975 (Johnstone 2008). The book presents a version—remember, this is the tribe's version—of the story Moskowitz Strain provided in her 2012 article mentioned previously, of the story describing how the animals created people. Where Moskowitz Strain says it was the Hairy Man—and, by implication, Bigfoot—who made people walk on two feet, tribal storytellers say something quite different: "Grizzly Bear said, 'People should be able to stand on their hind legs like me and they should have no tail'" (Johnstone 2008: 32). So, the ability of human beings to walk upright results from Grizzly Bear, not the Hairy Man, and actual grizzlies have the capacity to walk on their hind legs. Mind you, the Tule do tell stories of the Hairy Man—and they do identify him as Bigfoot—but in their book he's more a cautionary figure used to warn children not to stay out too late at night or the Hairy Man will get you.

Whatever the source of the Hairy Man stories and the pictographs, let's get something straight; if the Hairy Man painting—dated to sometime between five hundred and one thousand years ago—was intended by Native Americans to be depictions of Bigfoot (and not simply an upright grizzly bear), that's interesting and very cool, but not terribly surprising. Mayak Datat is an integral part of the Tule origin story. A native artist depicting a Hairy Man, specifically, or a Bigfoot more generally, therefore, is no more surprising or mysterious than a medieval European artist depicting cherubim, or angels with haloes and wings. Just as important, the artistic depiction of a Bigfoot, therefore, is no more evidence for that creature's existence than are those medieval paintings of angels evidence for the existence of angels. As noted in the introduction to this entry, to the Tule, Mayak Datat/Sasquatch isn't a living and breathing, flesh-and-blood critter. It isn't a primate or a human ancestor or a Neanderthal or a gorilla or any animal at all. It's a spirit being.

Whodunit?

The so-called Hairy Man pictograph is an authentic, beautifully rendered, and extraordinarily interesting piece of rock art. Some modern Bigfoot researchers have seized upon it, asserting that it must be real since the other critters depicted at Painted Rock are real. That's not a convincing argument, and a familiarity with, not just rock art, but, well, art, puts the lie to that argument. Again, even if we accept the claim that the Hairy Man and family pictographs were intended as depictions of the creature today called Bigfoot, that provides not even a scintilla of proof that Bigfoot was an actual animal.

Why?

As noted earlier, the evidence for a large, bipedal, hairy ape man living in North America in at least recorded memory is scant. I suppose that with little more than the aforementioned listing of eyewitness accounts, footprints, terrible photos, and worse video/film, and lacking convincing proof in the form of biological evidence, supporters need to fall back on whatever possible evidence they can muster. But again, an authentic and ancient work of art in California depicting a large, bipedal creature provides evidence only for something we already know: Native People included such an animal in their mythology. If you think the Hairy Man pictograph is sufficient proof of the actual existence of such an animal, then I have a unicorn, a griffin, and a hippogryph I'd be willing to sell you.

Fake-o-meter

The art is real, quite beautiful, and evocative. As evidence for Sasquatch actually walking around in southern California or anywhere else, nope: five.

Getting there

Painted Rock is located on the Tule River Indian Reservation; you'll need permission from the tribe to obtain access to the cave in which the pictographs are located. As I write this, Neil Peyron is the tribal chairman and was extremely gracious about arranging a tour of the site for me. And thanks to Zack for the tour. It's smart to call ahead: 559-791-2121.

From Route 190 in East Porterville, California, take a right onto Road 284, which becomes Indian Reservation Drive East, which becomes N Reservation Road or BIA Road 20/J42. You will enter reservation land in about 9.5 miles. Sure enough, there's an impressive wooden sculpture of the Hairy Man when you get there. Keep on the main road until you come to the first congested area; the tribal headquarters are on your right. You must stop there to get permission to see the rock art. Reservation lands are not public lands. Nontribal members should not go by themselves. The site is sacred to the Tule River people.

Category 9 Follies

$\mathcal{I}$f you type *follies* into any internet search engine, most of the top hits relate to the Stephen Sondheim Broadway musical by that name. That show is about a group of people who once performed in Vaudeville in a genre called *follies* (perhaps the most famous was the Ziegfeld Follies), extravaganzas of singing, dancing, and comedy. If you narrow your search a bit and include *architecture* along with *follies*, you'll find that it's an affectionate British term for a kind of mostly nonutilitarian, ornamental architecture, sometimes amusing, sometimes whimsical, sometimes captivating. Examples are fake Roman ruins far from Rome, castles built on a small scale appearing to be intended for elves or gnomes, Stonehenge knockoffs, and so on (Headley 2012). Though the term *folly* implies something foolish, as applied to architecture the term implies something a bit more gentle, with the designer or builder intending to generate a response more along the lines of "how interesting and amusing." Architectural follies often are anachronistic, eccentric, or, as author Gwyn Headley (2012) put it in the title of his book, *frivolous*, but in a good way. They are not intended to fool anyone, to prove a hypothesis, or force any textbook rewrites. They are intended merely to amuse and, perhaps, inspire thought.

There are a number of interesting archaeological oddities highlighted in this book that I am calling "follies," in a somewhat broader sense and again in a completely affectionate way: Cecil B. DeMille's **Lost Egyptian City** in California; **Carhenge** in Nebraska; a very self-aware archaeological parody, **The Dig**, in New York City; the transcendently beautiful, thought-provoking, and inspiring **Columcille Megalith Park** in Pennsylvania; and the **Maryhill Stonehenge**, a full-scale, concrete Stonehenge replica located in Washington State and that, while a folly by my reckoning, was intended for a very solemn purpose: a war memorial.

36. LOST EGYPTIAN CITY, GUADALUPE, CALIFORNIA

Archaeological perspectives

I have a very clear—and very early—memory of going with my parents to the theater in our town to see the epic movie *The Ten Commandments*. Made in 1956 (when I was only four years old), the movie featured a cavalcade of A-list Hollywood movie stars: Yul Brynner as the pharaoh Rameses; Edward G. Robinson (effecting precisely the same elocution he did in his many 1930s and 1940s gangster roles) as a Jewish overseer of Jewish slaves, and, of course, Charlton Heston in his signature role as Moses. This version of *The Ten Commandments* was directed and produced by the iconic Hollywood mover and shaker Cecil B. DeMille. It's a very impressive movie, at least in terms of special effects.

As impressive as that movie was, it certainly wasn't the first time someone had attempted to translate the Old Testament story of the Exodus to the screen. In fact, it wasn't even DeMille's first go at it. Thirty-three years earlier, in 1923, DeMille oversaw the production of a big-budget silent movie with the same title and source material as his 1956 epic. You can watch it here in five separate parts: https://www.youtube.com/watch?v=HYlz45iTpAg. (Though I was unable to find a standalone recording of the 1923 version, it appears as one of the bonus features on the DVD package of the 1956 movie.) The making of the earlier movie spawned an archaeological legend that, as it turns out, is actually true.

Here's what we know

For a movie made in the 1920s, the set, costumes, and special effects are absolutely stunning. By most measures, it was the most ambitious silent movie ever made, and certainly the most costly. However, as big as DeMille's budget was—ultimately totaling nearly $1.5 million (DeMille 1959: 258), a huge sum for the time—it wasn't big enough to transport a host of Hollywood stars to Egypt to film the movie in the real place with genuine, ancient Egyptian monuments in the background. Besides, as *The Ten Commandments* depicted a time when the temples, obelisks, sphinxes, and pyramids weren't ancient and decaying, filming in Egypt in front of ruins would have made little sense anyway. Instead, and rather sensibly for a Hollywood movie, DeMille filmed the exterior scenes in southern California, in what is today called the Guadalupe-Nipomo Dunes State Park.

There were more than enough sandy landscapes in the dunes for the area to pass as Egypt, but that meant that all Egyptian buildings and monuments—at least the fronts of those buildings and monuments—had to be replicated as inexpensively as possible using wood for support and primarily plaster in front (figure 11.1). In fact, it is estimated that the majority of the film budget was

Figure 11.1. A still taken from the 1923 movie *The Ten Commandments* directed by Cecil B. DeMille, showing a faux Egyptian building in the background and a portable sphinx being hauled by a gang of slaves. The scene occurs at an important point in the movie; a Jewish slave falls and, rather than stopping to save him, the pharaoh bids the others to continue moving the sphinx, crushing the fallen man to death.
Courtesy of the Guadalupe-Nipomo Dunes Center and director Douglas Jenzen.

expended on building those sets. According to the film's line-item budget, DeMille's construction team used more than half-a-million board feet of lumber and three hundred tons of plaster to produce the false fronts of buildings, more than twenty sphinxes, and four gigantic statues of the pharaoh Rameses (http://www.independent.co.uk/arts-entertainment/films/features/the-lost -city-of-cecil-b-demille-the-film-about-unearthing-a-1923-movie-set-that -took-30-years-to-a6787021.html).

Watch the movie for yourself. The backdrops are, indeed, quite impressive and convincing, especially so for a movie made nearly one hundred years ago. But don't look too closely. It's plain that what was built was relatively limited, and you can see that, in many outdoor scenes, the same sets keep showing up in the background with only distance and camera angle changing in an attempt to fool the audience into believing that there are more of those structures than DeMille's budget allowed him to have built.

As a result of DeMille's contract with the private owner of the property (this is before it became a state park), he had to haul off the set when he was done. He didn't quite do that and, instead, simply knocked down some of the larger parts of the set and abandoned the rest as is and walked away from it (Bahn 2014). Doug Jenzen (2018, personal communication), director of the Dunes Center in Guadalupe, California, and who is directing research at the site and designing a wonderful display about the dig at the Dunes Center, has tracked down photographs dating to the 1930s, long after the movie was released, showing at least some of the sphinxes in place and quite above ground. In fact, Jenzen related, two of those sphinxes were hauled off and placed at the entrance to a golf course.

The absurdity of the existence of the decaying remnants of a faux ancient Egypt archaeological site located in the dunes of southern California was recognized by DeMille (1959), who stated in his autobiography:

> If a thousand years from now, archaeologists happen to dig beneath the sands of Guadalupe, I hope they will not rush into print with the amazing news that Egyptian civilization, far from being confined to the valley of the Nile, extended all the way to the Pacific coast of North America. The sphinxes they will find were buried when we had finished with them and dismantled our huge set of the gates of Pharaoh's city. (1959: 253)

That's simply hilarious. In a sense, though no one has been fooled by DeMille's set, in a similar spirit it has, in fact, inspired a self-consciously whimsical archaeological excavation in southern California, not of ancient Egypt, but of DeMille's ancient Egyptian movie set.

Why are archaeologists skeptical?

There really isn't any skepticism to report here. The movie set is precisely where the movie was filmed and archaeologists are recovering remnants of that set.

Whodunit?

Well, we know that DeMille created the site, but it was a film school student who revealed its existence. Apparently, the lost Egyptian city of Cecil B. DeMille had become a film school legend, repeated and passed down over the years but never quite verified even though local people living near the dunes were aware of it and regularly found bits and pieces of painted plaster and fragments of the buildings and sphinxes made for the film. But when, in 1982, film school student Peter Brosnan was told the story by another student, Bruce Cardozo, who mentioned the reference to the story in DeMille's autobiography, Brosnan decided to play movie set archaeologist. Visiting the Guadalupe dunes in 1983 in an El Niño year where there had been a substantial amount of wind and dislocation of the dunes, Brosnan immediately saw chunks of the set on the surface.

This gave Brosnan an idea: Wouldn't it be interesting to obtain funding sufficient for an archaeological excavation of DeMille's movie set and at the same time produce a documentary movie focused on that excavation? Actually, that idea sounded genius to a lot of people, but the vicissitudes of funding two projects at the same time—a major archaeological dig and a documentary film—and issues with obtaining permits to excavate in what had become a designated state nature preserve held back the project for years. So many years, in fact, had passed since Brosnan had originally pitched the idea, he had given up hope of having his idea come to fruition. Finding little success in film, Brosnan abandoned that industry.

I have colleague Brian Fagan to thank for revealing the story of the buried DeMille movie set in an essay he wrote for *Archaeology Magazine* in 1991. That essay was the first I had heard of the tale, and I became obsessed with the story. The archaeological excavation of a 1923 ancient Egypt movie set seemed an obvious and fascinating way to apply archaeology to cinematic history. I remained hopeful that someone, at some point, would make an archaeological investigation of the DeMille set happen.

At the time, the idea of excavating the set was still just a pipe dream, but every great idea has its time, and in 2010 a private donor offered the money necessary for the excavation and film. After extensive negotiations with the state, a team of professional archaeologists in the company Applied Earthworks was hired, the dig began in earnest in 2012, and Brosnan and his old film school buddy Bruce Cardozo, who had introduced Brosnan to the story thirty years earlier, began filming as they excavated one of DeMille's sphinxes (figure 11.2). The resulting documentary was shown at film festivals in 2016 and was very well received (Brosnan 2016). I've seen it (I bought my copy at the Dunes Center), and it's fantastic. As I am writing this in late 2017, the ongoing project has just revealed a beautiful and pretty well-preserved chunk of another sphinx (Geggel 2017). Art restoration experts Christine Muratore Evans and Amy Higgins were working on that sphinx when I visited the Dunes Center in March 2018 (figure 11.3).

Why?

Obviously, we know why DeMille built and then abandoned the set. But what was the point, after all, of excavating a 1923 movie set? Brosnan points out that from the perspective of a film historian, the Guadalupe Dunes site represents a treasure trove of movie artifacts. There simply aren't many props or sets made for the silent-era movies that have been preserved for study, so the excavation of the

Figure 11.2. Archaeological excavations at *The Ten Commandments* movie set reveals the remains of one of the portable sphinxes constructed for the movie (see one of them in action in figure 11.1).

Courtesy of the Guadalupe-Nipomo Dunes Center and director Douglas Jenzen

Figure 11.3. Art conservators Christine Muratore Evans (left) and Amy Higgins (right) painstakingly work on the preservation and restoration of one of *The Ten Commandments* sphinxes at the Dunes Center in Guadalupe, California.

Ten Commandments set affords film historians a unique opportunity to examine the actual physical remnants of an important movie.

But I think there's another equally valid reason for the excavation and film. The tale of the lost Egyptian city of Cecil B. DeMille is just incredibly interesting, a unique and peculiar footnote to the career of an amazing man. And come on; fake Egyptian artifacts buried in a sand dune in California. Who wouldn't want to explore that?

Fake-o-meter

Zero stars. If you're looking for five stars, check out the truly awful, oops, I mean awesome movie *Sands of Oblivion* made in 2007. Archaeologists digging the DeMille set unleash ancient, evil, and supernatural Egyptian spirits from the underworld. Gory fun.

Getting there

As I write this, the actual location of the remnants of DeMille's Egyptian set are off limits in an effort to protect the breeding grounds of birds that live in the area around the dunes. However, you can see some of the artifacts recovered in the 2012 excavation of the site, as mentioned, at the Dunes Center located at 1065 Guadalupe Street, Guadalupe, California 93434 (http://dunescenter.org/visit-the-dunes/dunes-center/exhibits-and-activities-research/the-lost-city-of-demille/).

37. CARHENGE, ALLIANCE, NEBRASKA

Archaeological perspectives

Later in this guide, we'll visit a concrete replica of Stonehenge in Maryhill, Washington, where a philanthropist created a memorial to local men who had died in Europe fighting as soldiers in World War I. As serious as that monument is, Carhenge is the opposite; it's just plain silly. And brilliant and whimsical and in some very strange way, beautiful. It is, at least in part, a reflection of how fascinated we are in America by the 4,500-year-old stone monument in the south of England, so much so that there are, by the accounting of *Roadside America* (https://www.roadsideamerica.com/story/29025), about thirty reproductions of it, in various media, all across the United States.

Here's what we know

In America's heartland, secreted deep in the High Plains of western Nebraska, stand the silent sentinels of a mysterious monument made of metal, rubber,

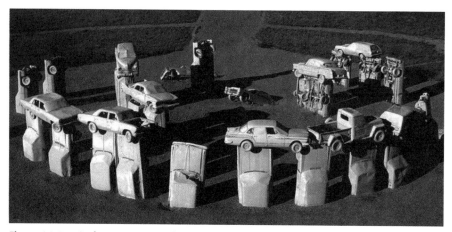

Figure 11.4.   Carhenge. It's Stonehenge. But made out of old cars. And in Nebraska. What more needs to be said?

Courtesy of Carhenge, Alliance, Nebraska, carhenge.com.

and glass (well, not so much glass anymore since vandals smashed all of the glass). So, metal, rubber, and shards of glass. It is a weathered and enigmatic ruin, a vague and incomplete circle of sixteen dull-gray uprights arching more than fifteen feet skyward and together encompassing a diameter of nearly one hundred feet. Balanced atop some of the adjacent uprights and connecting them are horizontal beams or lintels, also of metal. Within the incomplete circle stand another five pairs of metal uprights positioned, not in a circle concentric with the exterior uprights, but in the shape of a horseshoe, with each pair capped by its own lintel. Finally, standing isolated, far beyond the circle, a lone sentinel stands guard, as if directing the attention of the pilgrim standing in the center of this clearly sacred place to a point on the vast Nebraska horizon (figure 11.4).

What is this enigmatic enigma? What possessed the inhabitants of Nebraska to construct it in all its enigmaticness? Where did they obtain the strange (ha, you thought I was going to say enigmatic again) raw materials from which they constructed the monument? And what mysterious—okay, I'll say it, enigmatic—purpose did the builders have in mind when they placed this obviously sacred, holy monument here in what we now consider to be the American heartland? And why in the world did they build it all out of old, junked cars? You read that right. Unlike the real Stonehenge in England, which is made out of stone (you probably figured that out based on the name *Stonehenge*), Carhenge is made out of, as the name suggests, cars. Again, pretty obvious. And why is there not a running series on the *History Channel* exploring the great and unanswered—and perhaps unanswerable—mysteries of this place we call Carhenge because it looks like Stonehenge but it's made of cars? Is this silence on the part of cable TV channels attributable to a vast government conspiracy to keep the truth of Carhenge from the American public? Well, no.

Why are archaeologists skeptical?

Actually, archaeologists aren't at all skeptical. We know that Carhenge was intended as a folly, a funny parody of an iconic archaeological site. However, it seems that quite a few people in Alliance, Nebraska, were skeptical about its creation and, maybe especially its appearance, when it was built in 1987.

First, the owner of the property and the person who inspired its creation, Jim Reinders, received notification from the Alliance zoning board that the part of the farm where Carhenge was built was within city limits and, therefore, under the legal jurisdiction of city zoning ordinances. The property was zoned for farming and, apparently, members of the zoning commission viewed the construction as, not a whimsical work of art but a junkyard, which was an inappropriate use for the land. Of course, it wasn't a junkyard, and after quite a bit of back and forth, Reinders, who had refused to demolish the monument that had already gotten worldwide attention, convinced the city simply to redraw its boundaries, making the ten-acre parcel where Carhenge is located officially outside city limits. The result—city zoning regulations didn't apply and Reinders was in the clear. From city regulations.

But not state laws. The state got involved because so many people driving on the state highway near the farm would park illegally to get a closer look at the American heartland Stonehenge made of Detroit castoffs. The state felt that Reinders has created what is commonly called an "attractive nuisance," and Carhenge would have to go. Instead of demolition, Reinders responded by building a road and a parking lot where people could safely park and exit their cars to walk among the mighty metal sentinels (Mighty Metal Sentinels; a great name for a heavy metal band) of Carhenge. Mission accomplished, and the state backed off.

Now, perhaps like all art, everyone has his or her opinion about Carhenge. In an interview in a wonderful short movie about the site (*Carhenge: Genius or Junk*: https://vimeo.com/97151336), Reinders noted that among Alliance's nine thousand residents, seven thousand of them apparently are art critics. Truth is, some hate it (they think it's an eyesore, just a pile of junk). Some love it, appreciating the whimsy inherent in reproducing an ancient monument in modern junk. But love it or hate it, I think everyone in Alliance recognizes and appreciates this: each year Carhenge attracts between thirty thousand to eighty thousand visitors who, in all likelihood, would never visit Alliance if not for the existence of Carhenge. Those visitors purchase gasoline, stay in local motels, and eat at Alliance restaurants. It's a win-win for tourists who appreciate whimsy and for local businesses that appreciate, well, business.

Whodunit?

We know exactly "whodunit." Carhenge was the brainchild of a Nebraska native Jim Reinders, and it was constructed primarily by him and his family. Before he became an artist (a characterization, by the way, that he good-naturedly denies), Reinders had a career in the petroleum industry, and for a time he worked and lived in England where he visited the actual Stonehenge several times. He was fascinated by the place and, for some reason that I don't think even he can explain, he came up with the idea of building a replica of the real monument when he returned to Nebraska. There's just no explaining artistic genius.

Why?

Reinders retired quite young—he was only fifty-two—and returned to the family farm in Alliance, Nebraska, in the early 1980s around the time of his father's death. The extended family gathered in Alliance for the funeral, and there was a deep feeling of connection when they were all together. Jim suggested they all gather for a happier reason, a family reunion, back in Alliance in five years. In the meantime, Jim worked the family farm that he had inherited from his father.

It was the planned reunion that got Jim to thinking about a group activity that they might participate in, both as a memorial to his dad and as a bonding experience for the family. That's when he put it together: he had wanted to build a replica of Stonehenge, he needed a bunch of people to accomplish that, and, well, why wouldn't you want to build a replica out of junked cars? Family members enthusiastically agreed—that's a great family—and the die was cast.

Everyone pitched in and contributed whatever skills they had to produce what I think we can fairly call a wonderful piece of community art. Junk cars were collected, backhoes and tractors were assembled (especially once it became clear that, unlike the real Stonehenge example, mere human muscle power wasn't sufficient to raise the automobiles), and Stonehenge American Style rose from the Nebraska High Plains. The work included thirty-eight junk cars and was completed in less than a week. Painted gray to mimic the real stones of the real Stonehenge, the monument stands in silent testament to the wonderful and admirable weirdness of the American spirit.

Fake-o-meter

Zero. There's nothing fake about Carhenge. It's all about fun.

Getting there

Carhenge is located in Alliance, Nebraska, at 2151 County Road 59, about three miles north of its intersection with Highway 87. Unfortunately, I've not been able to visit the site. But it's certainly on my bucket list!

And there's more

As mentioned, *Roadside America* website lists about thirty faux Stonehenges in the United States. Carhenge is one of them. Another fake Stonehenge that I have seen is really quite amazing; it's a full-scale replica of the monument, not all fixed up, but as it looks today (see figure 1.2). What's funny, I think, is that although Mark Kline, the brilliant artist who produced it, clearly built a lot of whimsy into it (he jokingly has a mannequin of Merlin the Magician surfing on one of the stones as an example of a hypothesis actually proposed to explain how the monument was built by the use of magic), it's actually a very impressive replica, made of, of all things, styrofoam. Of course, it's called "Foamhenge." Originally located in Natural Bridge, Virginia, Foamhenge was evicted from that spot and is now located in Centreville, Virginia. Also in Natural Bridge, Kline has built an amusement called Dinosaur Kingdom II (https://www.facebook.com/dinosaurkingdom/). The primary theme there combines fighting dinosaurs and the Civil War. It's very weird. And hilarious. Did I already say it was weird?

38. THE DIG: GOVERNOR'S ISLAND, NEW YORK CITY

Archaeological perspectives

The archaeology of North America is filled with examples of fascinating and unexpected discoveries and the investigation of as-yet-unsolved mysteries of the American past. From the lost English colony of Roanoke in North Carolina to the abandoned La Navidad settlement of Columbus's shipwrecked men marooned on the island of Haiti, where the written record has failed us, the material record investigated by intrepid archaeologists succeeds in revealing historical secrets and solving enigmas.

An especially engaging and important example of the ability of archaeology to fill in the gaps in our history can be seen in the 2009 archaeological excavations on Governor's Island, a small patch of only 172 acres of land located a mere eight hundred yards off the coast of southern Manhattan in New York City. Excavations on Governor's Island have revealed another lost and forgotten story, a story ignored in our history books and missing from our school curriculums. Yet the tale it tells is central to the American narrative, and it has only recently been investigated by archaeologists—sadly, not Americans, but Belgians. I refer here to the seventeenth-century Dutch village of Goverthing (figure 11.5). You've never heard of it? Of course not, and that's a tragedy, one that I hope to remediate in this entry of *Archaeological Oddities*.

Figure 11.5.   The dig at the lost village of Goverthing on Governor's Island in New York City was briefly open to the public. Several signs were erected to help tell the story of this forgotten but fascinating part of American history.

Here's what we know

The Principal Investigator (PI) of the project was Professor Luc D'Hoe from Catholic University of Louvain, Belgium, who opened up the ongoing excavations to visitors in 2009 with an accompanying on-site museum for the display of some of the most interesting artifacts found in what he called "The Dig" (Kennedy 2009).

The story of Goverthing is moving and terribly sad. It began as an early seventeenth-century colony filled with a handful of hopeful settlers from the Netherlands. The colony flourished, and Belgian and French settlers rounded out the population of this multicultural island metropolis. As was the case for many early American towns, a single major industry came to dominate life in Goverthing. In my home state of Connecticut, the history and economy of the city of Waterbury was based on the brass industry. Also in Connecticut, New Britain, the location of my university, was defined as the small tool capital of the world, becoming the headquarters of Stanley Tools. Goverthing was no different, with a single industry dominating the economic landscape: snow globes. Yes, snow globes. Goverthing indeed became the snow globe capital of the world, ground zero for globes of snow, the Vatican, nay, the Jerusalem of snow globery. Several fine examples recovered during the excavations were on display at the onsite museum when I visited in 2009 (figure 11.6).

1938 — From a series of old children's tunes — 'I saw two bears'; but 'two bears have seen me' would have been a more appropriate title here.

Figure 11.6. The village of Goverthing's claim to fame is the fact that it became ground zero for the vast snow globe industry. This disturbing scene in this example recovered during the archaeological dig has a young child being mercilessly pursued by two polar bears; an R-rated snow globe, to be sure.

The economic fate of the colony rose and fell on the basis of the vicissitudes of the world's interest in snow globes, yet it managed to hang on to as late as 1954 even though the US Army had claimed ownership of the rest of the island, using the place for the storage of dangerous munitions. Fearing the worst as a strong electrical storm approached, the army forcibly removed the residents of Goverthing, many of whom hoped to ride out the storm and fearful that the army coveted the small corner of the island not yet in their hands. The residents' fears were well founded, and upon their removal the army buried the remains of their town in sand, where it lay in repose until archaeologists arrived, determined to retrieve our forgotten national memory of a time and place where America had once proudly been the snow globe capital of the world.

When I visited the still-active excavation, many artifacts from late in the village's existence were still in situ, in the precise place where archaeologists had discovered them in the sandy fill in which they were encapsulated. I witnessed the mournful scene of a handful of half-buried automobiles, barely upright street lights, eroding electrical towers, the ruins of houses with their chimneys still intact, a leaning church steeple, and even a partially intact human-powered mill (figure 11.7 and 11.8).

Life must have been difficult on Goverthing, and this can be seen no more clearly than in a handful of the artifacts on display at the museum. Saddest of all,

Figure 11.7. Artifacts dating to the final years of Goverthing's existence include automobiles buried by the US military when they forced the abandonment of the community.

Figure 11.8. The nearly intact foot-powered mill renovated by researchers during the excavation of the Goverthing site.

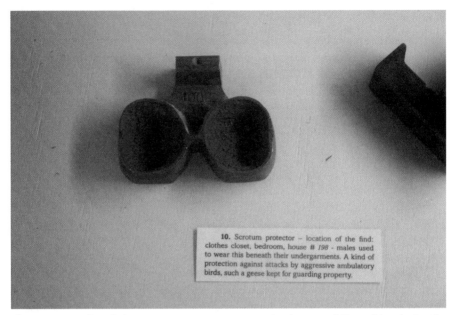

10. Scrotum protector – location of the find: clothes closet, bedroom, house # *198* - males used to wear this beneath their undergarments. A kind of protection against attacks by aggressive ambulatory birds, such a geese kept for guarding property.

Figure 11.9. A largely intact scrotum protector worn by the men of Goverthing during the period known as the Plague of the Birds. I'm doing my best to keep a straight face here. Goverthing was entirely a parody of archaeology, the brainchild of the brilliant Belgian artist Geert Hautekiet.

as a result of flocks of aggressive birds that attacked residents in the 1950s, during a time so troubling it is referred to in historical documents as the "Plague of Birds," men were obliged to wear metal scrotum cups to protect their manhood from vicious attack (figure 11.9). Indeed, the axiom that "the past is a foreign country, they do things differently there" is no better proven than by what I saw at The Dig. It was a truly moving experience.

Why are archaeologists skeptical?

Wait. What? The worldwide capital of snow globes? Scrotum cups? Are you kidding? Well, of course they were kidding. The Dig was a monumental and hilarious (to this archaeologist, anyway) parody—partially of archaeology, partially of American history—an absolutely amazing piece of performance art by the brilliant Belgian artist and musician Geert Hautekiet, who I had the great pleasure of meeting at the site when I visited. There was no Goverthing. There was no snow globe factory on Governor's Island. And, alas, there were no scrotum cups; and I have to tell you, the one on display at the museum didn't look like it would have been terribly comfortable, though I guess they would have been better than suffering the attacks of ball-biting birds.

Whodunit?

As just stated, the project was the brainchild of the wonderful Geert Hautekiet. The parody site was funded by a number of different Belgian sources and, locally, by the New York Historical Society and the Brooklyn Historical Society. The New York State National Department of Monuments and Archaeology was in on the joke. At least, that's what was posted at the site. But maybe all that was part of the joke.

Why?

The entire project was just, well, for fun. I asked Hautekiet about his motives or any deeper messages or aims. He just laughed at my question. However, he did tell a reporter for the *New York Times* that, just perhaps, the broader message of The Dig was that "you should never trust Belgians." Words to live by, I assume.

Hautekiet told me that The Dig on Governor's Island was, at the time, merely the most recent version of a number of fake archaeological sites he had crafted over the years. Because so much of the "performance" was presented in a serious manner, I asked if he was of the impression that some visitors thought his parody sites were the real deal, that Governor's Island really was the location of a colony of snow globe–making Belgians? He laughed and assured me that, in Europe, everyone he had ever encountered at one of his "sites" was well aware that the place was a work of art, a parody of archaeology. He then leaned in and told me that it was quite different in America where, by his estimate and after listening in on conversations both at the site and at the museum, about half of the visitors thought The Dig was entirely real. I shudder at that—again, seriously, scrotum cups and snow globes?—but I suppose that provides even further justification for the necessity of this book.

Fake-o-meter

Five, of course. I think Hautekiet would be insulted with anything fewer than five.

Getting there

The Dig was a limited engagement work of performance art. Governor's Island, which offers a quite lovely respite from the hustle and bustle of Manhattan, is accessible from Brooklyn Bridge Park's Pier 6 at Atlantic Avenue.

39. COLUMCILLE MEGALITH PARK, BANGOR, PENNSYLVANIA

Archaeological perspectives

I get it. Megaliths—large, crudely carved stones set upright, stacked one on top of another, or inserted into the landscape in circles or straight lines—are definitely cool. I have personally been transfixed by these ancient stone monuments located throughout western Europe and dating to as much as five thousand years ago: Swinside (see figure 4.10); Castlerigg; Long Meg and Her Daughters; the Merry Maidens; Carnac; Avebury; and, of course, Stonehenge (see figure 4.9). Even the names are evocative, sounding ancient, weird, even alien. Strange stories have been told to explain them. The "Merry Maidens" were young women seen dancing naked in the moonlight and turned to stone by a powerful warlock. The giant stones of Stonehenge were levitated to their locations and set in place by Merlin the Magician. Long Meg and her daughters were turned to stone by, yeah, that again, a powerful warlock angry at their naked dance under the moonlight.

At least in part as a result of the crudeness and irregularity of the stones that make up these monuments, I admit that there's definitely a strange, otherworldly, sort of *Lord of the Rings* vibe to them, especially to the modern eye. Megaliths including stone circles, individual upright stones (called *menhirs*), and stone burial chambers (called *dolmens*, *quoits*, or *cromlechs* depending on which local tradition of naming these monuments you ascribe to; see figures P.1 (bottom) and 4.14) are virtual icons of European antiquity, the equivalent of Egypt's pyramids or America's mounds. There are thousands of them, and many are rightly famous, attracting lots of visitors; for example, more than eight hundred thousand people visit Stonehenge each year. There's even a couple of atlases or gazetteers (Burl 2005; Cope 1998) as well as websites that discuss them and provide directions to people who'd like to visit (http://www.stonepages.com). People from all over the world are irresistibly drawn to them for their antique beauty as well as for what they might tell us about an ancient people removed from us by thousands of years and who are all the more fascinating because they possessed a culture apparently so alien to our own. So, I guess, if you're not able to travel all the way to Europe to see a fascinating megalithic site, it's a good thing that there's one in Bangor, Pennsylvania. I refer here to Columcille Megalith Park.

Here's what we know

Even in Europe where there are literally thousands of genuinely ancient megalithic sites, there nevertheless were attempts in the modern era to replicate "megalithic-ish" monuments (Daniel 1959). In 1820, for example, William Danby, a local landowner who had just employed a large number of workers to renovate his family's ancestral home at Swinton Park in England, shifted them over a couple of miles to construct a "Druid's Temple" consisting of stone circles, upright stones, dolmens, a stone chamber, and even a sacrificial table. In modern parlance, Danby's design picked up on nearly every imaginable "trope" of megalithic architecture and cobbled them all together at one relatively small site. Looking a bit like a hyperactive Stonehenge, Danby's Druid Temple wasn't intended to fool anybody; it was, using the term we're applying here, a folly. Danby merely wanted to keep "his" people busy creating something that was interesting and beautiful. I've not been there, but the photographs I have seen show clearly that in this he succeeded admirably (https://en.wikipedia.org/wiki/Ilton,_North_Yorkshire#/media/File:Druids_Temple_near_Ilton._-_geograph.org.uk_-_427.jpg).

It should come as no surprise, therefore, that right here in the United States we have our own version of a megalithic folly, called the Columcille Megalith Park, in Bangor, Pennsylvania. Though it technically is a folly—and I mean nothing negative by applying that term—no one there implies that the place represents the work of a displaced group of ancient Celts who made their way to central Pennsylvania in antiquity and spent their time as expatriates building a bunch of large stone monuments. It was built in the twentieth century, and the purpose was, I think, to create something of great beauty that, at the same time, is thought provoking. Mission accomplished (figure 11.10).

Why are archaeologists skeptical?

Well, there's nothing here really to be skeptical about. Columcille Megalith Park simply is a beautiful park established in the mid-1970s, characterized by a series of engaging stone monuments evocative of ancient megaliths, and now labeled an "outdoor sculpture park" by the Smithsonian Institution (figure 11.11).

Whodunit?

The stone structures at Columcille Megalith Park are the brainchild of Bill Cohea, a fascinating gentleman who, among other things, served in the navy, was a Presbyterian minister, founded an alternative high school, worked as a correspondent at the United Nations and White House, is a writer and poet, and called himself, rather wonderfully, the "Dream Manifestor of Columcille Megalith Park." That sounds about right. Cohea and his friend Fred Lindkvist began building stone monuments in the park beginning in 1979. To date, there are more than eighty stones incorporated into the megaliths of Columcille. Bill Cohea passed away on June 18, 2018, but his dream lives on.

Figure 11.10. The stone circle at Columcille built in Pennsylvania in the 1970s evokes memories of the ancient megalithic monuments I have seen in England and Scotland.

Figure 11.11. A trilithon at Columcille, two upright stones topped with a capstone, is reminiscent of the ancient trilithons of Stonehenge.

Why?

A great controversy erupted in 1977 when the artist Carl Andre unveiled a work of art he called the *Stone Field Sculpture* in Hartford, Connecticut. Andre's commission was for $87,000—he was and is a famous artist, and he doesn't come cheap. His Hartford work consisted of the placement of thirty-six large, stone boulders arrayed in a triangular pattern, sort of like that game with the pegs set in a board of wood called, appropriately enough, the "triangle peg game." That was it. Andre didn't sculpt any of the rocks, he didn't paint them, he didn't stack them. In fact, he basically just collected them and dropped them in place with a backhoe.

As you can imagine, a hue and cry was raised by the agency that paid him the eight-seven-large, feeling that they had been hoodwinked. Okay, Andre is known as a "minimalist," but couldn't he have created something a little less minimal just this one time? But a contract is a contract, and they ultimately paid the artist his money.

At the time I thought it quite absurd. I have long been an adherent to the philosophy that if I see a piece of art or hear a bit of music and think to myself: "Hell, I could have done that!" it must not really be art as I have no artistic or musical talent whatsoever. Then, by some strange twist of fate I found myself late one night in Hartford right across from the *Stone Field Sculpture*. I hadn't planned it, but there I was. So, of course, I crossed the street and walked into it, fully intending to laugh at the fools who paid an "artist" a ton of money to dump rocks in a little patch of urban space (figure 11.12). That didn't happen. I didn't laugh. I didn't chortle. I didn't even snicker. In fact, I was instantly transfixed by the boulder field. It was strangely beautiful and beautifully strange. In fact, I loved it. That raised the obvious question in my own mind: Why was I so moved by a triangular arrangement of thirty-six large stones?

I think that sometimes when enjoying art it is best not to even pose the question "Why?" and simply celebrate the beauty and mystery that clearly manifests in the work of the artist. Sure, Cohea wrote about his inspiration for Columcille: his encounters with the stones of the tiny island of Iona off the coast of Scotland; dreams in which the stones actually spoke to him and somehow inspired him to use their "energies" in his work (figure 11.13). Okay. But whatever his inspiration and whatever its source, I think I can agree with him—and applaud him—in the realization of his dream, his creation of, as he succinctly and accurately phrases it, "a place of myth and mystery" (Cohea 2000: 6). Indeed, Columcille is just incredibly cool; beautiful, serene, surprising, and evocative. It's a wonderful place to visit (figure 11.14).

Fake-o-meter

Well, as a "real," genuinely ancient megalithic site, this one merits a five. But Columcille is not presented as an actual, ancient site, so that's not fair. As a cool place to walk around and think about stuff, there's nothing fake about this place.

Figure 11.12. Though I laughed when I first read about the art installation called the *Stone Field Sculpture*. I was actually impressed and even moved when I experienced it for myself. What can I say, I'm an archaeologist. I like rocks. And I will admit that when I returned to see the installation on a sunlit day to take this photograph, it wasn't quite so evocative. Oh well.

Figure 11.13. The Megalith structures called *dolmens* (see figure 4.14) likely served as the inspiration for this dolmen at Columcille Megalith Park.

Figure 11.14.   Ancient, single, sometimes isolated, large, upright stones in Western Europe are called "menhir." This not-so-ancient menhir looms over the landscape at the Columcille Megalith Park in Pennsylvania.

Getting there

Columcille Megalith Park is accessible from State Road 191 in Bangor, Pennsylvania. On your GPS, punch in 2155 Fox Gap Road. There's a small parking area adjacent to the park just before you reach that address. You'll know you're there because you can see some of the megaliths from the road.

40. MARYHILL STONEHENGE, MARYHILL, WASHINGTON

Archaeological perspectives

Many folks—and if you're reading this book (which, of course, you are) you are among them—find archaeological sites fascinating and even captivating. In explaining the emotional attraction experienced by many to the physical remnants of antiquity, a colleague of mine, Jeb Card (2018), suggests that many perceive an underlying spookiness to ancient archaeological sites. In fact, the title of his recent book is *Spooky Archaeology* (Card 2018). Ancient, mouldering ruins, decrepit structures enfolded in dense vegetation indeed do seem to radiate a vibe of weirdness, strangeness, and yes, downright spookiness. Arthur Conan Doyle recognized this; a couple of his Sherlock Holmes stories (in particular, the *Hound of the Baskervilles* and the *Adventure of the Devil's Foot*) use "spooky" archaeological sites as the backdrops to stories that seem—until the great deductive reasoner solves the mysteries rationally—to be imbued with paranormal evil. H. P. Lovecraft may have been even more aware of the perceived spookiness of archaeological ruins; an evil entity seems to virtually emanate from an ancient circle of crudely carved, upright stones (that are also characterized by a terrible smell) in his story, the *Dunwich Horror*.

For some people, Stonehenge in England is an icon of archaeological spookiness (see figure 4.9; figure 11.15). The stones that constitute the monument are massive, deeply weathered, and each is uniquely irregular. Many of the stones have fallen and lie in repose where they fell. Some stones are missing entirely. Altogether, there's something that just seems weird, something simply "not right," even ghostly about the place, especially on the chilly, gray, and rainy day when I was there last. And maybe that's part of the attraction, that feeling of weirdness or otherworldliness about it.

The fantasy author Ray Bradbury in his book *The Martian Chronicles* described an ancient, abandoned, and decaying Martian city in this way: "Perfect,

Figure 11.15. Construction began on the real Stonehenge more than 4,500 years ago. The monument includes thirty "sarsens" placed in a nearly 100-foot-diameter circle topped by thirty lintel stones as the upright stones and five trilithons, sets of three stones, two uprights and one lintel in each. The largest of the trilithon uprights weighs close to 100,000 pounds.

Figure 11.16.   The Maryhill, Washington, version of Stonehenge isn't quite as old as Stonehenge, having been completed in 1929. Oh, and all of it was made from poured concrete.

faultless, in ruins, yes, but perfect, nonetheless." Is Stonehenge in this way "perfect" precisely because it is in ruins? Would Stonehenge be as emotionally evocative if it were, instead, physically perfect, with each stone looking exactly like its neighbor in the monument, as if they were all molded in a giant machine? Well, we don't have to speculate about that. There is, in fact, a full-scale, modern replica of Stonehenge you can visit that shows no signs of weathering, imperfection, or crudeness. I refer here to the Maryhill Stonehenge in Maryhill, Washington (figure 11.16).

Here's what we know

There's no intentional fakery, misinterpretation, or misrepresentation going on here, just an attempt to use the iconic appearance of the real Stonehenge in a modern monument. A local businessman, Samuel Hill, funded the Maryhill Stonehenge's construction as a memorial for the local soldiers killed in World War I (Tuhy 1983). A plaque at the site dedicates the memorial:

> In memory of the soldiers of Klickitat County who gave their lives in defense of their country. This monument is erected in the hope that others inspired by the example of their valor and their heroism may share in that love of liberty and burn with that fire of patriotism which death can alone quench.

Figure 11.17. The Maryhill Stonehenge was intended as a monument to World War I war dead.

The monument was dedicated and ground broken in 1918, and the concrete replica of Stonehenge was completed in 1929. Initially, Hill wanted to craft the model monument out of stone to better emulate the real thing. To save both time and money, instead the Maryhill Stonehenge ended up being made entirely of reinforced concrete. Though an attempt was made in casting each element of the monument to give their surfaces a rough appearance, it still looks like a giant Lego version of the 4,500-year-old original (figure 11.17).

Why are archaeologists skeptical?

There's really nothing to be skeptical about here. No trickery or chicanery. The one unfortunate detail about the Maryhill Stonehenge is that it doesn't work nearly as well as the real one at keeping track of the solstices. When Hill commissioned the monument, few researchers realized that Stonehenge served as a giant solar calendar, its stones—especially the so-called heelstone—marking important positions of the sun on the horizon at sunrise and sunset, especially at the solstices and equinoxes. Those locations of the sun on the horizon differ depending on where you are on Earth, especially latitude. Stonehenge is located at 50.18° North. Maryhill is at 45.7° North. That difference in latitude renders the Maryhill monument pretty much useless as a solar calendar. But the concrete Stonehenge was never intended as a calendar, so that's perfectly okay, of course.

Whodunit?

We know that the monument was the brainchild of businessman and philanthropist Sam Hill. Apparently, Hill had visited the real Stonehenge in 1915. He clearly was inspired by the ancient monument and used it as a model for the World War I memorial he commissioned in 1918.

Why?

Hill was a Quaker, a religion that is underlain by a pacifist philosophy. When Hill visited Stonehenge in 1915, the prevailing explanation for the monument was that it had been used for human sacrifice by the ancient Druids. Today we know that's not true, but ostensibly, Hill's guide to the site told him: "Here the ancients 4,000 years ago offered bloody sacrifices to their heathen gods of war" (Tuhy 1983: 191). Hill's biographer stated that Hill was deeply moved by the notion that warfare afflicted humanity even four thousand years ago, and this inspired his desire to replicate Stonehenge in America as a memorial to fallen soldiers. His construction of a Stonehenge-themed war memorial was, as stated by this biographer: "to remind my fellow man of [that] incredible folly" (Tuhy 1983: 191); in other words, the folly of war.

Fake-o-meter

Zero. Nobody is trying to fool anyone here.

Getting there

The Maryhill Stonehenge is located along the Lewis and Clark Highway (Route 14), east of the town of Maryhill. About a mile east of the intersection of Highway 97 and 14, there is a road on the right called, not coincidentally, Stonehenge Drive. Turn right and head to the parking lot for the monument. The memorial is today administered by the Maryhill Museum of Art. There is no fee to view the monument, although donations are appreciated.

An Epilogue (of Sorts)

$\mathcal{A}$t last we have visited, if only on the pages of this field guide, all forty of what I have included in my listing of the strangest, most engaging, and, in some cases, most amusing archaeological sites, artifacts, features, and archaeologically themed locations in North America.

As we have seen, some of these places are entirely fake. Truly, the Cardiff Giant does not represent the actual, petrified remains of a biblical Nephilim. It was a cynical—and briefly successful—attempt by its perpetrators to make a pot of money by exploiting human gullibility. It's a fun story, and it is wonderful that the tale of a 150-year-old archaeological humbug—that's nineteenth-century for "fake news"—can be revisited by an actual visit to the giant himself. If you go, say "hi" to him for me.

At the same time, while the Columcille Megalith Park isn't a genuine archaeological site, that doesn't detract in the least from its beauty. It is truly an inspirational, engaging, and even moving place. Maybe that's just me—I do like rocks—but I think others would find it so as well. Visit it for yourself, have a walkabout, bring a picnic lunch, and sit in the shadows of its wonderfully raw stone sentinels. I think you'll love the place as much as I did. Well, almost as much; I am, after all, a rock nerd.

We've also visited a bunch of places in North America where demonstrably Native American rock art along with out-and-out modern fabrications etched into the surfaces of boulders, rock slabs, pebbles, and pieces of slate have been presented as evidence that ancient Europeans and Middle Easterners visited America in antiquity. Some interpretations of rock art are even more extravagant, suggesting the ancient presence here of foreigners from places a bit further removed like, you know, elsewhere in the galaxy. It's all nonsense, but it is undeniably interesting nonsense.

Then there were those misinterpreted and misrepresented paintings of what their misinterpreters and misrepresenters call dinosaurs—proving, to them at least, that human beings and dinosaurs were contemporaries—in Utah, of all places—only a few thousand years ago. Such interpretations are wrong, but the art is certainly worth a look. Further, it is important to consider the reasons why some people interpret them to mean something they demonstrably do not.

I suppose, if there's a broader context in which to view the fake, misinterpreted, and misrepresented sites highlighted in this guide, it is through the lens of fake news. As shown here, there's nothing new about fake news. There have always been people who have had an agenda, here about the human past, but it certainly isn't restricted to antiquity, and who have attempted to convince others of the rightness—and maybe even the righteousness—of their worldview. They support, even proselytize their beliefs, philosophies, and agendas through confirmation bias (focusing only on evidence that fits their preconceived opinions and filtering out whatever doesn't), cherry-picking data, pareidolia (seeing patterns in random, natural images), apophenia (seeing connections between entirely unrelated events, sites, or places), paranoia, and even flat-out fakery. The Cardiff Giant, ancient paintings of dinosaurs in Black Dragon Canyon, and Gungywamp are, in this view, comrades in arms with pizzagate, crisis actors, and Jewish bankers conspiring with extraterrestrial reptilians.

Scientists, including archaeologists, aren't completely objective automatons. We have philosophies, agendas, and preconceptions. But those philosophies are about the importance of understanding what truly happened in the human past to better understand the human condition. Those agendas are about collecting data and testing hypotheses about human antiquity and rejecting those hypotheses—perhaps not gleefully, but rejecting them nonetheless—when the data don't support them. And those preconceptions we may harbor about what happened and when in human antiquity simply cannot withstand the power of those "stubborn facts" John Adams talked about and that I noted in chapter 1.

Now, I fully recognize that some of you might be peeved at me for how I have characterized sites that you may interpret differently from how I and most of my archaeological colleagues do. Take this story for what it's worth. By sheer coincidence, the parents of one of my students were friends with the owners of one of the sites I mention in this book. The owners were very aware of and not particularly happy about my disagreement with their interpretation of the place. According to my student, the owners of the site actually recommended to her parents that she withdraw from my university because of my opinions about their site. Seriously? Well, I'm glad they didn't take my viewpoint personally.

You too may disagree with my skepticism about some of the sites presented here, but that's the beauty of science. Throughout this book I have pointed out the rules of archaeology, explicitly enumerating the kinds of physical evidence that must be found in order to support claims of ancient Celtic settlements (or Norse or Hebrew or extraterrestrial) in North America or the existence of hidden remains of millennia-old civilizations in Illinois, Missouri, or Arizona. Find irrefutable evidence, publish it, and have it reviewed by archaeologists and historians. At that point I will happily congratulate you, pat you on the back, and begin work on a new, updated edition of this book. Until then . . .

The Sego Canyon pictographs do not contain within them depictions of extraterrestrial visitors to Earth. But you definitely should consider a visit to that canyon and stand in the presence of its truly impressive rock art. The Kensington Runestone and the Heavener Runestone aren't objects genuinely inscribed by Viking travelers to the New World, but they are fascinating historical artifacts nonetheless. The Acton, Upton, and Peach Pond stone chambers aren't ancient celestial observatories or hell mouths or gateways to other planes of reality, but they are incredibly cool historical features and interesting to explore. I seriously doubt that you can achieve spiritual enlightenment by bathing in the positive vibes emanating from the remnants of a couple of ancient houses (Palatki and Honanki) in Sedona, but I bet you can gain a visceral appreciation for Native American culture by visiting them, and that's even better.

I will leave you, gentle reader, at that point. I heartily encourage you to hike, bike, explore, and engage in the wonderful places described in this book. Even things that contradict "stubborn facts" about the human past in North America can be worthwhile—and fun—to contemplate.

References

Adovasio, J. M., J. Donahue, and R. Stuckenrath. 1990. The Meadowcroft Rockshelter radiocarbon chronology 1975–1990. *American Antiquity* 55: 348–53.

Alrutz, Robert W. 1980. The Newark Holy Stones: The history of an archaeological tragedy. *Journal of the Scientific Laboratories, Denison University* 57: 1–57.

Andres, Dennis. 2009. *What Is a Vortex?: Sedona's Vortex Sites: A Practical Guide.* Meta Adventures, Sedona.

Argüelles, José. 1987. *The Mayan Factor: Path beyond Technology.* Bear and Company, Santa Fe.

Bahn, Paul. 2014. *The Archaeology of Hollywood: Traces of the Golden Age.* Rowman & Littlefield, Lanham, Maryland.

Barger, Lucas. 2013. *Life on a Rocky Farm: Rural Life Near New York City in the Late Nineteenth Century.* State University of New York Press, Albany.

Barnes, F. A., and Michaelene Pendleton. 1979. *Canyon Country Prehistoric Indians: Their Cultures, Ruins, Artifacts, and Rock Art.* Wasatch Publishers, Salt Lake City.

Barnhart, Terry A. 1986. Curious antiquity? The Grave Creek controversy revisited. *West Virginia History*: 103–24.

Begley, Christopher. 2016. The lost white city of the Honduras: Discovered again (and again). In *Lost City, Found Pyramid: Understanding Alternative Archaeologies and Pseudoscientific Practices*, edited by Jeb Card and David S. Anderson, pp. 35–45. University of Alabama Press, Tuscaloosa.

Bell, Thomas. 2011. Hoax or history: The Michigan Relics. http://eyewondermedia.com/content/michigan-relics

Bierce, Ambrose. 1911. *The Devil's Dictionary.* Dover, New York.

Bird, Roland T. 1939. Thunder in his footsteps. *Natural History* 43: 254–61, 302.

Brosnan, Peter. 2016. *The Lost City of Cecil B. DeMille.* Documentary film.

Burgess, Don. 2009. Romans in Tucson?: The story of an archaeological hoax. *Journal of the Southwest* 51: 3–102.

Burl, Aubrey. 2005. *A Guide to the Stone Circles of Britain, Ireland, and Brittany.* Yale University Press, New Haven.

Card, Jeb. 2018. *Spooky Archaeology: Myth and Science of the Past.* University of New Mexico Press, Albuquerque.

Carlson, Barbara. 1966. Dinos gum up the works. *Hartford Courant.* August 26, p. 1.

Catlin, George. 1838. Letters from correspondents: The Dighton Rock. *New York Mirror*: 213.

Chartier, Craig, S. 2007. *Report on the Site Examination Testing and Monitoring of the Reconstruction of the Acton Stone Chamber.* Town of Acton and the New England Antiquities Research Association, Acton, Massachusetts. http://www.plymoutharch.com/wp-content/uploads/2010/12/actonstonechamber.pdf.

Cline, Eric H. 2007. *From Eden to Exile: Unraveling Mysteries of the Bible.* National Geographic, Washington, D.C.

Cohea, David. 2000. *Columba & Oran: Excavating a Mystery.* Columcille, Inc., Bangor, Pennsylvania. http://static1.1.sqspcdn.com/static/f/1571723/19618897/1343419943267/Columba+and+Oran+PDF.pdf?token=MS9KW8ASC5sehOzJA9NKc6E3B%2Bg%3D.

Colavito, Jason. 2001. Archaeological cover up? http://www.jasoncolavito.com/archaeological-cover-up.html.

Connah, Graham. 1987. *African Civilization: Precolonial Cities and States in Tropical Africa; An Archaeological Perspective.* Cambridge University Press, Cambridge, England.

Cope, Julian. 1998. *The Modern Antiquarian: A Pre-Millenial Odyssey through Megalithic Britain.* Thorsons, London.

Daniel, Glyn. 1959. Some megalithic follies. *Antiquity* 33: 282–84.

Darwin, Charles. 1859. *On the Origin of Species by Means of Natural Selection.* Appleton, New York.

Delabarre, Edmund Burke. 1928. *Dighton Rock: A Study of the Written Rocks of New England.* Walter Neale, New York.

———. 1936. Miguel Corte Real: The first European to enter Narragansett Bay. *Rhode Island Historical Society Collections* 29.

DeMille, Cecil B. 1959. *The Autobiography of Cecil B. DeMille.* Prentice Hall, Englewood Cliffs, New Jersey.

Dillehay, T., and M. Collins. 1988. Early cultural evidence from Monte Verde in Chile. *Nature* 332: 150–52.

Doleman, William H., Thomas J. Carey, and Donald R. Schmitt. 2004. *The Roswell Dig Diaries.* Pocket Books, New York.

Drabelle, Dennis. 1996. Ancient Egypt on the Pacific. *Preservation* 48: 38–46.

Dudley, Gary P. 2001. *The Legend of Dudleytown: Solving Legends through Genalogical and Historical Research.* Heritage Books, Bowie, Maryland.

Fagan, Brian. 1991. Digging DeMille. *Archaeology* 44: 16, 18, 20.

Farlow, J. O., et al. 2010. Dinosaur trackways of the Paluxy River Valley (Glen Rose Formation, Lower Cretaceous), Dinosaur Valley State Park, Somervell County, Texas. *Actas de V Jornadas Internacionales sobre Paleolog√≠a de Dinosaurios y su Entorno*: http://paleo.cc/paluxy/Farlow%20et%20al%202012%20Paluxy%20River%20tracksites.pdf.

Farquharson, R. J. 1876. Recent archaeological discoveries at Davenport, Iowa, of copper axes, cloth, etc. supposed to have come down to us from a prehistoric people, called the mound-builders. In *Proceedings of the Davenport Academy of Sciences*, pp. 119–43. Women's Centennial Association, Davenport, Iowa.

———. 1876. On the inscribed tablets found by Reverend J. Gass in a mound near Davenport, Iowa. In *Davenport Academy of Natural Sciences*, pp. 103–16. J. D. Putnam, Davenport, Iowa.

Feder, Kenneth L. 1994. *A Village of Outcasts: Historical Archaeology and Documentary Research at the Lighthouse Site.* Mayfield Publishing, Mountain View, California.

———. 1994. The Spanish *entrada*: A model for assessing claims of Pre-Columbian contact between the Old and New Worlds. *North American Archaeologist* 15: 147–66.

———. 2010. *Encyclopedia of Dubious Archaeology: From Atlantis to Walam Olum*. Greenwood, Santa Barbara, California.

———. 2010. *Linking to the Past: A Brief Introduction to Archaeology*. Oxford University Press, New York.

———. 2014. Connecticut's hidden animals? *The Skeptical Inquirer* 38: 56–57.

———. 2017. *Ancient America: Fifty Archaeological Sites to See for Yourself*. Rowman & Littlefield, Lanham, Maryland.

———. 2018. *Frauds, Myths, and Mysteries: Science and Pseudoscience in Archaeology*. Oxford University Press, New York.

Fell, Barry. 1976. *America B.C.: Ancient Settlers in the New World*. Demeter Press, New York.

Flavin, Richard. 2012. Falling into Burrows Cave. http://www.flavinscorner.com/falling.htm.

Gage, Mary E., and James E. Gage 2008. *A Handbook of Stone Structures in Northeastern United States*. Powwow River Books, Amesbury, Massachusetts.

Gass, Rev. Jacob. 1876. A connected account of the Explorations of Mound No. 3, Cook's Farm Group. In *Proceedings of the Davenport Academy of Natural Sciences*, pp. 92–98. Davenport, Iowa.

Geggel, Laura. 2017. 94-year-old "Ten Commandments" sphinx unearthed in coastal dunes. *Live Science*. https://www.livescience.com/61045-hollywood-sphinx-found-in-dunes.html.

Godfrey, William S. 1951. The archaeology of the old stone mill in Newport, Rhode Island. *American Antiquity* 17: 120–29.

Goodwin, William. 1946. *The Ruins of Great Ireland in New England*. Meador, Boston.

Gorman, F. J., John Pendergast, Diana Doucette, Virginia Ross, and Charles Panagiotakos. 1986. *Intensive Archaeological Survey of Druid Hill, LeBlanc Park, Lowell, Massachusetts*. Environmental Archaeology Group, Boston, Massachusetts.

Halsey, John R. 2009. *The "Michigan Relics": America's Longest Running Archaeological Fraud*. Iowa City, Iowa.

Hamilton, M. Colleen, and Joseph M. Nixon. 2016. Archaeological excavations at Cecil B. DeMille's 1923. *The Ten Commandments* Film Set, Guadalupe-Nipomo Dunes, California. *Journal of Ancient Egyptian Interconnections* 8: 110–21.

Hayden, D. L. 1993. The great Burrows Cave scam. *American Institute for Archaeological Research Newsletter* 9: 13–15.

Headley, Gwyn. 2012. *Follies: Fabulous, Fanciful, and Frivolous Buildings*. National Trust Books, London.

Hertz, Johannes. 1997. Round church or windmill: New light on the Newport Tower. *Newport History* 68: 55–91.

Hitt, Jack. 1998. How the Gungywampers saved civilization. *GQ* 68: 128–35.

Hodgman, Rev. Edwin R. 1883. *History of the Town of Westford*. The Westford Town History Association, Westford, Massachusetts.

Hoffman, C. 2019. Stone Prayers: Native American Constructions of the Eastern Seaboard. Arcadia Publishing, Mt. Pleasant, South Carolina.

Huddleston, Lee. 1967. *Origins of the American Indians: European Concepts 1492–1729*. University of Texas Press, Austin.

Hunter, Douglas. 2017. *The Place of Stone: Dighton Rock and the Erasure of America's Indigenous Past*. University of North Carolina Press, Chapel Hill.

Imbrogno, Philip, and Marianne Horrigan. 2000. *Celtic Mysteries in New England*. Llewellyn Publications, St. Paul, Minnesota.

Ingstad, Anne Stine. 1977. *The Discovery of a Norse Settlement in America*. Universiteforlaget, Oslo, Norway.

Ingstad, Helge. 1964. Viking ruins prove Vikings found New World. *National Geographic* 126: 708–34.

Ingstad, Helge, and Anne Stine Ingstad. 2000. *The Viking Discovery of America: The Excavation of a Norse Settlement in L'anse aux Meadows, Newfoundland*. Breakwater Books, St. John's, Newfoundland.

Isaacs, Darek. 2010. *Dragons or Dinosaurs: Creation or Evolution*. Bridge Logos Foundation, Alachua, Florida.

Jackson, Nancy, George A. Jackson, and William Linke Jr. 1981. The "trench ruin" of Gungywamp, Groton, Connecticut. *Bulletin of the Archaeological Society of Connecticut* 44: 20–29.

Jaworski, Rita. 1977. Letters to the editor: Questions age of dino tracks. *Hartford Courant*. October 19, p. 18.

Jenzen, Doug. 2018. Personal communication.

Johnstone, E. B. 2008. *Bigfoot and Other Stories*. Tulare County Board of Education, Vasalia, California.

Joltes, Richard E. 2003. Critical enquiry: Burrows Cave, a modern hoax. http://www.critical enquiry.org/burrowscave/burrows.shtml.

Kehoe, Alice Beck. 2005. *The Kensington Runestone: Approaching a Research Question Holistically*. Waveland Press, Lovegrove, Illinois.

Kelsey, Francis W. 1908. Some archaeological forgeries from Michigan. *American Anthropologist* New Series 10: 48–59.

Kennedy, Randy. 2009. Uncovering a small town (and some tall tales). *New York Times*. http://www.nytimes.com/2009/09/19/arts/19archaeology.html.

Korff, Kal K. 1997. *The Roswell UFO Crash: What They Don't Want You to Know*. Prometheus, Amherst, New York.

Kuban, Glen J. 1996. The Paluxy dinosaur/"man track" controversy. http://paleo.cc/paluxy.htm.

Lafayette Wonder, The. 1869. *Syracuse Daily Journal*, October 20.

Lang, Joel. 1978. Dinosaur State Park to reopen. *Hartford Courant*. May 11, p. 59.

Le Quellec, J-L., Paul Bahn, and Marvin Rowe. 2015. The death of a pterodactyl. *Antiquity* 89: 872–84.

Leakey, Mary D. 1984. *Disclosing the Past*. Doubleday and Sons, New York.

Lenik, Ed. 2002. *American Indian Rock Art in the Northeast Woodlands*. University Press of New England, Lebanon, New Hampshire.

———. 2008. *Making Pictures in Stone: American Indian Rock Art of the Northeast*. University of Alabama Press, Tuscaloosa.

Lepper, Bradley T., James R. Duncan, Carol Diaz-Granádos, and Tod A. Frolking. 2018. Arguments for the age of Serpent Mound. *Cambridge Archaeological Journal*: 1–18.

Lepper, Bradley T., and Jeff Gill. 2000. The Newark Holy Stones. *Timeline* 17: 16–25.

Liban, David. 2005. *Carhenge: Genius or Junk?*. Tinyfist Films. https://vimeo.com/97151336.

Lucas, Fred. 2013. *The Zeno Voyage: Anatomy of a Hoax*. JasonColavito.com Books, Albany.

Macoy, Robert. 1870. *General History, Cyclopedia, and Dictionary of Freemasonry*. Masonic Publishing Company, New York.

Magnusson, M., and H. Paulsson (editors). 1965. *The Vinland Sagas*. Penguin, New York.

Mahan, Shannon A., F. W. Martin, and C. Taylor. 2015. Construction ages of the Upton Stone Chamber: Preliminary findings and suggestions for future luminescence research. *Quaternary Geochronology*: 1–9.

Mainfort, Robert C., and Mary L. Kwas. 1991. The Bat Creek Stone: Judeans in Tennessee? *Tennessee Anthropologist* 16: 1–19.

———. 1993. The Bat Creek fraud: A final statement. *Tennessee Anthropologist* 18: 87–93.

———. 2004. The Bat Creek Stone revisited: A fraud exposed. *American Antiquity* 69: 761–69.

Mallery, Garrick. 1894. *Picture Writing of the American Indians*. Washington, D.C. Bureau of American Ethonology.

Marsh, Othniel C. 1869. The Cardiff Giant a humbug. *Proceedings of the Massachusetts Historical Society* 1869–1870: 161–62.

Mason, Rev. Elias. 1874. *Gazetteer of the State of Massachusetts*. B. B. Russell.

Mather, Cotton. 1689. The wonderful works of God commemorated. http://quod.lib.umich.edu/e/eebo/A50176.0001.001?rgn=main;view=fulltext.

McCulloch, J. Huston. 1988. *Tennessee Anthropologist* 13: 79–123.

McGlone, William R., Phillip M. Leonard, James L. Guthrie, Rollin W. Gillespie, and James P. Whittal Jr. 1993. *Ancient American Inscriptions: Plow Marks or History*. Early Sites Research Society, Sutton, Massachusetts.

McIlvaine, Charles. 1839. Preface. In *An Inquiry into the Origin of the Antiquities of America*, by John Delafield Jr., pp. 5–11. N. G. Burgess & Co., Cincinnati.

McKusick, Marshall. 1991. *The Davenport Conspiracy*. Iowa State University Press, Ames.

Miguel Corte Real: The first European to enter Narragansett Bay. 1936. *Rhode Island Historical Society Collections* 29.

Moreno-Mayar, J. Victor, et al. 2018. Terminal Pleistocene Alaskan genome reveals first founding population of Native Americas. *Nature* 553: 203–207.

Moskowitz, Kathy. 2004. Mayak Datat: An archaeological viewpoint of the Hairy Man pictograph. http://www.bigfootproject.org/articles/mayak_datat.html.

Moskowitz Strain, Kathy. 2012. Mayak Datat: The Hairy Man pictographs. *The Relict Hominoid Inquiry* 1: 1–12.

Nelson, Vance. 2012. *Untold Secrets of Planet Earth: Dire Dragons*. Untold Secrets of Earth Publishing, Red Deer, Alberta, Canada.

New York Times 1925. Puzzling "relics" dug up in Arizona stir scientists. *New York Times* 1, 27.

Oestreicher, D. M. 2008. Unpublished manuscript.

Pflock, Karl T. 2001. *Roswell: Inconvenient Facts and the Will to Believe*. Prometheus, Amherst, New York.

Poole, Buzz. 2007. *Madonna of the Toast*. Mark Batty, New York City.

Quinion, Michael B. 2008. *Cider Making*. Shire Publications, Oxford.

Raff, Jennifer A., and Deborah A. Bolnick. 2015. Does mitochondrial haplogroup X indicate ancient trans-Atlantic migration to the Americas? A critical evaluation. *PaleoAmerica* 1: 297–304.

Rasmussen, M., et al. 2014. The genome of a late Pleistocene human from a Clovis burial site in western Montana. *Nature* 506: 225–29.

Ringborn, A., et al. 2003. Dating ancient mortar. *American Scientist*. 91: 130–137.

Rodwell, Warwick. 1989. *The Archaeology of Religious Places: Churches and Cemeteries in Britain*. University of Pennsylvania Press, Philadelphia.

Romacito, Rick. 1993. American Indians and the New Age: Subtle racism at work. *The Skeptical Inquirer* 18: 97–98.

Sagan, Carl. 1963. Direct contact among galactic civilizations by relativisitic interstellar spaceflight. *Planetary Space Science* 11: 485–98.

Senter, Phil, and Sally J. Cole. 2011. "Dinosaur" petroglyphs at Kachina Bridge site: Naturual Bridges National Monument, southern Utah: Not dinosaurs after all. *Palaeontologia Electronica* 14: 1–5. http://palaeo-electronica.org/2011_1/236/index.html.

Severin, Tim. 1977. The voyages of Brendan. *National Geographic* 152: 770–97.

Silverberg, Robert. 1989. *The Mound Builders.* University of Ohio Press, Athens, Ohio.

Simonson, J. 1947. Black Dragon Canyon. *Utah Magazine* 9: 24–25, 45.

Smith, Brian. 2002. Early Henry Sinclair's fictitious trip to America. *New Orkney Antiquarian Journal* 2.

Stamps, Richard B. 2001. Tools leave marks: Material analysis of the Scotford-Soper-Savage Michigan Relics. *BYU Studies Quarterly* 40: 210–38.

Sutherland, Patricia. 2000. The Norse and Native Americans. In *Vikings: The North Atlantic Saga*, edited by W. W. Fitzhugh and E. I. Ward, pp. 238–47. Smithsonian Institution Press, Washington, D.C.

Sykes, Bryan C., et al. 2014. Genetic analysis of hair samples attributed to Yeti, Bigfoot and other anomalous primates. *Proceedings of the Royal Society B* 281. http://rspb.royalsociety publishing.org/content/281/1789/20140161.

Talmage, James E. 1911. The "Michigan Relics": A story of forgery and deception. *Deseret Museum Bulletin, New Series* 2: 2–30.

Thomas, Cyrus. 1885. The Davenport Tablet. *Science* 6: 564.

———. 1894. *Report on the Mound Explorations of the Bureau of Ethnology.* Bureau of American Ethnology, Washington, D.C.

Tompsen, Lyle. 2011. An archaeologist examines the Oklahoma Rune Stones. *The Epigraphic Society Occasional Papers* 29: 5–43.

Tribble, Scott. 2009. *A Colossal Hoax: The Giant from Cardiff That Fooled America.* Rowman & Littlefield, Lanham, Maryland.

Tuhy, John E. 1983. *Sam Hill: The Prince of Castle Nowhere.* Timber Press, Portland, Oregon.

Vescelius, Gary. 1956. Excavations at Patee's Caves. *Bulletin of the Eastern States Archaeological Federation* 15: 13–14.

Walker, Tim. 2015. The Lost City of Cecil B. DeMille: The film about unearthing a 1923 movie set that took 30 years to make. *Independent.* http://www.independent.co.uk/arts -entertainment/films/features/the-lost-city-of-cecil-b-demille-the-film-about-unearthing -a-1923-movie-set-that-took-30-years-to-a6787021.html.

Wallace, Josh. 2015. Oklahoma runestone is impressive but not from Vikings, Swedish scholar says. *The Oklahoman.* http://newsok.com/article/5416047.

Warner, J. S., and J. E. Warner. 1995. Some horizontal sunrise markers in Black Dragon Canyon. *Utah Rock Art: Some Papers Presented at the Annual Symposium of the Utah Rock Art Research Association* 4: 92–101.

Waters, Michael, et al. 2011a. Pre-Clovis mastodon hunting 13,800 years ago at the Manis site, Washington. *Science* 334: 351–53.

Waters, Michael, et al. 2011b. The Buttermilk Creek Complex and the origins of Clovis at the Debra L. Friedkin site, Texas. *Science* 331: 1599–1603.

Whitley, David S. 1996. *A Guide to Rock Art Sites: Southern California and Southern Utah.* Mountain Press Publishing Company, Missoula, Montana.

Whittall, James. 1984. A cluster of standing stones on Druid Hill, Lowell, Massachusetts. *Early Sites Research Society Bulletin* 11: 19–33.

Williams, Vance. 2012. *Untold Secrets of Earth: Dire Dragons.* Untold Secrets of Earth Publishing Company, Alberta, Canada.

Wilson, Joseph A. P. 2012. The cave who never was: Outsider archaeology and failed collaboration in the USA. *Public Archaeology* 11: 73–95.

Wolter, Scott. 2009. *The Hooked X: Key to the Secret History of North America*. North Star Press, St. Cloud, Minnesota.

———. 2010. Archaeopetrography on a "Burrows Cave" white marble artifact. *Ancient American* 14: 14–16.

Zeno, Nicolo. 1558. The discovery: Of the islands of Frislana, Eslanda, Engronelanda, Estotilanda, and Icaria: Made by two brothers of the Zeno Family viz: Messire Nicolo, the Chevalier, and Messire Antonio. http://www.jasoncolavito.com/voyage-of-the-zeno-brothers.html.

The Zeno Brothers' fantastic voyage. 2013. *Jason Colavito: Historical Researcher & Skeptic*. http://www.jasoncolavito.com/blog/the-zeno-brothers-fantastic-voyage.

Index

About the Author

Kenneth L. Feder, professor of anthropology at Central Connecticut State University, specializes in the archaeology of North America. He is author of several books, including *Ancient America: Fifty Archaeological Sites to See for Yourself.* Feder has appeared on numerous television documentaries on the National Geographic Channel, the BBC's Horizon, the History Channel, the Discovery Channel, and the SyFy Channel and has been featured in episodes of the Canadian-based William Shatner's *Weird or What?*